An Introduction to Latin American Philosophy

Latin American philosophy is best understood as a type of applied philosophy devoted to issues related to the culture and politics of Latin America. This introduction provides a comprehensive overview of its central topics. It explores not only the unique insights offered by Latin American thinkers into the traditional pre-established fields of Western philosophy, but also the many "isms" developed as a direct result of Latin American thought. Many concern matters of practical ethics and social and political philosophy, such as Lascasianism, Arielism, Bolívarism, modest and immodest feminisms, republicanism, positivism, Marxism, and liberationism. But there are also meta-philosophical "isms" such as originalism and perspectivism. Together with clear and accessible discussions of the major issues and arguments, the book offers helpful summaries, suggestions for further reading, and a glossary of terms. It will be valuable for all readers wanting to explore the richness and diversity of Latin American philosophy.

Susana Nuccetelli is Professor of Philosophy at St Cloud State University, Minnesota. She is the author of *Latin American Thought* (2002) and co-author of *Latin American Philosophy: An Introduction with Readings* (2004). She co-edited the *Blackwell Companion to Latin American Philosophy* (with Ofelia Schutte and Otávio Bueno, 2009) and is a contributor to the *Stanford Encyclopedia of Philosophy*.

An Introduction to Latin American Philosophy

SUSANA NUCCETELLI

St. Cloud State University

CAMBRIDGE
UNIVERSITY PRESS

CAMBRIDGE
UNIVERSITY PRESS

University Printing House, Cambridge CB2 8BS, United Kingdom

One Liberty Plaza, 20th Floor, New York, NY 10006, USA

477 Williamstown Road, Port Melbourne, VIC 3207, Australia

314–321, 3rd Floor, Plot 3, Splendor Forum, Jasola District Centre, New Delhi – 110025, India

79 Anson Road, #06–04/06, Singapore 079906

Cambridge University Press is part of the University of Cambridge.

It furthers the University's mission by disseminating knowledge in the pursuit of education, learning, and research at the highest international levels of excellence.

www.cambridge.org
Information on this title: www.cambridge.org/9781107067646
DOI: 10.1017/9781107705562

First published 2020

Printed in the United Kingdom by TJ Books Limited, Padstow Cornwall

A catalogue record for this publication is available from the British Library.

Library of Congress Cataloging-in-Publication Data
Names: Nuccetelli, Susana, author.
Title: An introduction to Latin American philosophy / Susana Nuccetelli, St Cloud State University, Minnesota.
Description: Cambridge, United Kingdom ; New York, NY, USA : Cambridge University Press, 2020. | Series: Cambridge introductions to philosophy | Includes bibliographical references and index.
Identifiers: LCCN 2020026168 (print) | LCCN 2020026169 (ebook) | ISBN 9781107067646 (hardback) | ISBN 9781107705562 (ebook)
Subjects: LCSH: Philosophy, Latin American. | Philosophy – Latin America.
Classification: LCC B1001 .N83 2020 (print) | LCC B1001 (ebook) | DDC 199/.8–dc23
LC record available at https://lccn.loc.gov/2020026168
LC ebook record available at https://lccn.loc.gov/2020026169

ISBN 978-1-107-06764-6 Hardback
ISBN 978-1-107-66718-1 Paperback

To Gary Seay

Contents

Tables

Preface

Identifiable as a part of mainstream Western philosophy, Latin American philosophy is a relative newcomer, a discipline still defining itself and the subject of lively debates over basics. Thus it poses a special challenge for those who would write introductory works about it. In this book, I do not aim to introduce the whole discipline of Latin American philosophy. Rather, my aim is simply to present some of Latin American philosophy's debates and movements, in particular those that have proved to be the most contested and original. Furthermore, the topics are not arranged in any strict historical order. In two previous books about the discipline, my discussions were arranged that way, but I see no reason to insist on that detail here.

The chapters of the book focus on some major issues that still need to be worked out if scholars are to make headway in the subject. Among them are meta-philosophical issues concerning the nature and quality of Latin American philosophy. *What is* Latin American philosophy? How does it differ from Latino philosophy? Who are we to count as practitioners of either of these disciplines? And what's the right identifying adjective: "Latin American," "Hispanic," "Latino," or something else? Since these issues can be better addressed once the reader has some acquaintance with the sort of philosophical inquiries distinctive of Latin American philosophy, I discuss them in the last chapter of the book. All other chapters concern "isms" that have developed in Latin American philosophical thought, some borrowed from European and North American thought, some indigenous. Thus there is Lascasianism and Scholasticism, but also Arielism, Bolivarism, feminism, republicanism, positivism, Marxism, and liberationism, among others. How is the reader to make progress given this rather forbidding forest of terminology?

Well, I do believe that it is possible to make progress for the patient reader of these chapters to make progress. I have written them with an eye to clarity and included a glossary in the back of the book, where technical terms are defined. In addition, I include information about the nationality and dates of birth and death of any given thinker the first time they occur, but only for those whose views bear on the discussion at hand. Thus readers may find "Karl Marx (German, 1818–1883)" but only "Fulgencio Batista" when the latter is merely mentioned. In the case of present-day philosophers, I have included dates only when they are available in the public domain.

In thinking about the issues of this book, I have benefited from conversations I have had at some points with a number of people, including Jorge J. E. Gracia, Renzo Llorente, and Eduardo Rabossi. And there are others whose suggestions and criticisms have been very helpful in the writing of various chapters, including Jordan Curnutt, Claus Dierksmeier, Ana Diz, Lori Gallegos de Castillo, Alex Guerrero, Vicente Medina, Paul Neiman, Daniel Trapani, Luz Triana-Echeverria, Cosimo Zene, and students in a senior seminar in Latin American Philosophy at St. Cloud State University. I have also learned from the responses of audiences at meetings of the American Philosophical Association and the Ontario Society for the Study of Argumentation at the University of Windsor. I am especially grateful to Gary Seay for his comments on all chapters, which he patiently read and edited. However, any remaining errors or infelicities are not his but mine.

1 Setting the Scene: The Iberian Conquest

In Latin America, a number of philosophical doctrines developed as responses to the mainstream views of the Iberian colonial period – which extended, roughly, from the mid-1500s to the early 1800s. This chapter looks closely at four doctrines whose central themes can be traced to that period. It begins by examining the doctrines of Bartolomé de las Casas (1474–1566) and Francisco de Vitoria (1486–1546) on the moral status of the actions of Spain, their native nation, during the early stages of the European modern expansion. From these doctrines of practical ethics and political philosophy, the chapter turns to José de Acosta (ca. 1539–1600) and his objections to Scholasticism in epistemology and philosophy of science. Pressured by the new physical and social realities of the Americas, these Spanish thinkers came to question the Spanish and Portuguese philosophical establishment. As shown in the discussion here, in their different ways they challenged some applications of the official philosophy of Roman Catholic Church, Thomism, that were common in these countries during the sixteenth century. A fourth doctrine considered below, that of twentieth-century Mexican philosopher and historian Edmundo O'Gorman (1906–1995), offers an anti-realist rejection of some established beliefs about the "discovery" of America. Although O'Gorman's anti-realism is not altogether original, its application to this issue is. It also suggests that the end of the colonial period was far from marking the end of philosophical reflection on the Iberian expansion.

1.1 A Moral Challenge: Las Casas and Vitoria

The history of ideas sometimes reveals interesting questions with philosophical implications – for example in practical ethics and political philosophy. Of this sort are the questions raised by those Spanish thinkers of the sixteenth century who reflected on the moral permissibility of the Iberian conquest of the Americas. Might that historical event be morally justified in spite of the harms inflicted upon the indigenous peoples of New Spain (Mexico), the West Indies, and Central and South America? The disagreement over how to answer this question was a substantive one, even if in the twenty-first century it may be difficult to imagine that there could be any disagreement about the moral wrongness of the Iberian colonial expansion, and more generally, the expansion of other European empires of the time. It is hardly imaginable that anyone might defend the way conquerors and settlers exploited the Amerindians, or the colonial system of slavery they imposed on Afro-Latin Americans. But to the Europeans of the time, the natives of America were beings stranger than any encountered before. Moreover, some of these people practiced cannibalism and human sacrifice, and some Spaniards and Portuguese might have acted from genuine moral concern when they rejected those practices and expressed a sense of moral obligation to interfere for the sake of the victims. Giving those who left a record of such reactions the benefit of the doubt, for at least some conquistadors and settlers, the world of the Amerindians must have seemed a kind of moral chaos from which the indigenous peoples needed to be rescued by enlightened Catholic Christians. But of course such feelings and beliefs cannot rid them, either then or today, of moral accountability.

Although many European thinkers of the time, especially Spanish thinkers, understood the issue of accountability associated with the colonial expansion, they disagreed among themselves about whether those who carried it out deserved praise or blame. Their debate over the morality of the conquest took place largely in terms of what we now call 'human rights,' since the chief issue was whether the Amerindians had sufficient personhood to qualify for such rights, which in the sixteenth century were called 'natural rights.' Nearly all European philosophers of the time who discussed these rights did so in terms of the methodology developed three centuries earlier by the medieval Italian theologian and philosopher St. Thomas Aquinas (1225–1274), a great interpreter of the Greek philosopher Aristotle (384–322 BCE). Aquinas produced important works on nearly all the central branches of philosophy, but they are essentially an extensive development and revision of Aristotelian ideas, fitting them into the framework of Christian theology. Among these ideas is the notion that standards for evaluative judgments of 'good' and 'bad,' 'right' and 'wrong,' are built into the order of nature itself. Thus, according to Aquinas' natural law theory, to act rightly is to act in whichever way best promotes certain values that are necessary for human flourishing, because they correspond to the true nature of human beings. Questions of justice are also settled in terms of human nature: people are treated justly when they are treated as they deserve in accordance with their nature.

When Iberian philosophers of the sixteenth century discussed natural rights, they debated nearly always as Thomists who were committed to Aquinas' conception of natural law and to his conception of human nature as essentially rational. On this view, humans are by nature rational beings with inalienable natural rights to life and freedom from gratuitous harm. Although the three thinkers to be considered next all agreed on these points, they disagreed on a position widely held by Thomists of the colonial period concerning Aristotle's "theory of natural slaves," with only one of our philosophers holding that the native peoples of the Americas are such "natural slaves." According to that theory, race and ethnicity determine normative worth so that some groups of people, owing to their ethnicity or their race, are barbarians by nature, and thus fit only for servitude. The expression 'normative worth' in connection with this theory refers to the significance or importance of a being in a broad range of domains, including morality, knowledge, and rationality. Aristotle's *Politics*, the work in which he advanced this theory, fails to provide any empirical evidence for its core claim: namely, that the importance of persons in any of these domains may vary according to ethnicity or race.[1] As a result, the theory reflects nothing more than Aristotle's own ethnocentric bias and should be rejected on moral grounds.

---

[1] Parts 1.2 and 1.5 of the *Politics*. According to this doctrine, there are two types of slaves, natural slaves and conventional slaves, and only the latter can be freed. A common objection to this theory is that Aristotle gave no directions as to how to tell who's who. In addition, he used the vague term 'barbarians' to refer to either non-Greeks or irrational people. These groups need not overlap, since he considered Carthaginians to be rational but they were, of course non-Greeks.

1.1.1   Lascasianism

Lascasianism developed as a reaction to the view that Amerindians are less human and may therefore exemplify the sort of people Aristotle had in mind with his theory of natural slaves. Widely accepted during the European expansion of sixteenth century, a pseudoscientific theory along Aristotle's lines denied Amerindians full personhood, and therefore full human rights. Juan Ginés de Sepúlveda (Spanish 1490–1573), an eminent clergyman in his country, held that theory. In his moral defense of the conquest, Sepúlveda took it to apply to the native peoples of the Americas. He believed that he could show that Amerindians and Europeans did not have equal rights, and therefore, that the Spanish invasion of America was morally justified. Sepúlveda's chief reasons for these claims were clearly articulated in a famous debate with Las Casas at the Spanish city of Valladolid (1550), in which he argued that the evidence of the Amerindians' behavior and habits of life (especially their practices of human sacrifice and idolatry) revealed that they were barbarous by nature, and thus their fittingness only to be 'natural slaves.' In accordance with Aristotle's view that some people were by nature suited to rule and others only to be slaves, the Amerindians were clearly of a slavish nature. Thus, Sepúlveda argued, although fully rational human beings do have natural rights to life and security in their persons and property, Amerindians cannot claim those rights.

Note that Sepúlveda denied neither that the Indians were rational beings nor that they could improve under Spanish rule. In his dispute with Las Casas (Las Casas and Sepúlveda 1994/1550), he argued instead that their rationality on average could not compare with that of the Spaniards. He believed Spain should shoulder the moral obligation of waging war against the natives because force is more effective than persuasion and conversion, rationality comes in degrees, and natural law dictates that barbarians must be ruled by those who are comparatively more rational. His reasons for these claims boiled down to:

1. The natives of the Americas are barbarians owing to (i) the rudeness of their character (ii) the servility of their minds, and (iii) the fact that they

have committed grave crimes against natural law, as shown by their practice of idolatry and other "sins" against nature.

2. Spain had a duty to save innocent victims and to evangelize the natives.

In support of (2), Sepúlveda deployed a lesser-evil strategy, claiming that human sacrifice among the Amerindians was resulting in 20,000 deaths per year, and in support of (1) he invoked some of the attacks carried out by Amerindians on Spanish missionaries and the Spaniards' virtues of prudence, justice, and religiosity – together with some "facts" that he considered evidence of the superiority of Spaniards. These included the fact that the Spaniards led by Cortés had defeated the Aztecs and that they were first to arrive in the "New World." To the objection that the native peoples lived in well-organized societies, he responded that communities of bees and spiders also have highly structured societies without this amounting to a sign of rationality. Finally, he invoked an outmoded principle of civil law according to which those who have been defeated are slaves of the defeater.

None of these reasons was of any weight for Sepúlveda's rival in the debate at Valladolid, the Spanish Dominican friar and Bishop of Chiapas Fray Bartolomé de las Casas (1474–1566). Known even today as the 'Apostle of the Indians' for his devotion to the causes of the natives of Latin America, Las Casas differed dramatically from Sepúlveda in that he had direct knowledge of these peoples on whose behalf he advocated locally and in Spain. He traveled widely in the Spanish American colonies, where he spend most of his life, and crossed the Atlantic many times during his long life to defend their human rights before the Spanish authorities. In his writings he invariably attempted to persuade his readers that the Amerindians were indeed rational human beings with full natural rights that should be respected, the same as Europeans, and that therefore enslaving them was wrong. "The only way" of winning them over to Christianity, Las Casas argued, was to respect their humanity and acknowledge them as fellow children of God. Although his method of arguing consisted mostly in the standard Scholastic appeal to authority (namely, the Old Testament, Greco-Roman authorities, the early Christian Fathers, and Aquinas), he introduced the novel arguments summarized below to reject some of his contemporaries' contentions that the

Amerindians were cruel and inhuman peoples or savages who could not govern themselves or be converted to Christianity.

Las Casas was unsparing in his criticism of Spanish conquerors and settlers, recording their cruelties toward the natives in language that makes clear his own moral revulsion.[2] In his widely translated *Short Account*, he writes that his countrymen were responsible for the destruction of whole villages of native peoples, who were either killed or forced into involuntary servitude under harsh conditions. As a result, a vast number of Amerindians died from violence, starvation, or inhumane working conditions. With startling candor, Las Casas also described his own early hypocrisy on the question of an *encomienda* which he held by inheritance, which he ultimately came to recognize as wrong.[3] He also left abundant textual evidence of another example of his own moral evolution, one that happened after learning of the unspeakable toll in human suffering endured by Africans as a result of the Atlantic slave trade. In a published apology, he noted with regret his own complicity with that unjust institution, which stemmed from his previous support of a petition for the transportation of African slaves to America. By means of his apology, Las Casas publicly renounced his participation in the petition and denounced it as a grave moral error (Las Casas 1993: 85–87).

In *The Only Way* and many other writings Las Casas gave details of his commitments to campaigning for the human rights of the Amerindians. After returning his *encomienda*, this cause became the central focus of his

[2] Note that it is Spanish Dominican Friar Antón Montesinos who is standardly credited with the first public defense of the rights of the Amerindians. He did so in 1511 on the occasion of two sermons that he gave in Santo Domingo, in which he defended the rationality of Amerindians against the Spanish settlers who had enslaved them. Montesinos's sermons influenced others, especially some priests of the Dominican order in Latin America like Las Casas, who went on to argue that the rationality of the Amerindians conferred on them certain inviolable natural rights.

[3] The *encomienda* was a title for the ownership of a number of enslaved Amerindians given to a settler by the Spanish King, under the commitment that the settler would teach them the Roman Catholic doctrine. It may be considered a servitude system by which some Amerindians were theoretically, "granted" as a loan to a Spaniard, not in perpetuity. It was introduced in Hispaniola (the Caribbean archipelago known as the Greater Antilles) and later to other Spanish territories. The *encomendero* (grant holder) had the right to benefit from the Amerindians' labor or their tribute, with the obligation to teach them Christianity, protect them, and preserve their rights to their own property.

life. Driven by the sense of an imperative to speak out against a monumental injustice, he pleaded the case of the Amerindians before local congregations as well as civil and religious authorities. With the same cause in mind, he requested audiences with two kings of Spain. On one occasion, he obtained an audience at court before Emperor Charles V. According to his own account of his speech before the Emperor, as provided in *The Only Way*, he described to him straightforwardly the enormity of the crimes committed by Spain in its American colonies. On another occasion he sent a letter (1555) to the confessor of the successor of Emperor Charles V, Philip II, in which he contended not only that the King should block the colonists' petition in Peru to make the Amerindian slavery system perpetual but that, in addition, Spain faced duties of reparation. In effect, this letter advanced the radical view at the time that the Spaniards, to make up for past injustices, should free the Amerindians, accept only a token tribute from their leaders, and completely withdraw from the Americas (1993: 169–173). He later argued more explicitly that Spain should pay reparations to the Amerindians (1993: 161).

His entreaties did bear fruit since ultimately, Charles V was moved to decree the New Laws outlawing the enslavement of Amerindians. *The Only Way* also drew the attention of the Pope himself, who used it as the basis for an encyclical, *Sublimis Deus*, which vindicated the humanity and rationality of the Amerindians and their natural right to liberty. Yet it is important to bear in mind that Las Casas was himself a man who struggled continually with his own conscience as he strove to navigate the moral minefield of colonialism, and was willing to revise his views on his moral obligations and feel regret over his moral failings.

In arguing for such radical doctrines at the time, Las Casas often departed from traditional Scholastic strategies. Against those who took the practice of human sacrifice by some Amerindians to undermine their status as rational beings, he argued (in this case, conflating explanation with moral justification) that the practice was a natural result of their intense religiosity, which led them to offer to their gods the best they had (Las Casas 1993: 162–167). Against the objection that the Amerindians committed idolatry, he devised the 'doctrine of probable error,' according to which these peoples, though *in error* because they held "idolatrous" beliefs that were false, were nevertheless *justified* in holding them because those beliefs resulted from following the advice of their own wise men, who were *usually not wrong*. Clearly, this argument might confer some degree of epistemic justification on the beliefs at stake, but it falls short of doing the work Las Casas needed it to do in order to give a sound rebuttal of the Spaniards' "idolatry" objection against Amerindians. Also fallacious was his attempt to morally justify the practice of human sacrifice among some natives by appealing to the fact that such practice was not uncommon among some respected peoples of antiquity. After all, argued Las Casas, according to the Bible, God did ask Abraham to sacrifice his own son. In addition to rejecting the common charge of barbarism against Amerindians, Las Casas never doubted their full rationality. Given the natural law theory commonly assumed in this debate, if they were fully rational, then that was sufficient grounds for their possession of human dignity and natural rights.

1.1.2 Vitorian Thomism

If Las Casas was a man of action arguing in order to obtain respect for the natural rights of Amerindians while issuing eloquent attacks on the practices of settlers and rulers, Francisco de Vitoria (Spanish 1486–1546) was a dispassionate scholar whose position arguably falls in the same side of the debate over the morality of the conquest. Nevertheless, Vitoria reacted more tentatively to claims that Amerindians had a somewhat diminished rationality, and therefore humanity. For example, he remained agnostic about whether they were fit enough to govern themselves – a common charge at the time geared to justify their subjection, and which Las Casas had rejected altogether.

At the same time, Vitoria was less interested in the practical implications of the debate over the moral justification of the conquest and more interested in the moral and political implications of the European modern expansion. Like Las Casas, Vitoria too had a Thomist conception of natural rights, but he went further to develop his own version of Thomism as well as an absolutist, realist view of the rights of Amerindians and Spaniards in a series of lectures delivered at the University of Salamanca, a great center of sixteenth-century Thomist scholarship, where he was professor. Unlike Las Casas, he devoted most of his efforts to constructing a carefully reasoned proof in order to decide whether the various actions involved in the Spanish conquest were morally justified.[4]

In a series of magisterial lectures collected by his students under the title, *De Indis et Ivre Belli Relectiones*, Vitoria offered a number of moral-theological arguments that bear on the issue at hand. Salient among them are "On the American Indians" (1991: 231–292) and "On the Law of War" (1991: 293–227). In "On the American Indians," he set out to determine whether or not there were sound reasons for the moral justification of waging a war against the Amerindians in order to forcibly convert them to Christianity. To do this, he chiefly invoked elements of canon law grounded in the definition of 'just war' first developed by St. Augustine and subsequently refined by other scholars of moral theology. Vitoria reasoned by means of frequent citations of Scripture and appeals to authority, and the method of counterexample.[5] Equipped with these elements of the Scholastic method, his reflections led him to conclude that, although the Spaniards had 'legitimate jurisdiction' in the Americas (by which he meant that they were at liberty to travel abroad), they had no right to wage war against Amerindians, or to enslave them and take their lands and other property. This conclusion was quite radical at the time for someone in Vitoria's position at the University of Salamanca.

In the course of offering grounds for that conclusion, he raised issues that are still interesting to us today, concerning the moral justification of the use of coercive force by the armies of powerful nations against native peoples in traditional societies. Note that Vitoria did not begin his lecture by assuming that the conquest was a morally bankrupt undertaking. Rather he analyzed major arguments for and against its moral permissibility, and concluded from that analysis that although sometimes such wars are justified and other times they are not, the reasons commonly provided for waging war against the Amerindians were insufficient. Furthermore, he appeared to make no effort at persuasion, although from what he wrote, he

---

[4] The actions at stake in the debate over the morality of the Conquest included waging war against the native peoples, invading their territories, imposing new rulers, and preaching a new religion.

[5] Vitoria also addresses some issues of philosophical ethics in these lectures which are not relevant for our topic here. Prominent among them is his discussion of the nature of moral obligation and its relation to knowledge and free will.

was committed to the conclusion that his fellow Catholic Christians could not claim to be both devoted to the tenets of their faith and also in favor of the conquest.

As in the case of most of those concerned at the time with the right of Amerindians, for Vitoria too the question turned largely on the facts in terms of their rationality. But unlike Las Casas, he reflected the prevalent ethnocentrism of his time by regarding them as somewhat 'dull' and in need of tutelage. Yet he saw no reason to judge them *irrational*. Moreover, he questioned the right of Spaniards to wage war against them, arguing that 'slaughter of the innocent' is contrary to natural law. In the absence of provocation – and lacking good moral reasons – war against other nations is morally wrong. From these principles he concluded that there could not be a just war against the Amerindians, for no wrong had previously been done to Spain by these peoples. In "On the Law of War" (1991: 293–27), he was more hesitant: there may be legitimate reasons for waging war against the local peoples, but only when they violate some of the sociability rights of citizens of a foreign nation, which included rights to travel freely in the local people's land, acquire citizenship, and preach their own religion. Other legitimate reasons for war included being attacked by another nation (in which case the war is always defensive and should end with the aggressor's withdrawal), and where there is a need to interfere with customs such as cannibalism and human sacrifice. Nevertheless, for Vitoria, the fact that Amerindians rejected the Gospel, a common reason invoked at the time to justify war against them, was not a sufficient reason.

1.2   An Epistemic Challenge: Acosta

Let us now turn to another philosophical thinker of the Catholic Church who rejected some claims and methods that were common among the Iberian Scholastics of sixteenth century. In his case, the relevant question involved epistemology and philosophy of science. José de Acosta was a Jesuit missionary who spent some sixteen years in what are now regions of Peru and Mexico. In his *Historia Natural y Moral de las Indias* (*Natural and Moral History of the Indies*) of 1590, Acosta challenged some of the Scholastics' beliefs and methods in empirical matters that concerned the biogeography and climatology of the region.[6] He did so by invoking his perceptual experiences in America, together with the accounts of Western explorers and navigators. These he used in arguing by counterexample, and testimony from evidence, against certain mainstream beliefs among Iberian Scholastics about those matters, thereby also challenging their attempts to draw conclusions about climatology and geography by means of appeal to authority and the method of disputation.

To understand how Acosta used the empiricist method of reasoning from evidence to challenge Scholasticism effectively, we need to have some facts about his intellectual context in view. Before the sixteenth century, philosophers did not distinguish, as we now do, between their own subject matter and that of science. Rather, nearly all of what we now refer to as the natural and social sciences they counted as part of 'philosophy.' And the reigning construal of philosophy was embodied in Scholasticism, which amounted to Spain's philosophical and scientific paradigm. After all, it comprised not only a method of inquiry but a whole set of fundamental assumptions about truth and knowledge: it was the sole accepted manner of learning about what really exists and how we know it. Moreover, whereas we would today regard philosophy and theology as completely independent practices, Scholastics usually held them to be not only compatible but equivalent. Their worldview conceived of nature as Divine Creation, which could be understood through prayerful attention to Scripture and to the writings of great figures such as Thomas Aquinas, Augustine, and the Fathers of the Church. Chiefly through the writings of Aquinas and Augustine, the Scholastics learned about the classics of Greek and Roman philosophy, especially Aristotle and Plato. They were familiar with both the Judeo-Christian tradition in theology and with ancient philosophy, which included the natural sciences. Their method, the Scholastic method of inquiry, had two building blocks. On the one hand, it assumed that claims about nature, as any other claims in philosophy and theology, admit of proof by appeal to the texts of eminent philosophical or theological authorities. On the other, it strongly relied on

---

[6] Although Acosta's challenge to Scholasticism, often neglected in the relevant literature, has not gone unnoticed (Ford 1998; Nuccetelli 2002), the new English translation of his *Historia Natural y Moral de las Indias* might help to draw deserved attention to it, especially among scholars interested in the modern revolution in science and philosophy.

syllogistic reasoning to draw conclusions about any particular new case at issue from premises based on authority. As a result, the acceptance of a theory in, say, astronomy, became contingent on Ptolemy's views, one in physics on Archimedes' views, and so on. Although this kind of armchair justification in science appears very odd to us today, it was not odd for our medieval ancestors. In their time, science (from the Latin word *scientia*) was *what admits of proof or demonstration*, and this included theology. After all, they believed that the tenets of the Christian faith could be 'proved' by Scripture. Given this conception of what is demonstrable or provable, there is no significant difference in method between theology, geometry, and philosophy on the one hand, and physics and biology on the other.

What changed all this, of course, was the great revolution in the natural sciences that swept many European universities in the sixteenth and seventeenth centuries, with the work of Copernicus, Kepler, and Galileo in astronomy, Newton in physics, Harvey in anatomy, and many others. A true paradigm shift in the Kuhnean sense, this development brought a redefinition of 'science,' like none that had occurred since antiquity, for it changed what might count as a demonstration or proof. No longer could it be a mere appeal to reason alone, or to the authority of Scripture or the writings of ancient Greek authorities or the Fathers of the Church. Now many believed that the natural sciences required empirical methods such as the direct observation of natural phenomena. Even some rationalist thinkers of the modern period such as René Descartes came to acknowledge that understanding biological phenomena requires some experimental element. As a result of the revolution that took place during this period, when we speak of the 'natural' or 'empirical' sciences today, we mean the sciences whose objects of inquiry are observational at least in principle. Biogeography and climatology are among these sciences. Their theories can be settled by appeal only to empirical evidence, and inference and testimony based on evidence of that kind.

While the modern upheaval in the natural sciences was remolding the intellectual life of most of Europe, however, the Spain and Portugal of the Counter-Reformation clung stubbornly to the old paradigm of Scholasticism. Dominated by a conservative hierarchy in the Church and devout Catholic Monarchs, Spain and Portugal remained hostile to the ideological incursions of empiricism in philosophy and the sciences. For their American colonies, the spread of Scholasticism meant that an altogether stagnant paradigm was to prevail in their educational institutions for about three centuries. It also meant the isolation of its philosophers from the rest of the world, since there was censorship preventing the introduction of more up-to-date philosophical ideas stemming from rationalism and empiricism. Some such ideas, however, managed to circulate underground, though most of them were hardly known in the American colonies. Typically, representatives of the Iberian rulers and their local acolytes determined which theories could enter the colonies. But Church officials also played a role in the censorship, as did the vast bureaucracies of local government and the recently established universities.

There was a close relation between the establishment of Scholasticism in the American colonies of Spain and a parallel elimination of the indigenous peoples' worldview. Octavio Paz (1914–1998), a prominent contemporary Mexican thinker and literary figure, has captured this relation well in the following passage:

> The decadence of European Catholicism coincided with its apogee in Spanish America: it spread out over new lands at the very moment it had ceased to be creative. It offered a set philosophy and petrified faith, so that the originality of the new believers found no way of expressing itself . . . . Catholicism offered a refuge to the descendants of those who had seen the extermination of their ruling classes, the destruction of their temples and manuscripts, and the suppression of the superior forms of their culture; but for the same reason that it was decadent in Europe, it denied them any chance of expressing their singularity. (Paz 1961: 105)

Nevertheless, Paz was probably also aware that, in colonial Latin America, some philosophical or scientifically curious intellectuals found their way *out* of Scholasticism. Salient among them was Acosta, whose experience in Peru and Mexico triggered an insightful reflection on how the empirical evidence about the nature of the "New World" differed from what he had learned from his Iberian Scholastic peers. His "History" points out numerous errors in the writings of some of the most esteemed Scholastic authorities of the time, who though trained only in philosophy, had ventured their uninformed opinions about the biogeography and climate of Central and South America. Acosta made clear that, on his view, both of these disciplines involve empirical matters, which as such, are knowable only from experience. Accordingly, he wrote that in matters of that sort "experience should be of more force than all Philosophical demonstrations."

A case in point was the exact shape of the Earth, whose roundness "we who now live in Peru see . . . visibly." In addition, its shape could be inferred from the evidence provided by the crew of Magellan's ship *Victoria*, who first circumnavigated the globe and deserved "the honor and praise to have best discovered" this fact.[7] Acosta also wrote that from his location in Peru, he was able to see the heavens *in a new way*, and that this evidence, together with some accounts of the modern voyages of discovery, led him to believe that the earth is in fact spherical. He appeared to recognize that such a belief would challenge the official opinion of some eminent Doctors of the Church.

Even Aristotle himself came under Acosta's challenge: there was suspicion that "the Philosopher" (i.e., Aristotle) was sometimes mistaken, he boldly noted. He was wrong, for example, in holding that the region between the tropics is a "torrid" or "burning" zone, utterly uninhabitable for humans and nonhumans owing to its extreme heat. Acosta charged that anyone who had actually been in the tropics of America knew of its pleasant climate for any human and nonhuman living things. Challenging Aristotle by counterexample, Acosta charged that this part of the world ("the Antipodes") is "very well peopled and inhabited by men and other sorts of creatures, being a region of all the world the most fruitful of waters and pastures, and very temperate . . . To conclude, we must believe that the burning zone is well inhabited, although the ancients have held it impossible" (Acosta 1604/1590: 4). In addition to providing evidence of the flora

---

[7] Acosta (1604/1590: 4). Note that in the face of powerful foreign opposition, Charles V sponsored the explorer Ferdinand Magellan (Portuguese, ca. 1480–1521), who hypothesized there was a passage from the Atlantic to the Pacific in South America that would enable him to circumnavigate the globe. After finding this passage off Cape Horn on October 21, 1520, in the strait that now bears his name, he made his way up the west coast of South America and then westward into the islands of the South Pacific, only to meet his death there at the hands of native Polynesians. Yet one of his vessels, the *Victoria*, commanded by Juan Sebastián del Cano (Spanish, ca. 1476–1526) completed the voyage on September 6, 1522, thereby accomplishing under the flag of Spain the first circumnavigation of the globe. As evident in Acosta's quote, Acosta took notice of the impact of this achievement for modern geography.

and fauna of America's tropics, Acosta hypothesized (more than a century before the discovery of the Bering Strait) that the natives of the Americas had migrated from Asia. In sum, Acosta did not hesitate to challenge the mainstream view in matters of biogeography and climate. His challenging attitude is explicit even in the many subtitles of his *Historia*, for example those that read

- "That the Heaven is round on all parts, moving in his course of itself"
- "Containing an Answer to that which is objected in the holy Scriptures against the roundness of the earth"
- "Of the fashion and form of Heaven, at the newly found world"
- "The reason why S. Augustine denied the Antipodes"
- "Of Aristotle's opinion touching the new World, and what abused him to make him deny it"
- "Of the opinion which Plato held of the West Indies"
- "That the burning Zone abounds with waters and pastures, against the opinion of Aristotle, who held the contrary[.]"[8]

Note that Acosta was thus taking a huge risk. After all, in the Spain of the Renaissance, largely untouched by the philosophical and scientific innovations of other parts of Europe, the subversive import of his claims was considerable, and the risks were numerous. For one thing, the King might not have given permission for publication of his book (a requirement for publication at the time), the Spanish Inquisition might have censored its contents, and/or he might have been the victim of persecution and punishment. But none of these bad things happened to Acosta, perhaps because in the *Historia* he set some safeguards such as excusing the Scholastic authorities for errors committed as a result of a devotion to issues of "greater importance" concerning theology. As for the ancient philosophers in his list, before objecting to their mistaken beliefs, Acosta somehow excuses them by writing that "whatever the Ancients say or hold … it must not trouble us, for … it is well known and verified that they have not been so studious in the knowledge and demonstrations of Philosophy … " (Acosta, 1604/ 1590: 3).

---

[8] Acosta (1604/1590) book I, chapters 2, 4, 5, 7, 9, and 12, and book II, chapter 6.

1.3 A Metaphysical Challenge: O'Gorman

By the seventeenth century, the Western world had begun a slow but steady change of mind in its assessment of the legacy of Christopher Columbus (Genoese, 1451–1506). His reputation evolved from a widespread condemnation of his treatment of native peoples into the ascription of a hero role as the "discoverer" of America, the "Admiral of the Ocean Sea." Contributing to this change of mind were advances in geographical knowledge, especially regarding the surface of the earth, which enabled Europeans to learn that the so-called New World was in fact a continent distinct from all other land masses on earth. Furthermore, with more than a century of European expansion in America achieved, concerns about the morality of this expansion were giving room to self-interested considerations about the wealth Spain stood to obtain from its colonies. The Western world was open to the claim that Columbus had "discovered" America, even if, as is now known, he died without ever realizing that he had not landed in South Asia, as he thought. But of course we all now know that the basis for the belief that Columbus had discovered America was then as shaky as the basis for Aristotle's belief, in antiquity, that there could be no life in the torrid zone owing to its persistent heat.

Prominent among early challengers of the myth that Columbus had discovered America was Edmundo O'Gorman, a historian and philosopher who explicitly rejected it in his 1960 monograph *The Invention of America*. For O'Gorman, that Columbus discovered America amounts to a misleading legend that was cemented during the nineteenth century through the work of American writer and historian Washington Irving (1783–1859). O'Gorman offered a mix of historical and philosophical reasons for disputing that Columbus had discovered America. But his reason for disputing it involves neither ascribing to another European the role of "discovering" America, nor condemning the myth because of the implicit ethnocentrism in its failure to take into account one momentous fact: that it was during the Encounter of 1492 that Europeans and Amerindians met each other.

O'Gorman, it must be said, had a historian's interest in debunking the Columbus legend, together with an interest in debunking a realist view of the reference of geographical terms such as 'America.' Given O'Gorman's anti-realism about the reference of these terms, they refer to nothing at all except notions that depend on our conceptual framework. Furthermore, what we think actually happened in any historical event, such as the Encounter, depends on how we construe the "facts." Indeed, it may be that there are no "facts" uncontaminated by such interpretations. Persons with very different worldviews may understand the same set of "facts" in completely different ways.

At the same time, O'Gorman's argument against the legend of Columbus' discovery relies heavily on historical evidence that Columbus was unaware of having landed in a "new" continent. There is solid evidence for this claim, stemming chiefly from two early biographies of "the Admiral," one by his son Ferdinand Columbus, the other by Bartolomé de las Casas.[9] In light of this evidence, to say that Columbus 'discovered America' is to shape the facts of 1492 to make them fit an interpretation of them that originated many years later.

Under a straightforward reconstruction, O'Gorman's argument is in fact very plausible. After all, if someone stumbles on a foreign object but has no idea what it is, we would hardly say that such a person has 'discovered' it. We would use *that word* only for someone who had some idea about what that object was. If they do not, then they have merely stumbled into it. That is, the 'discoverer' must be someone who has some awareness of the identity of what has been found. But if Columbus did not discover America, what exactly was his achievement? We know where he landed, but he did not. He thought that he had reached Asia; hence his use of the term 'Indies' to refer to America and his belief that its inhabitants were 'Indians.' His voyage has a certain meaning for us that it did not have for him.

From this historical evidence, O'Gorman concluded that Columbus did not discover America. In addition, he noted that, when introduced, the concept of 'America' was associated with the emerging concept of the 'continent,' which Europeans did not have until modern times. In their conception, the earth consisted of a sole mass of land ('the island of the earth') surrounded by water. On the basis of such data, O'Gorman also concluded that terms such as 'America' denote something that admits only of invention, not discovery (1960/1961: 81–84). Can anything be said

---

[9] The relevant biographies here are *The Life of the Admiral Christopher Columbus: By His Son Ferdinand* (ca. 1500) and *Historia de las Indias* by Bartolomé de las Casas (1550–1563).

for this claim? After all, it conflicts with the ordinary, realist understanding of those objects named by geographical proper names such as 'America,' 'Asia,' and 'Europe.' After all, we ordinarily take them to refer to certain masses of land on the surface of the earth.

To sum up, O'Gorman offered two arguments against the belief that Columbus discovered America. One is a strong argument that can be construed as proceeding from historical evidence concerning Columbus's ignorance about the discovery attributed to him, together with the plausible premise that *to invent* and *to discover* are success verbs and as such they presuppose some awareness by the agents of whatever they discover or invent. Compare the verb *to remember*: no one can remember that P without having awareness that P, and the same is true for other success verbs such as *to know*, *to recall*, *to learn*, and so on. As result, an appeal to a common intuition in philosophy of language about verbs of this sort supports O'Gorman's argument: Columbus neither discovered nor invented America. He stumbled into it.

However, O'Gorman further contends that America could not have been discovered by anyone, simply because it was invented by the Europeans. If so, then it did not exist before its invention. After all, if a thing was invented, then it *did not exist* before the intervention of a certain agent. By contrast, if a thing was discovered, then it did exist all by itself. I have maintained that this argument by O'Gorman, unlike the previous one, challenges ordinary intuitions about the reference of geographical proper names such as 'America,' 'Asia,' and 'Europe.' Since we ordinarily believe that they have certain mind- and language-independent referents, O'Gorman begs the question against this common intuition by assuming without argument that, just as Thomas Edison invented the incandescent bulb, we simply invented America.

1.4   The Upshot

As we have seen, some Thomist philosophers and theologians played an active role in a controversy over the morality of the conquest that took place in Spain and its American colonies during the mid-sixteenth century. Although the participants who objected to the moral justification of the conquest left testimony of their deep concern about the human rights of

Amerindians, the arguments they provided can be easily applied to other European expansions of the time. Those arguments found a receptive audience at the highest levels of the Spanish Court and the Catholic Church.[10] By the seventeenth century, however, Spain was ready to trade philosophical inquiry into what is morally just or right for the benefits of exploiting its American colonies. The Thomists of that century were not able to advance the understanding of human rights, especially the rights of indigenous peoples, beyond the insights already on offer from Vitoria and Las Casas. Vitoria deserves credit for his contribution to practical ethics and political philosophy on the issues of just war and the international rights of nations. His doctrine of just international intervention played a foundational role in the constitution of modern international law. By contrast, Las Casas was a man of action interested in writing only to undo what he rightly considered the great injustice inflicted on the Amerindians by the conquest. But in pursuing this cause, he introduced reflections on a wide variety of topics that have exerted great influence on later thinkers and their doctrines. For example, Simón Bolívar's *mestizaje* theory of Latin American identity (see Chapter 3) and the present-day liberation theology of Gustavo Gutiérrez and others (see Chapter 9). It was natural, of course, that Lascasianism should have an influence on liberation theology, an ongoing theological-philosophical movement that emerged in the 1960s, first among Catholic priests in Latin America and later among members of non-Catholic clergy of the Americas. After all, the liberation theologians have two chief points of agreement with Las Casas. First, they too rely on a version of Thomism that recommends the promotion of any ways of life conducive to human flourishing and the avoidance of those ways of life that undermine it or destroy it. Second, they too have an agenda of sociopolitical change for Latin America, designed to help eliminate the pervasive injustices that undermine the humanity of its peoples, especially of the poor.

In addition to triggering these contributions to practical ethics and political philosophy, the conquest has triggered other philosophical reflections of the sort also considered in this chapter. One was Acosta's empiricist

[10] To my knowledge, this philosophical reflection on the moral status of the European modern expansion was a phenomenon unique to sixteenth-century Spain. No reflection of a comparable dimension took place during that century in Britain, France, or any other colonial power.

reflection on certain consequences of the Iberian geographical explorations of the sixteenth century that bear on the method of science. For the reasons discussed above, his *Natural & Moral History of the Indies* deserves a place in the modern rejection of Thomism in science, its armchair assumptions about the geo-climate of the Southern hemisphere, and its use in science of the obsolete Scholastic method of disputation. Note, however, that in spite of these problems, the prevalent paradigm in Spanish and Portuguese universities remained Thomistic for centuries.

Acosta also acknowledged some facts concerning the Iberian contribution to the modern revolution in cosmography and climatology. These facts are regularly neglected in historical accounts of the philosophy of science, which focus chiefly on the revolution in cosmology and other branches of physics. Prominent among the facts in Acosta's mind were the advances in geographical and climatological knowledge produced by the explorations around the world of Spanish and Portuguese navigators. I have already mentioned the first circumnavigation of the globe completed by the crew of Magellan, a Portuguese navigator who organized the successful expedition under the Spanish flag. But there are many more. Consider for example Vasco da Gama (1469–1524), a Portuguese navigator sponsored by Manuel I of Portugal, who commanded the first fleet of Europeans to reach India by sea (in 1497–1499). And in Spain, of course, the Catholic Monarchs sponsored Columbus, whose voyages of exploration led to important geographical breakthroughs and set the stage for further expeditions to the Americas.

Finally, as discussed in the previous section, O'Gorman might have a good argument for rejecting the traditional belief that Columbus discovered America. But he failed to make a plausible case for the counterintuitive claim that America was instead invented by Europeans. It is plausible that since Columbus had no clue where he was when he landed in America, and died without ever learning it, he stumbled on America, but could not have discovered what he never got to know. After all, as discussed in the section above, 'to discover' is a success verb. But the claim that America was *invented* rather than discovered runs headlong into common-sense realism about the masses of land and water and their distribution on the earth. To say that Europeans have 'made up' the continents is a provocative metaphysical claim, to substantiate which O'Gorman owes us a compelling argument.

1.5 Suggested Readings

Acosta, José de. 1604/1590. *The Natural & Moral History of the Indies*. London: Hakluyt Society.

First published in Seville in 1590 under the title, *Historia Natural y Moral de las Indias*, this "bestseller" was soon to be translated into other languages and now comes with a new English translation (the first since 1604) by Frances Lopez-Morillas (Duke University Press, 2002). In this book, Acosta launched a critique of the Scholastic paradigm that should be understood in the context of the modern scientific revolution.

Canteñs, Bernardo J. 2009. "The Rights of the American Indians," pp. 23–35 in Susana Nuccetelli, Ofelia Schutte, and Otavio Bueno, eds., *Blackwell Companion to Latin American Philosophy*. Oxford: Wiley-Blackwell.

Well-informed survey of the novel work in political morality, human rights, and international jurisprudence carried out by Spanish philosophers and theologians of 'the Second Scholasticism.' This label refers to some prominent academic thinkers who at the time of the conquest grew concerned with those issues. Thomists trained at the universities of Salamanca in Spain and Coimbra in Portugal, they made ample use of the Scholastic method of reasoning. Canteñs takes their central questions to be (i) whether there was a moral justification for the Spaniards to wage war against the Amerindians, and (ii) which rights (if any) might the latter have as persons and as nations. A good source for those curious about how the Scholastic method of disputation works on issues of applied ethics and political philosophy.

Columbus, Christopher. 1960. *The Journal of Christopher Columbus*. New York: C. N. Potter.

One of Christopher Columbus's many diaries. It registers not only some of his deeds but also some of his attitudes and feelings toward the indigenous peoples of the Americas. From it we learn a number of interesting facts, such as that he had sought sponsorship for his "Enterprise of the Indies" in other European countries before obtaining it from Spain, where he finally persuaded the Catholic Monarchs only after eight years of earnest argument. Furthermore, he thought of his project in part as one of expansion of the Christian faith, a kind of sacred war similar to the religious crusades of the Middle Ages and Spain's wars against "infidels." The *Journal* also contains disparaging references to the customs and appearance of the native peoples, strongly illustrating the conflict of values and ways of life created by the modern European expansion. It also supports O'Gorman's thesis that Columbus was unaware of having landed in America.

Fernández Retamar, Roberto. 1989. *Caliban and Other Essays*. Minneapolis: University of Minnesota Press.

Warns against accepting the 'Black Legend,' a spurious sixteenth-century account of the violations of human rights committed during the Spanish conquest. This legend aimed at smearing Spain, and thus at indirectly benefiting the colonialist interests of the British Empire, which were falsely presented as being more humane. But in rejecting this legend Fernández Retamar illustrates a tendency among twentieth-century intellectuals in Latin America to embrace Iberian roots for the region and claim them to be superior to the Anglo-Saxon roots of North America, while neglecting to denounce the moral wrongs of the Iberian conquest. For more on that tendency, see Chapter 7 in this book.

Ford, Thayne R. 1998. "Stranger in a Foreign Land: Jose de Acosta's Scientific Realizations in Sixteenth-Century Peru," *The Sixteenth Century Journal* 29(1): 19–33.

Argues that Acosta's theses in *Historia* are a response to the inconsistency of received Scholastic opinion made with empirical data that he had gathered himself during his stay in Latin America. Although his methods are now obsolete, at the time they produced significant results and deserve credit for their contribution to the modern scientific revolution in the areas of geography and climatology.

Hale, Charles A. 2004. "Edmundo O'Gorman, Mexican National History and the 'Great American Dichotomy,'" *Journal of Latin American Studies* 36(1): 131–145.

Detailed account of O'Gorman's life, views, influences, and polemics. Contends that during his career, O'Gorman opposed an understanding of history along positivist lines and vindicated instead historiographical research that was rooted in philosophy – especially the philosophy of German neo-idealism and phenomenology, introduced in Latin America by Ortega y Gasset. The early O'Gorman became familiar with these movements while studying philosophy in his native Mexico. But O'Gorman's legacy as "a historian of the national experience" is complex and difficult to evaluate. (For O'Gorman's own assessment of it, see Rodríguez de Lecea 1997 and Alvaro Matute 1997.)

Las Casas, Bartolomé de. 1990. *Memorial of Remedies for the Indies*, ed. V. N. Baptiste. Culver City, CA: Labyrinthos,

1992a/1537. *Bartolome de las Casas: The Only Way*, ed. H. Rand Parish. Mahwah, NJ: Paulist Press.

1992b/1542. *A Short Account of the Destruction of the Indies*. London: Penguin.

1993. *Witness: Writings of Bartolomé de las Casas*, ed. George Sanderlin. Maryknoll, NY: Orbis Books.

Classic sources for the applied moral philosophy of Las Casas.

Las Casas, Bartolomé de and Juan Ginés de Sepúlveda. 1994. "Aquí se contiene una disputa o controversia," pp. 372–379 in Jack J. Himelblau, ed., *The Indian in Spanish America: Centuries of Removal, Survival, and Integration*. Lancaster, CA: Labyrinthos (trans. pp. 39–54 in Nuccetelli and Seay 2002).

Best source for Sepúlveda's defense of the moral permissibility of the Spanish conquest. Translation pp. 39–54 in Nuccetelli and Seay (2002).

León-Portilla, Miguel. 2016. "Extending Christendom: Religious Understanding of the Other," pp. 62–76 in Virginia Garrard-Burnett, Paul Freston, and Stephen C. Dove, eds., *The Cambridge History of Religions in Latin America*. New York: Cambridge University Press.

Provides textual evidence that the Spanish friars who participated in the Iberian expansion of the sixteenth century kept a conception of humanity from the Middle Ages, which they mixed with the humanism of the period. At the beginning of that century, many of them had grim and even contradictory views about the rationality of the native peoples of the Americas. But eventually they came to ascribe to them at least "some level" of rationality. Shows that Las Casas's moral evolution toward a conception of Amerindians that was sympathetic to their dignity as persons was not an isolated case, especially among friars of the Dominican order working in the Americas.

Marks, Greg C. 1992. "Indigenous Peoples in International Law: The Significance of Francisco de Vitoria and Bartolomé de las Casas," MA thesis, pp. 131–151 in The Australian Yearbook of International Law. Australia National University. www5.austlii.edu.au/au/journals/AUYrBkIntLaw/1991/1.pdf

Contends that the writings of Las Casas and Vitoria are still relevant to scholars interested in current theories of the rights of the indigenous peoples, even if the assumptions these thinkers had and their context are considerably different from those needed today. Their well-informed analyses can help resolve problems facing the protection of the rights of present-day indigenous peoples around the world.

Medina, Vicente. 2013. "The Innocent in the Just War Thinking of Vitoria and Suárez: A Challenge Even for Secular Just War Theorists and International Law," *Ratio Juris* 26(1): 47–64.

Points out a problem for just-war theorists like Vitoria and Suárez, who held that killing the innocent in a just war was morally wrong, but that punishing them, even with death, *after* a just war was morally permissible. Since Vitoria took Amerindians to illustrate "the innocent," the tension noted in this essay may explain at least in part Vitoria's hesitation to condemn Spain's actions during the conquest.

O'Gorman, Edmundo. 1961/1960. *The Invention of America: An Inquiry into the Historical Nature of the New World and the Meaning of its History*. Bloomington: Indiana University Press.

Best source for the author's arguments discussed in this chapter. For a more plausible anti-realism in the case of art, see his recently translated "Art or Monstrosity," (2017/1960).

Rabossi, Eduardo. 2004. "Notes on Globalization, Human Rights, and Violence," pp. 139–155 in Ricardo J. Gómez (ed.), *The Impact of Globalized Neoliberalism in Latin America: Philosophical Perspectives*. Newbury Park, CA: Hansen House Publishing,

Argues that the current phenomenon of globalization in fact started with the European expansion of the sixteenth century. Although today the "global civil society" might be able to exert some control over the levels of violence generated by that expansion in places such as Latin America, just as in the sixteenth century, it cannot control the prevalence of poverty and malnutrition. These amount to an "indirect" form of violence that continues to undermine the protection of human rights in the region.

Talbot, William. *Which Rights Should Be Universal?* Oxford: Oxford University Press, 2005.

Contains a chapter entirely devoted to Las Casas's moral evolution as evident in his change of mind about the *encomienda* (also discussed above). Talbot frames that moral evolution in terms of the Rawlsian notion of reflective equilibrium.

Todorov, Tzvetan. 1992. *The Conquest of America: The Question of the Other*. New York: Harper Torch.

Interesting narrative about the Europeans' "discovery" of America and the "other." Focused mostly on the figure of Christopher Columbus, it questions the standard account of Columbus's motives while portraying him as an ambivalent figure who was at once a religious fanatic and a modern explorer. Given his religious fundamentalism, the goal of his explorations was to wage a crusade. But given his modern ambitions, he was willing to engage in the discovery of anything "other" – from lands to plants. Like Columbus, other *conquistadors* were transitional figures with one foot in the world of medieval values conducive to, for example, imposing their own religion on others, and the other foot in the world of modern values such as those fueling quests for wealth and fame.

2   Modest and Immodest Feminism

Machismo (from *macho*, literally, 'male'), the standard term in Latin America for *male chauvinism*, refers to a pervasive bias that permeates the cultures of the region. There is a long history of talented women whose lives and careers have been impeded or even destroyed by this bias. Most famous, of course, is the case of Juana Inés de la Cruz (Mexican, 1651–1695), whose pioneer affirmation of the rights of women is one of the topics of this chapter. But many other women in the intellectual history of the region have encountered *machismo*, for example, Clorinda Matto de Turner (Peruvian, 1852–1909), Alfonsina Storni (Argentinean, 1892–1938), and Frida Kahlo (Mexican, 1907–1954). In 1945 the Chilean poet Gabriela Mistral (1914–1957) became the first Latin American to win the Nobel Prize for Literature, but she was well aware that many other talented Latin American women writers had never been recognized in their life-times for their work. And there can be little doubt that that was owing to the widespread bias of *machismo*.

The antidote to *machismo* is, and has been, an equal-rights type of femin-ism, both as a practice and as a philosophical inquiry traditionally falling within the scope of moral and political philosophy. The last thirty years, however, have seen the rise of more ambitious types of feminism in these and other branches of philosophy. In what follows, I group these different aspirations of feminists into two categories: modest and immodest femin-ism. I call 'modest' any feminist philosophical inquiry whose claims fall within the scope of moral and social and political philosophy because they aim chiefly at vindicating the equal worth of women and men. And I call 'immodest feminism' any feminist inquiry whose claims have wider scope, from ethics and political philosophy to symbolic logic, epistemology, and so forth. Although modest feminist theories qualified originally as quite radical, today they seem moderate by comparison with the immodest theories, which advocate for radical social change to accommodate the distinctiveness of women. Both groups of feminist theories are well represented in the Americas.

2.1 *Machismo* **Defined**

As I construe *machismo*, it turns out to be a special case within a family of harmful moral misconceptions best construed by adapting Peter Singer's definition of the bias of speciesism. Thus construed:

> *Machismo* is a type of sexism in Latin America according to which men have greater normative worth than women.
>   Sexism is a bias affecting any action, omission, or psychological state that can be associated with the content that sex determines normative worth.

The sort of normative worth at stake here concerns chiefly moral and rational categories. But it may also designate other kinds of normativity such as epistemic, scientific, or artistic. *Machismo* and other kinds of sexism manifest themselves in people's actions and psychological attitudes, which include beliefs and other cognitive attitudes as well as desires and other noncognitive attitudes. As the literature on social bias suggests, a bias can be explicit or implicit depending on whether or not the agent consciously embraces it.

Given that morality provides some of the most authoritative reasons for action and attitude, *machismo* is best construed in terms of moral worth. Furthermore, the notion of *moral worth* is particularly relevant to feminist issues, since to say that a being has moral worth is to say that it has moral standing. When a being or thing has moral worth, there is a duty to treat it with a certain consideration. This duty may range from preventing harm to providing certain benefits. Although some nonhumans may have some moral worth (e.g., whales or the Grand Canyon), anything that qualifies for personhood has *full* moral worth, which is sometimes called 'dignity.'[1]

---

[1] As usually noted in discussions of moral worth, the concepts 'person' and 'human' must not be conflated since not all persons might be humans (e.g., intelligent aliens if there are any) and not all humans might have full personhood (e.g., the controversial cases of fetuses, the permanently unconscious, and the severely cognitively impaired).

A culture dominated by *machismo* is a male-centered culture where women are not granted full moral worth, and thus, not granted full personhood or dignity. A culture of this sort may treat women as mere means, directly harm them, deny them equal opportunity, assign to them subservient roles, and so on. There is abundant evidence that *machismo* has had such consequences in Latin America. Among contemporary philosophers who noticed this phenomenon in the early 1970s is Enrique Dussel, for whom *machismo* took hold of the region with the arrival of the Iberian conquerors, because before this event "[t]he Aztecs, Chibchas, Incas and almost all the Tupi-Guarani were matrilineal but not matriarchal" (1973b: 92). By contrast, the conquerors assumed that the father is at the origin of everything and considered Spain their fatherland (not their motherland). Although Dussel does not provide historical evidence for his claim about the origin of *machismo*, it is plausible that this bias has its historic roots in the Spanish conquest. After all, it is well documented that the Spanish conquerors behaved as if they had an entitlement over the native women, whom they treated as instruments.[2] The relationship between Hernán Cortés (1495–1547), the Spaniard who successfully invaded Mexico, and Doña Marina or 'La Malinche,' one of twenty Amerindian women presented to him as human "gifts," counts as evidence of the onset of *machismo* that Dussel seems to have in mind. La Malinche traveled with Cortés as his companion and translator of the native languages – thus becoming instrumental in the fall of the Aztecs and ultimately of Mexico itself to the hands of the Spaniards (Townsend 2006). Among feminists in Latin America, the case of La Malinche has achieved a certain iconic status as an illustration of the subservient roles assigned to women during the Iberian conquest and colonization of Latin America.

Ingrained in colonial culture, *machismo* survived under different guises in later periods and is still felt today. To illustrate present-day *machismo*, Dussel rightly points to evidence from popular culture, in particular from the Argentinean music genre and dance known as 'tango.' The tango is a good illustration of twentieth-century *machismo* because its lyrics typically portray upper-class men "taking" lower-class women, who willingly accept

---

[2] Columbus left abundant evidence of this sense of entitlement in his diaries, where he often referred to the native women he encountered as if they were indeed animals. In his *Journal* (1960: 200), for example, he wrote that his men "brought seven head of women, small and large, and three children."

exchanging sexual favors for improvements in their socioeconomic status. In addition, the traditional rules for dancing the tango allow only men to lead.[3] But there are countless other manifestations of *machismo* in present-day Latin American society – for example, the high degree of violence against women and the subservient roles assigned to them.

2.2 Modest Feminism

2.2.1 Juana Inés de la Cruz's Proto-Modest Feminism

2.2.1.1 *Life and Work*

Just as Acosta embraced empiricism in the course of critically assessing some dominant doctrines of the colonial period, in the seventeenth century Juana Inés de la Cruz advanced feminist views in the course of challenging some prevalent biases affecting nuns and more generally women during the same historical period.[4] Often referred to simply as 'Sor (Sister) Juana' and 'Juana Inés,' this self-educated Mexican nun achieved great celebrity as a poet and playwright of the Spanish Baroque artistic movement in Latin America. Sor Juana's plays were well known in the intellectual circles of colonial Mexico and her poetry was published in Spain.[5] But the success

---

[3] In explaining how women come to accept unjust treatment in society, Dussel in fact engages in a bit of armchair social psychology: "All this starts with the education a woman receives as a child. The male is encouraged to fight his way bravely upward, whereas the female is encouraged to play with dolls. Right from the beginning she is trained to be alienated for her future husband. Her whole acculturation brings her to this point. What then is a woman?" (Dussel 1973b: 94).

[4] Born in San Miguel Nepatlan, in 1651, Juana Inés de Asbaje y Ramírez de Cantillana grew up on a farm in the south of Mexico, the child of a woman who seems to have been quite independent, since she had several children out of wedlock and ran the farm on her own. When Juana Inés was still a girl of about ten, her mother took up with a man and sent her to live with her grandfather in Mexico City. But this turn of events appears to have been fortunate in the end, for according to Sor Juana (De la Cruz 1988/1691) her grandfather had a library where she could satisfy an intellectual curiosity that, as she acknowledged, would have been unusual in any child of her age, but especially so in a girl. After responding to the reprimand of Bishop Fernández, she abandoned any secular pursuits.

[5] The recognition of Sor Juana's talent increased after her death. To this day, it is the object of praise in the Spanish-American world and beyond. It is not uncommon for her achievements to be celebrated by referring to her as 'the Tenth Muse,' 'the Phoenix of

that matters to us here belongs to the secular arts: this brought her respect as a feminist thinker and also ultimately elicited a reprimand from her confessor and some religious superiors that ended her career as both a literary writer and a philosophical thinker. Plotting against her, a development we will consider in what follows, high-ranking officials of the Catholic Church in Mexico City objected to her intellectual pursuits on the grounds that they were inconsistent with the religious commitments of a nun.

Sor Juana responded to these objections in two of her writings, the *Autodefensa Espiritual* (*Spiritual Self-Defense*), a letter of about 1681 that remained unpublished until recently, and the "Respuesta a Sor Filotea" ("Reply to Sor Philotea"), a short essay that she published before renouncing her intellectual and literary pursuits. The letter was written to end her relationship with her confessor, while the essay was a rejoinder to an objection to her pursuits by a "Sor Philosotea de la Cruz," who was in fact Manuel Fernández de Santa Cruz, the Bishop of Puebla. In these documents Sor Juana offered a defense of her secular pursuits by referring to some facts about her life, together with some general premises about women's rights to knowledge and an education. She argued that her own case shows that women can learn and excel at such practices as much as men, and therefore deserve an equal opportunity to do so. In response to the charge that she had engaged in pursuits unsuitable for a nun, she provided biographical details explaining how her passion for empirical science and the humanities had developed over many years as a natural curiosity that was too strong to suppress. During her childhood, she declared in the "Respuesta" (p. 210), instead of playing with dolls, she had been interested in reading and writing from the age of three. Later, she had learned Latin by means of a few lessons, and even contemplated trying to attend the university disguised as a man. When that scheme failed, she had to content herself with being an autodidact, a project in which she achieved great success.[6]

Mexico,' and other such epithets. See for instance, Alfonso Reyes, *The Position of America* (New York: Alfred A. Knopf, 1950).

[6] In her "Respuesta," Sor Juana also noted that she learned facts about the natural world through reflection on her own sensory experiences, for instance, while cooking. Or that even during a period when doctors prescribed that she avoid reading books, nothing could stop her intellectual curiosity, which was aroused by the experience of nature

The "Respuesta" also describes her decision to enter the cloistered life of a religious order, thinking that the rigorous demands of convent life would distract her from her 'temptation' to study. In this, however, she was mistaken, for the order of nuns with which she finally settled allowed her ample time for study, at least at first.[7] These were the nuns of the Convent of Santa Paula, who provided her with an environment suitable for continuing her intellectual and literary pursuits. Sor Juana had with her her own collection of books, one of the finest libraries in Mexico at the time, which she amassed throughout her life. Later she sold them, under pressure from her superiors. The rules of this order similarly presented no impediment to Sor Juana's social life. Although they required her to participate in the community's religious ceremonies and perform a communal service (in her case, keeping the convent's financial records), she could remain in her cell most of the time. But this "cell" was no dank monastic chamber with a cot and crucifix but rather a private apartment with various rooms where she could study, take her meals, and receive visitors. She often entertained high-ranking visitors, including the viceroy of Mexico and his wife, who were the official representatives of the King in the viceroyalty of New Spain, a vast colonial domain with its capital in Mexico City. She also presided over animated *tertulias*, or literary salons, often frequented by intellectuals and prominent figures of the local society.

These details about Sor Juana's life at the convent support the hypothesis that, from Sor Juana's perspective, joining the nuns had little to do with religious devotion, and more with pursuing her secular talents by the only means available to her in the circumstances (Paz 1988). After all, being an illegitimate daughter with no dowry, she had no future at the Mexican court of the vice-regina, the Marquise of Mancera, from which she resigned to enter the convent at age sixteen. In spite of her known talents, without a dowry she did not qualify for a marriage of the kind that might have

---

itself. Applying reason to the sensory data acquired by observation, she then managed nonetheless to learn about nature without the aid of books.

[7] In 1667 Sor Juana entered the order of Discalced Carmelites but the obligations of monastic life in that convent were more severe than she had anticipated, and three months later she returned to live at the court of the Viceroy's wife in Mexico City. Two years later she again took vows, this time in the less severe order of St. Jerome, remaining there until her death in 1695.

allowed her to pursue her interests. Of course, Sor Juana was well aware that the ecclesiastical authorities regarded her scholarly interests and secular writing as unseemly in a woman, and worse yet in a nun. She later recounted in the "Respuesta" an episode in which reading books was declared off-limits to her by a local prelate. But no ban on studying, it seems, could stop her inherent impulse toward reflection, and without texts to occupy her attention, she turned to the simple observation of everyday phenomena – while cooking, while conversing with her sisters in the order, while watching children play with their toys. By means of observing the ordinary workings of things, she could learn even without reading books. On the other hand, in her "Respuesta" she also appealed to cases from the Bible and classical antiquity of women who had distinguished themselves by their wisdom and learning. The assumption here is that her efforts might not be censured by the Church if they could be framed within the tradition of Western thought. Sadly, she was to be disappointed in this, for she had powerful enemies in the hierarchy of the Church in Mexico. Ultimately, she was silenced and forced to give up her study entirely. Driven into a forced seclusion, she died during an outbreak of the plague. But her writings remained eloquent defenses of a woman's right to knowledge and an education. As such, they are among the first expressions of feminist writing in Latin America and beyond. But what kind of feminism do they defend? Before addressing this question, let us outline the plot that led to her sad end.

2.2.1.2   The Plot and the Arguments

Sor Juana's circle of acquaintances in Mexico included Manuel Fernández de Santa Cruz, the Bishop of Puebla. Octavio Paz (1988: 389–410) and other critics who have been attracted to the figure of Sor Juana have ventured some hypotheses about the Bishop's role in a plot that led to her downfall. On Paz's hypothesis it unfolded this way: first, Bishop Fernández encouraged Sor Juana to publish a letter, the "Carta Antenagórica," which almost certainly would have provoked the extremely conservative new Archbishop of Mexico, Francisco Aguiar y Seijas. According to Paz, Bishop Fernández resented that it was Aguiar y Seijas and not himself who had recently been appointed to the Archbishop position. Be that as it may,

Bishop Fernández published the "Carta," in which Sor Juana took issue with an obscure Scholastic philosopher who was well regarded by Aguiar y Seijas. More specifically, she objected to a sermon that the Portuguese scholar Antonio de Vieyra, of the Jesuit order, had presented some forty years earlier.[8] A great storm ensued, at least in part because Bishop Fernández himself under a pen name ('Sor Philotea de la Cruz') included in the same publication his admonishment of Sor Juana. Fully aware of the identity of 'Sor Philotea,' Sor Juana set out to write a rejoinder, the "Respuesta," in which once again she advocated that the full moral worth of women be acknowledged and that their corresponding rights to education, learning, and to engage in other secular practices be recognized. She offered reasons of two kinds: autobiographical particular reasons of the sort illustrated above, and general reasons for considering such practices morally permissible. Her autobiographical reasons suggests a strong but modest argument that applies to Sor Juana and any woman with inclinations relevantly similar to hers. This argument runs as follows:

1. I cannot help my interest in learning and knowledge.
2. *Therefore* it is permissible for me as well as for any other similarly situated women to engage in learning and knowledge.

Assuming the plausible Kantian rule that 'ought' implies 'can,' any person who truly cannot refrain from doing something is under *no* moral obligation to omit doing it. If a woman cannot refrain from engaging in the practices of learning and knowledge, it follows that she is under *no* moral obligation to refrain from engaging in these practices. In the "Respuesta," Sor Juana made a case for her inability to abstain from learning and

---

[8] Since it was known in Sor Juana's circles that Archbishop Aguiar y Seijas sympathized with Vieyra's Scholastic views in philosophy and theology, by offering some arguments against Vieyra her "Carta" indirectly criticized the Archbishop. Its central argument objects to a sermon of Vieyra about how to interpret Christ's advice to the apostles that they should love one another as he had loved them. Contra Vieyra, Sor Juana argued that Christ's greatest *fineza* (proof of love, or benefaction) had been to refrain from interfering with human volition, so that individuals might exercise their free will. The polemic, framed in Scholastic terms, addresses an issue that was of little interest for philosophers of the time. Furthermore, her objection to Vieyra would have been outdated, since he had given the targeted sermon forty years earlier and had by now left Portugal for Brazil, where he probably never learned of her "Carta."

knowledge by appeal to the autobiographical, anecdotal evidence mentioned above. She recalled numerous episodes of her life, suggesting that it was in her very nature to be curious about almost any discipline, and that this consuming hunger for knowledge was something she had been unable to avoid since childhood.

But Sor Juana also went beyond particular reasons of this sort to invoke cases in the history of Western thought that might support more general conclusions about women's rights. This line of reasoning differs from the argument above since it maintains:

1. There is a long and varied history of women who have shown a capacity for learning and knowledge analogous to that of men.
2. The cases of those women illustrate capacities generally present in women.
3. People with relevantly similar capacity for learning and knowledge have an equal right to engage in these practices.
4. Therefore, women have an equal right to engage in learning and knowledge.

Assuming a compelling rejection of *machismo*, defined as above, once you establish empirically that women's and men's capacities for learning and knowledge do not differ significantly, it follows from the other premises in this argument that women and men have an equal right to these intellectual activities. In the "Respuesta," Sor Juana strove to produce that evidence by appeal to real and fictional examples of women in history whose intellectual capacities were widely recognized.[9]

Bishop Fernández's admonishment of Sor Juana targeted the engagement in secular pursuits of women in general, and of nuns in particular. It considered any such engagement a sign of arrogance. But Sor Juana held fast to her defense of the right of women to secular education. If the reprimand by Bishop Fernández is not enough evidence that Sor Juana

[9] Sor Juana also offered a rhetorical argument according to which the view in the reprimand that a nun should devote herself to religious issues assumes that she had the general ability to understand such issues. That was too much to assume in her case, since she might be among those unable to comprehend the mysteries of revealed religion. Yet in the context of the general tone of the "Respuesta," this line of argument is nothing more than the expression of false modesty on the part of Sor Juana.

was under pressure from high-ranking officials in the Mexican Church, here is an eloquent paragraph from the letter sent to her confessor, Antonio Núñez of the Society of Jesus, in which she contends,

> My studies have not been to the harm or detriment of any person, having been so extremely private that I have not even enjoyed the direction of a teacher, but have learned only from myself and my work, for I am not unaware that to study publicly in schools is not seemly for a woman's honor ... [B]ut private and individual study, who has forbidden that to women? Like men, do they not have a rational soul? Why then shall they not enjoy the privilege of the enlightenment of letters?[10]

Eventually abandoned by her confessor and friends, Sor Juana finally submitted to the discipline of her superiors and abandoned her intellectual and literary activities altogether. She also sold her books and passed her days in quiet seclusion, completely devoted to the religious and communal practices of her convent. When an epidemic of plague struck, she contracted it while helping to nurse the sick and died at the age of forty-four. But what might have been Sor Juana's motivation to write the "Carta" that started all this? Plausibly, as Octavio Paz suggests, that the new Archbishop of Mexico had made enemies in Sor Juana and her friend, the Bishop of Puebla.[11] What is still puzzling is that her "Carta Antenagórica" appeared in print preceded by Bishop Fernández's reprimand. Was he betraying Sor Juana by publishing her *Carta* without her consent? Had they both staged the whole episode to humiliate the Archbishop of Mexico City? We may never know the answer to these questions.

Although in the context of present-day feminism, the intrigue leading to Sor Juana's downfall makes little sense, it is unquestionable that her defense of women's rights earned her a place within equal-rights feminism. Even if moderate today, this type of feminism was quite radical at her time.

---

[10] Sor Juana's "The Letter," included in Paz (1988: 498).

[11] Sor Juana had a number of reasons to dislike Francisco Aguiar y Seijas, the new Archbishop of Mexico. For one thing, it was common knowledge at the time that this man disliked women, avoided any contact with them, and disapproved of women's involvement in intellectual practices. Furthermore, she had authored two plays, *The Truth of a Household* and *The Greater Labyrinth is Love*, and it was common knowledge in her circles that he opposed the literary genre of drama.

Another type of Latin American modest feminism is the topic taken up next.

2.2.2   Roxana Kreimer's Scientific Feminism

2.2.2.1   *The Case against Hegemonic Feminism*

A right is an entitlement that creates in others a strong duty to honor some interest of the right-holder. Although a human right is a modern concept, by Sor Juana's time the concept of a natural right was already well entrenched in philosophy and the law. It had its roots in Roman jurisprudence and had been incorporated into ethics in the Middle Ages by way of natural law theory. By the seventeenth and eighteenth centuries, natural rights were important concepts in reasoning about how law and civil society must be organized. Having a right to something was already equated with having a strong claim that created in other people the legal or moral duty to honor that right by either performing, or refraining from performing certain actions. Commonly recognized as rights were claims to life, liberty, and property. With the emergence of liberal democracies in the West, the state and positive law acquired the function of protecting those rights. In this way they evolved into legal rights codified in documents such as the American *Bill of Rights* and the French *Declaration of the Rights of Man*.[12] Together with freedom of speech and religion, they are paradigm negative rights, which are the rights to be left alone or not to be interfered with. By contrast, positive rights count as entitlements of the right-holder to be provided with something – for example, healthcare or an education. If Sor Juana had a negative right to express her objections to Antonio de Vieyra in the "Carta," her superiors failed to honor their duty of forbearance toward her (i.e., of not interfering with her free expression). But if she

---

[12] As standardly observed, moral rights must not be conflated with legal rights. While the former are taken to have universal authority, the latter are a more geographically local product of legislative enactment, civil decree, or case law. Legal rights require no grounding in moral rights, nor moral in legal. Rather, the two types may be seen as different kinds of rights in systems parallel to each other but each substantially independent, thereby allowing the system of moral rights to serve as a basis for questioning existing conventions of legal rights or, alternatively, providing them with a rational defense.

had a positive right to an education, others had a duty to provide her with it – for example, the government, by allowing her access to institutions of education.[13]

Contemporary modest feminists such as Roxana Kreimer are in full agreement with Sor Juana on the claim that, if women and men have the same right-engendering capacity, they must have the same moral rights grounded in that capacity.[14] Let's take this to be a core thesis of modest feminism, a position that we can now characterize as follows:

> Modest feminism: Whenever women are equal to men in some right-engendering capacity, they are morally entitled to have the same rights, whether these be negative or positive rights.

Sor Juana and Kreimer both vindicate women's rights to free speech, knowledge, and education. But while Sor Juana emphasized the common humanity of women and men, Kreimer invokes recent developments in Darwinian biology and the social sciences to contend that there are some significant differences between women and men that explain and may even morally justify certain inequalities. Based on scientific data gathered during the last twenty years, Kreimer proposes a kind of empirical feminism that is consistent with the equal-rights feminism I have ascribed to Sor Juana but conflicts with a family of feminisms that now prevail in the university curriculum. Kreimer calls these feminisms "hegemonic" and rejects them on the ground that (1) they are pseudoscientific and (2) they put at risk the fight for equal rights for women and men. These feminisms are pseudoscientific because their proponents fall mostly into one of the following groups: they are professionals in the social sciences with no background knowledge in biology, or biologists with no background knowledge in the social sciences (of course, they could also be philosophers with background knowledge in neither). Since Kreimer doubted the

---

[13] Negative rights are generally considered more stringent than positive rights, because the duties they create in others are more easily fulfilled: they may be discharged just by refraining from acting – that is, by doing nothing. But there is some controversy about this.

[14] See Luiza Lopes Franco Costa et al. (2019); Kreimer (n.d., a and b), and the articles listed on Kreimer's website *Feminismo científico*, https://feminismocientific.wixsite.com/misitio.

veracity of the academic feminists' claims about the consequences of male chauvinism in Argentina and elsewhere, she gathered a fact-checking team whose data turned out to be bad news for the academic feminists – to whom she refers as "hegemonic" feminists. In addition to the falsity of their claims, Kreimer believes that they implicitly have either an irrationalist or relativist metaphysical conception of what there is. Be that as it may, she is correct in noticing that hegemonic feminism chiefly gravitates in institutions of higher education, a fact also noticed by Robert Almeder (1994) in his discussion of contemporary feminism in the United States. In any event, as I read Kreimer's scientific feminism, it has two building blocks: a critique of academic feminism, and a theory of the rights of women that is skeptical about the common belief that women's interests are not considered equal to men's. Its skepticism about the inequities facing women today rests on empirical data from the social sciences. From these data, Kreimer concludes that there is no proof of discrimination against women today since, for example, the representation of each sex in high-status or salaried positions appears to be proportional to that of each sex in non-high-status or salaried positions in the same area. Furthermore, according to Kreimer, some theories of evolutionary biology and scientific psychology suggest that women are less inclined to consider competitive jobs because they have a genetic preference for motherhood and jobs that involve relationships with others. They are also less inclined on average to prefer impersonal jobs and jobs that are at odds with these preferences because of their location or schedule. These facts fit well with cognitive and evolutionary psychologists' belief that we are born with certain innate tendencies and some group preferences are adaptations. A likely example of such a preference, Kreimer holds, is the higher "competitive nature of men in the search for status, a feature that from the perspective of evolution has increased their reproductive success."[15]

The other building block of scientific feminism also aims at undermining academic feminism by charging that this set of doctrines neglects to take into account the violations of the rights of men in Argentina, and by

[15] In "Evidencias en contra del 'techo de cristal,'" Kreimer (n.d., b) also contends that "among the lower status jobs there is also a male overrepresentation, so if we average the job positions of all men and women, it is likely that women's status on average is slightly higher than men's" (p. 1, my translation).

extension, the rest of the Western world. Kreimer alleges that, compared with women, men suffer a number of injustices, including:

1. A shorter life span;
2. A higher incidence of death by suicide and murder;
3. A higher incidence of substance abuse;
4. A greater number of work and car accidents;
5. A lower chance of completing their education;
6. A later retirement age;
7. A higher inequality before the law, as reflected in sentences involving child custody, false accusations of sexual misconduct, longer sentences for the same crime, and less credibility reporting domestic abuse.

2.2.2.2   Evaluating Scientific Feminism

I believe that although Kreimer should be credited for her appeal to scientific evidence, her objection to academic feminisms becomes an *ignoratio elenchi* when it draws attention to the rights of men – which are not at issue in the debate about the rights of women. Furthermore, there is room to reject the moral relevance of some of the injustices faced by men in Kreimer's list, especially those concerning their shorter life span, which are quite weighty given the special value of life and the badness of death. Compared with the value of other goods, life's value is more basic than, say, the value of paid leave and education, since plainly these are of no use to the dead. On this matter, Kreimer's contention faces two major problems. She first conflates an inequality with an inequity (i.e., an unjust inequality), and second, presents only the hard data that help support her *ignoratio elenchi*. Let's consider each of these problems in turn.

First, not all inequalities are inequities. There is consensus in social and political philosophy that only some inequalities amount to injustices. That in most countries women live longer than men on average is an inequality, but it falls short of being an *inequity* and is therefore morally *irrelevant*. No equal right has been violated, no correlative duty arises for society. Why? Because the unequal longevity between men and women is not a controllable factor and in matters of morality, ought implies can.

Second, given that health is especially valuable because some level of it is necessary for having a decent opportunity to pursue one's goals in life, if something could be done to improve the high level of morbidity among women, a failure to do it would be a serious moral wrong. Kreimer notes that women on average live longer than men, but neglects to mention the greater incidence of morbidity among women. Longevity does not equate in their case with better health. As shown by solid data provided by the World Health Organization, the global burden of ill-health falls mostly on women.[16] *Controllable* factors concerning unequal access to information, healthcare, and basic health practices have led to a higher incidence among women of suffering from physical and sexual violence, sexually transmitted diseases (STDs), and HIV/AIDs, as well as malaria and pulmonary disease. In 2009, bioethicist Ruth Macklin gathered data showing that:

1. Reproductive and sexual ill-health accounted for 20 percent of the global burden of ill-health for women compared with 14 percent for men.
2. Half a million women, 99 percent of whom are from developing countries, die every year of preventable causes.
3. In developing countries, the total disease burden of STD and HIV/AIDS was 8.9 percent for women and 1.5 percent for men.

Consistent with these data, other surveys point to striking differences in the distribution of morbidity, not only between men and women but also between developed and developing regions of the world. Factors causing these inequities include female genital cutting, men's refusal to have protected sex, women's vulnerability to violence, restrictions on abortion and contraception, and poor healthcare infrastructures, especially for assisting women during pregnancy and childbirth. Unlike some of the inequalities cited by Kreimer, these do seem unjust because they all originate in economic, social, or cultural factors that are controllable. This objection does not, of course, entail that men face none of the "injustices" on her list. She might be right that, for example, on average men receive longer sentences than women for the same crimes. If so, their rights to equality before the

---

[16] World Health Organization, 2011, "10 Facts about Women's Health," www.who.int /features/factfiles/women/en/.

law are indeed violated, and they have a strong legal and moral claim that must be honored. But even so, Kreimer's appeal to men's rights against immodest feminism still misses the point. Yet I agree that immodest feminism, a set of feminist doctrines now prevalent in academic settings, must be rejected on philosophical grounds, to which I now turn.

2.3   Immodest Feminism

2.3.1   Ofelia Schutte's Liberationist Feminism

On the issue of the moral wrongness of *machismo*, modest and immodest feminists are in full agreement. Feminists of both types may even accept a conditional version of the formal principle of justice discussed above, according to which *if* women and men are sufficiently alike in a characteristic that is moral-right conferring, then they have the same right conferred by that characteristic. But unlike the modest feminists, the immodest feminists contend that women differ from men in many normatively relevant characteristics. Thus, the modest and immodest feminists hold doctrines that cannot be both true, though they could both be false. Although immodest feminists subscribe to many different philosophical persuasions, we can construe their core doctrines as holding that

a. Women are inherently different from men in ways relevant not only to morality but also to other normative domains such as knowledge, the method of science, and logic.
b. Male chauvinism, of which *machismo* is its Latin American variety, cannot be eliminated unless the region undergoes some drastic social, economic, and political changes.

Given (a), there is a strong reason for thinking that women can and must develop their own perspectives in ethics, epistemology, and other branches of philosophy as well as in science. In the United States, a claim of this sort is central to, for example, care ethics (Gilligan 1982, Noddings 1984, Held 1993). Its proponents regard the impartialist view of major ethical theories as resulting from a male-dominated perspective that should be rejected because it ignores the partialism that is typical of the ethical perspective of women. On the alternative view of care ethicists, what matters most to women in making ethical decisions and judgments are not considerations about what is most just or rational from an agent-neutral perspective, but certain agent-relative considerations regarding the self and its relationships. Be that as it may, of concern to us are some Latin American feminists whose philosophical doctrines turn out to be more radical than those of the care ethicists, since in addition to doctrine (a) above, they also hold theses consistent with (b). If these doctrines are on the right track, whole areas of philosophical inquiry such as social and political philosophy and epistemology would be reduced to practical issues of political advocacy – or so I will show by looking closely at the liberationist feminisms of Ofelia Schutte and Enrique Dussel.

A close look at the "liberationist feminism" of Ofelia Schutte (Cuban American, b. 1945) can provide abundant textual evidence that such is *in fact* the result sought by the Latin American immodest feminists.[17] Schutte regards her proposal as one of practical feminist philosophy that is suitable for Latin America because it can free the region from the bias of male chauvinism that, on her view, is the effect of "Euro-/Anglo-centric privilege." For anyone receptive to these claims, she recommends the adoption of the following approach:

> To proceed, then, first, one would look for a critical conception of knowledge. Second, one would look, if not for an explicit, at least for an implicit move to connect theory and practice. Third, one would take into account the ways in which the methods support a generally progressive project of liberation (which is a way of restating the two former points). Fourth, and perhaps most importantly, at stake in employing these methods is the enacting of a transformative politics of culture. (Schutte 2011a: 791)

To get this liberationist feminist program in epistemology off the ground, Schutte adopts a strategy not at all unfamiliar within academic settings in North America. Schutte makes clear that her strategy requires interdisciplinarity (i.e., it is not limited to philosophy) and practical activism (i.e., it is not limited to gaining knowledge but aims at effecting radical social change). Let us now consider the steps she suggests in the above quote for the development of such a liberationist, feminist agenda. The first step quoted above is

---

[17] Schutte (1998, 2011a). For an overview of a number of immodest feminisms in Latin American philosophy, see Stephanie Rivera Berruz (2018).

epistemic, since it concerns the development of a conception of knowledge with these two features: it is feminist, and characteristically Latin American. It must therefore be a conception sensitive to the Latin American context on the issues at hand while avoiding male-centered and "Euro-/Anglo-centric" values. Regarding the feminism part of Schutte's proposal, she believes that neither a standard postmodernist conception nor a positivist's conception of knowledge can be of use because each rests on values of those kinds.[18] Although positivism in Latin America had beneficial effects in terms of promoting higher education for women, Schutte states, it has also helped to preserve "the venerated maternal role of women in the home" and has "privileged Western constructs of knowledge over indigenous and Afro-descendant thought, thereby reinforcing the ideology of Eurocentrism as a necessary component of progress" (ibid). Her alternative conception of knowledge, vaguely identified as consisting of "critical social theory and post-structuralist approaches," has no such shortcomings (ibid.: 792). Yet beyond hammering the point that her proposal avoids the biases of *machismo*, racism, ethnocentrism, and so on, Schutte provides *no* details about her conception. As a result, the proposal seems more an ideological call for action than a piece of philosophical reflection, a perception that is reinforced by her use of emotive language – as evident in her quote of a passage by Nelly Richard that reads, "Latin America now appears as a margin demanding attention, it is up to Latin Americans and, in this case, Latin American feminists to insert their voices into these new openings."[19]

[18] What Schutte defines as positivism is in fact a caricature made up of stereotypes about this important philosophical movement in Latin America. For she construes it as "the view that there are a certain number of positive, observable or scientifically verifiable facts in the world, and that the role of knowledge is to accumulate and order them in such a way as to reach hypotheses with predictable and efficacious outcomes, which in turn will lead to new facts subject to the ongoing processes of observation, gathering of new hypotheses, testing, and application for maximum efficiency and utility" (2011a: 791). Cf. Chapter 5 of this book.

[19] Schutte (2011a: 793). Note that in including this quote from Richard, Schutte does not follow her own recommendation that, in developing any Latin American conception of knowledge it is better to avoid outside views – or in her own words, "strong precautions must be taken when importing and applying theories from the global North to the global South" (p. 796). Here is another example, featuring Schutte herself making use of emotive language: "This is a region of the world where freedom has been as much curtailed and destroyed as it has been fought for and enacted" (2011a: 797).

Since emotions generally fall short of counting as philosophical reasons, the feminist epistemology of Schutte's proposal remains without any philosophical support. What about her grounds for the claim that liberationist feminism must have a conception of knowledge that is characteristically Latin American? They amount to a feminist variety of Leopoldo Zea's perspectivism, which in Chapter 10 of this book I show to be quite shaky. And Schutte's attempt to support it fails because it consists in an appeal to weak anecdotal evidence: namely, an episode during an academic seminar in Ecuador on "queer studies" during which the participants were able to "resignify the notions and give them new names linked to local experiences" (Schutte 2011a: 796). They allegedly did so by using the Spanish term *transfeminista* for 'queer' so that 'queer studies' became *estudios transfeministas*. But to my knowledge, this illustrates a mere English-to-Spanish translation, rather than any creative 'resignification.' In any event, I shall not discuss the perspectivism of Schutte's proposal here because I show the weakness of that framework in my discussion of Zea.

If the ideological, dogmatic character of this feminist proposal is not yet clear, some statements meant to support the other steps of the approach would make it indubitable. I already illustrated Schutte's practice of appeal to emotive language, which is to be avoided in professional philosophical writing. Yet she explicitly recommend this practice on the basis that it might help academic feminists to advance their cause. "A philosophically grounded personal narrative," writes Schutte, "can be a powerful agent of consciousness-raising and change" (ibid.: 796). In fact, she considers such personal and emotional narratives to be part of the new Latin American conception of knowledge. After all, the goal of "decolonization" amounts to "a constant challenge for those of us seeking a proper sense of epistemic inclusion as we insist on the recognition of our more complex and so far marginalized or invisible/inaudible epistemic locations in a world where discrimination against global South women and women of color continues to be a matter of serious concern" (ibid.: 801). But emotions are not, of course, reasons. Schutte's feminist epistemology promises to deliver a new conception of knowledge that she hardly spells out or supports with arguments. As far as we can understand her conception of knowledge from what she writes, it is primarily a political ideology, contrary to the truth-seeking critical thinking that is fundamental to philosophical inquiry.

2.3.2   A Brief History of Immodest Feminism

The problems facing Schutte's feminist epistemology are indicative of the uphill battle faced also by other academic feminisms. As shown by Susan Haack (1993, 1998), Robert Almeder (1994) and others, academic feminism rejects standard methods of inquiry in epistemology and other areas of philosophy on the basis of assumptions and without engaging in reasoned argument with anyone who holds an opposite view. In objecting to some versions of feminism of this sort in epistemology, Susan Haack (1993: 38) plausibly argues that no such epistemology appears based on sound reason or evidence, and must therefore be "in the propaganda business" rather than the business of philosophy. An objection along similar lines seems fitting in the case of Schutte's feminist epistemology, discussed above. If I am right, there is a sharp line separating immodest feminism from the modest feminism of, say, Sor Juana, who defended the right of women to knowledge without claiming a right to any feminist or Latin American kind of knowledge. Like any other philosophical thinker, she invoked reasons and evidence to argue against the bias of *machismo* and its consequences for women in epistemology and the sciences. But Sor Juana's struggle was one of equal rights more generally, and as such, it prefigured the struggle of modest feminists of the late 1800s and the early 1900s who aimed at obtaining for women in Western societies the same rights that those societies had already recognized for men, such as the rights to vote, have a college education, and inherit or buy property. Latin American modest feminism, sometimes called 'first-wave feminism,' held the first international congress of feminism in Buenos Aires in 1910, which was attended also by Latin American feminists of an equal-rights persuasion broader than, but consistent with, that of Sor Juana. By the 1960s, the feminist thinking sometimes referred to as 'the second wave' of feminism went from activism for equal rights to theorizing in academic settings about the special rights of women. This became an ideological type of feminism, according to which success in the fight for the rights of women requires some deep socio-political-economic change. During this period, the feminists of Latin America embraced the fight for radical change but were not active in academic settings.[20] In general, when it came to entering the academic world in Latin

---

[20] Latin American feminists of this period continued to be mostly devoted to activism, with the possible exception of Graciela Hierro (1928–2003), whom Schutte and

America, feminism would have to wait until the 1990s, and the advent of the so-called third wave of feminism (Schutte and Femenías 2009).

This standard talk of "waves" of feminism may however obscure the real philosophical difference that separates the two types of feminism of concern here. On the one hand, there is the feminism of Sor Juana and the turn-of-the-twentieth-century feminists, which emphasizes the similarity between men and women and vindicates their equal rights. On the other, there is the ideological feminism of the turn of the twenty-first century, which emphasizes the differences between men and women and accordingly vindicates women's need of their own moral theory, philosophy of science, epistemology, and so on. In addition, academic feminists associate *machismo* and other prejudices based on sex or gender with the existence of an unjust sociopolitical and economic order. They take the elimination of such biases to be contingent on the elimination of the order that causes them.

In Latin America (as elsewhere), beyond these common claims, the 'academic' or "third-wave" feminists have much that they disagree on among themselves. For women in the region make up a very diverse group in terms of their race, ethnicity, class, geographical location, and philosophical persuasion, and since the academic feminists wish to capture that diversity, there are numerous strands of academic feminism. To name but a few, these include Afro-Latin American feminism (e.g., Segato 2003; Curiel 2007); Borderlands feminism (e.g., Anzaldúa 2003); Indigenist feminism (e.g., Rivera Cusicanqui 1996); liberationist feminism (e.g., Dussel 1978; Schutte 2011a); transnational feminism (e.g., Alvarez 1990, 1998a, 1998b); and postcolonial feminism (e.g., Schutte and Femenías 2009).

2.3.3 Dussel's Liberationist Feminism

I have examined above the case of Schutte's liberationist feminism. But hers is not the only strand of such feminism. Among other strands is that of Enrique Dussel (Argentine, b, 1934), one of the founders of a more general "liberation" movement in Latin American philosophy considered

Femenías (2009) credit with having introduced feminism as an academic subject in Mexican universities.

in Chapter 9. The views on women rights that he published in 1978 include the hypothesis about the origins of *machismo* in Latin America that we found plausible earlier in this chapter. Although most of these feminisms are proposed by theorists from the social sciences with almost no background in philosophy, the liberationist feminism of Schutte or Dussel stands out, because these are philosophers by training. Since I have already discussed Schutte's feminism and found it open to criticism on a number of grounds, let us consider whether Dussel's feminism scores better.

According to Dussel, what I am here calling 'modest feminism' (i.e., the equal-rights feminist model) is characteristic of early Latin American feminism and all waves of "North American" feminism. Although this claim is inaccurate, since contemporary feminism in North America equally emphasizes the distinctiveness of women, we may ignore this problem in order to focus on Dussel's contention that modest feminism should be rejected because it neglects to consider the distinctiveness of women, which derives from the distinctiveness of their sexuality – something that does not simply render them different from men, but which has an equal and independent value that is totally independent of men's validation. Dussel claims that women need to gain their sexual freedom in order to defeat machismo and achieve their liberation. "Women's liberation," writes Dussel (1978: 95),

> entails an opening of woman to the realm of distinctiveness. Distinctive is not the same as different. What is different is within the same or within the man–woman totality, it is machismo; woman is the non-phallus, the castrated one. Distinctive is what is originally other. True women's liberation consists in announcing that machismo is unrealistic because the phallus is not the only expression of sexuality.

Since there is nothing in *machismo* that is really natural, Latin American cultures today must rid themselves of this bias that privileges the man and keeps the woman in subjection to him. That is a perversion of nature which, as we saw, Dussel traces to the European expansion and specifically to the Iberian conquest.

The good news is that, on his view, *machismo* can be eliminated and women can achieve their liberation, though these victories would take a drastic change in the socio-political-economic order requiring nothing short of a Marxist, or at least a socialist, revolution. For all his "liberationist" talk, Dussel now takes a very conservative turn by arguing that nuns would play a key role in the struggle for liberation. But they must remain celibate to consecrate themselves to that struggle and to better the lives of the Latin American poor and dispossessed (Dussel, 1978: 96–98). Even in a church dominated by a male hierarchy, nuns are especially positioned to help defeat the bias of *machismo* by claiming "a sexuality that is originally feminine," thereby showing that "the phallus is not the only expression of sexuality" (ibid.: 95). The elimination of the phallic domination of men would bring about the end of machismo. Nuns find themselves in a particular advantageous position for leading such a "renewal" and "reconceptualization" of the distinct sexuality of women and men because they are not the victims of subjection by men either sexually or socially by being assigned typical subservient roles as housekeepers, educators to children, and so on.

Ironically, however, Dussel recommends that nuns think of their celibacy as the necessary mode of a life consecrated to the liberation of a suffering world. Because they are free of family obligations, they can be devoted entirely to changing the world politically, economically, and socially, so that a more just society can come into being. Their commitment must thus be to the poor, who are their 'family.' At the end of the day, then, Dussel's liberationist feminism is of help to neither nuns nor other women, for they are all told that they must acknowledge their sexual distinctiveness and join the fight for a more just society. That is, they must wait for their rights, either subordinating their feminist demands to other more urgent demands for radical change, or worse, postpone them altogether. Now Dussel's liberationist feminism appears indistinguishable from most versions of academic feminism – including Schutte's and the Afro-Latin American, Indigenous, Marxist, and socialist feminisms. In fact, all varieties of academic feminism rest on the central claim that in the current socio-political and economic order, women cannot successfully eliminate *machismo*. To change it, they must assert their various kinds of distinctiveness, reconceptualize social roles, and develop practical agendas for change at all levels, including theoretical and applied branches of philosophy. Standard moral theory and human rights theory are unsuitable for this purpose.

2.4   The Upshot

In light of the results obtained so far, I am sympathetic to two of Kreimer's claims, though I recast them to read: first, feminist issues in Latin America, as anywhere else, are issues of practical philosophy whose resolution needs to be properly informed by science, especially cognitive and evolutionary psychology. Second, contemporary immodest feminisms believe in the truth of either normative relativism or nihilism, which entails the rejection of major ethical theories. To avoid the charge of dogmatism, such a belief must be supported with argument. Modest feminism, as characterized in this chapter, is a doctrine of human rights that may be supported by appeal to a number of ethical theories – from the natural law theory whose heyday in Latin America was in Sor Juana's time, to more contemporary theories of distributive justice based on utilitarian, Rawlsian, or libertarian principles. Although any such vindication of equal rights for women requires the rejection of *machismo*, it need not claim that equal rights are contingent on any drastic change of the sociopolitical and economic order. For this reason, Sor Juana's feminism, though very radical at the time, falls in the same category as the modest feminism of the turn of the twentieth century and Kreimer's scientific feminism. However, for the reasons pointed out above, the modest feminism of Kreimer is in fact pseudoscientific and should be significantly revised. I suggest a reassessment of what really follows from the fact that some of the rights of men are violated in our societies – which is not the conclusion that "hegemonic" feminism is false.

In addition, Kreimer's vindication of the rights of men should take into account non-biased scientific data about women and eliminate the claim that inequalities between the sexes concerning factors such as life span amount to inequities or unjust inequalities. With respect to immodest feminism, my analysis of the liberationist versions of Schutte and Dussel suggests that they are closer to ideological propaganda than to philosophical inquiry.

2.5 Suggested Readings

Almeder, Robert. 1994. "Liberal Feminism and Academic Feminism?" *Public Affairs Quarterly* 8(4): 299–315.

Offers a classification of contemporary feminist theories useful for locating the feminisms of Latin America. Within the category of 'liberal feminism' falls any vindication of equal rights for women that assumes they are achievable to a satisfactory degree without any radical change of the socioeconomic order. Academic feminism comprises a variety of feminist doctrines sharing the rejection of liberal feminism – from Marxist feminism to postmodern feminism. Almeder supports liberal feminism, and charges that academic feminism is nothing more than a political ideology of radical egalitarianism.

Carbonero Gamundí, María Antonia, and Silvia Levín, eds. 2014. *Injusticias de género en un mundo globalizado: conversaciones con la teoría de Nancy Fraser.* Colección Politeia, Rosario, Argentina: Homo Sapiens Ediciones.

Good example of the sort of armchair inquiry into social issues inspired by the "decolonizing" framework of US feminist philosopher Nancy Fraser, who is quite popular among Latin American feminists today. The editors claim without proof that the injustices faced by Latin American women are the result of globalization and neoliberalism.

Curiel, Ochy, 2007. "Los aportes de las afrodescendientes a la teoría y la práctica feminista: desuniversalizando el sujeto mujeres," pp. 163–190 in M. L. Femenías, ed., *Perfiles del feminismo Iberoamericano*, vol. 3. Buenos Aires: Catálogos.

An example of the concerns of academic feminism of the Afro-Latin-American variety. Objects to generalizations about groups of women in feminist theory. Such generalizations fail to capture diversity even among the diversity of Afro-Latin Americans. The aim of feminism for this group should be to resist biases (racism, heterosexism, and class exploitation) without making generalizations that tend to homogenize groups.

de la Cruz, Juana Inés. 1988/1691. "Respuesta a Sor Filotea" ("Reply to Sor Philothea"), pp. 166–243 in Octavio Paz, ed., *A Sor Juana Anthology*. Cambridge, MA: Harvard University Press.
   1998/1681. *Autodefensa Espiritual: Letter of Sor Juana Inés de la Cruz to Her Confessor.* San Antonio, TX: Galvart Press.

Locus classicus for the feminist views of Sor Juana.

Dussel, Enrique. 1978. *Ethics and the Theology of Liberation*. Maryknoll, NY: Orbis, (references to selection pp. 92–98 in Susana Nuccetelli and Gary Seay, eds., 2004. *Latin American Philosophy: An Introduction with Readings*. Upper Saddle Brook, NJ: Prentice Hall.)

Clear statement of the agenda of one of the versions of liberationist feminism considered in this chapter.

Fuller, Amy. 2015. *Between Two Worlds: The Autos Sacramentales of Sor Juana Inés de la Cruz*. Cambridge, UK: Modern Humanities Research Association.

Chapter 1 of this book looks closely at the historical context of Sor Juana's feminism. Provides background information that suggest a continuity between the feminism of her "Respuesta" to Bishop Fernández.

Haack, Susan. 1993. "Epistemological Reflections of an Old Feminist," *Reason Papers* 18: 31–43.

Defends equal-rights feminism while objecting to immodest feminism on the grounds that it is imperialistic, since it does not restrict itself to its original scope (social and political philosophy) and lacks a unified feminist approach (something evident in the literature on epistemology). This precludes the existence of a "woman's point of view" or "women's ways of knowing." Haack finds such phrases reminiscent of sexist stereotypes. In the end, her analysis agrees with Almeder's in that both charge that academic feminism fails to engage in philosophical inquiry.

Kreimer, Roxana n.d.(a). "Es sexista reconocer que hombres y mujeres no son idénticos? Una evaluación crítica de la retórica neurofeminista." Universidad Nacional de Tucumán, undated MS. Available via Facebook group "Feminismo científico." https://es-la.facebook.com/groups/feminismocientifico/permalink/273421369955768/

Charges that academic feminism neglects to take into account scientific data gathered in the last twenty years and which is relevant to its central claims. Proposes as an alternative a "scientific" feminism that recognizes the rights not only of women but also of men.

Merrim, Stephanie, ed. 1991. *Feminist Perspectives on Sor Juana Inés de la Cruz*, Detroit, MI: Wayne State University Press.

Collection of previously unpublished essays by scholars of Hispanic American literature who are broadly sympathetic to a variety of radical feminisms. Their unifying question is what to make of the widely accepted view that Sor Juana was the first feminist of the Americas, given that hers was an equal-rights feminism.

Paz, Octavio. 1988. *Sor Juana: Or, the Traps of Faith*. Cambridge, MA: Harvard University Press.

An excellent analysis of Sor Juana's feminism. Dismisses with good reasons a number of historically inaccurate interpretations of facts about her life and work while proposing some new hypotheses based on strong evidence. Particularly relevant to Paz's interpretation of the kind of feminism at stake in her work is the appendix, "Sor Juana: Witness for the Prosecution" (pp. 491–502).

Rivera Cusicanqui, Silvia. 1996. "Los desafíos para una democracia étnica y genérica en los albores del tercer milenio," pp. 17–84 in S. Rivera Cusicanqui, ed., *Ser mujer indígena, chola o birlocha en la Bolivia postcolonial de los años 90*. La Paz: Ministerio de Desarrollo Humano.

A sample of Indigenous feminism, written by a scholar in social theory who suggests that Amerindian women still suffer from a kind of alienation caused by the colonial order, which shows in the fact that these women prioritize ethnic and class struggle over feminist struggle. It is more important for them to overturn racial and ethnic discrimination than *machismo*. The author takes this descriptive claim to entail that, to eliminate *machismo*, Latin American feminists must fight first for "decolonization" and against the ills associated with colonialism, such as multiculturalism'.

2002. "Ch'ixinakax utixiwa: A Reflection on the Practices of Discourses of Decolonization," *The South Atlantic Quarterly* (Winter 2002): 96–109, www.adivasiresurgence.com/wp-content/uploads/2016/02/Silvia-Rivera-Cusicanqui-Chixinakax-Eng1.pdf

A clear example of the sort of ideological inquiry carried out by postcolonial, Indigenous feminists. The author subsumes the oppression of indigenous women in a more general picture of the oppression of the native peoples resulting from neoliberal capitalism and globalization.

Schutte, Ofelia. 2011a. "Engaging Latin American Feminisms Today: Methods, Theory, Practice," *Hypatia* 26(4): 783–803.

The source for Schutte's liberationist feminism discussed above.

Schutte, Ofelia, and María Luisa Femenías. 2009. "Feminist Philosophy," pp. 397–411 in Susana Nuccetelli, Ofelia Schutte, and Otavio Bueno, eds., *Blackwell Companion to Latin American Philosophy*. Oxford: Wiley-Blackwell.

One of the clearest outlines of feminist philosophy in Latin America from the 1980s to the present, but mostly descriptive. Contends that in the 1990s, feminists were devoted to political activism. Although the authors make a number of unsubstantiated claims, the strength of their article resides in the fact that it provides an overview of the implosion of ideological feminisms in Latin American academia.

Segato, Rita Laura. 2003. *Las estructuras elementales de la violencia*. Buenos Aires: Prometeo and Universidad Nacional de Quilmes.

Another illustration of the sort of doctrine advanced within Afro-Latin-American feminism, written by a Brazilian anthropologist, who claims to have evidence that in some cases, Afro-Brazilians and white Brazilians differ in terms of crucial beliefs about family and gender identifications. The evidence suggests to Segato that feminism must take into account differences among women based on class, race, and ethnicity.

Yugar, Theresa A. 2014. *Sor Juana Inés de la Cruz: Feminist Reconstruction of Biography and Text*. Eugene, OR: Wipf and Stock.

Critical survey of Sor Juana's life and writings. Argues that there is a continuity in her challenges to prejudice against women within the Catholic Church. By challenging her confessor in the *Autodefensa*, since he belonged to the most powerful Catholic order in Mexico at the time, the Society of Jesus, she was challenging both the Church and the Inquisition.

3 The Authoritarian Republicanism of Bolívar

Bolivarism is a set of doctrines in the applied moral and political philosophy of early-nineteenth-century Latin America.[1] It fueled ongoing populist phenomena then as well as today, as illustrated by the "Bolivarian" revolution of Hugo Chávez and Nicolás Maduro of the turn of this century in Venezuela. Bolivarism also continues to be a moral force behind some present-day movements striving to obtain not only political and economic reform elsewhere in Latin America, but also the recognition of the distinct racial and ethnic identity of the people of the region. In this chapter, I reconstruct and assess the core doctrines on these issues of Bolivarism. But this task requires taking account of certain historical and biographical facts that can help explain the emergence and significance of those doctrines, to which I turn first.

3.1 Historical and Personal Context

3.1.1 Wars of Independence

By the end of the eighteenth century, descendants of Spaniards born in the "New World," the so-called *criollos*, were eager to have a say about the form of polity that would work best in Latin America. Although, as this chapter makes clear, they disagreed deeply about what that form was, they agreed about one thing: namely, that the substantive social, economic, and political changes necessary for the region could not occur under Iberian rule.

---

[1] As I use the term "Bolivarism" here, it is a doctrine of applied political philosophy that must not be conflated with the term used to refer to the socialist revolution of Hugo Chávez and Nicolás Maduro in Venezuela: viz., "Bolivarianism."

Luckily for them, with the next century came an event in Europe that opened the way for their nations to gain independence.

In the first decade of the nineteenth century there was social unrest and low morale in Spain following its defeat by Britain's Royal Navy at the Battle of Trafalgar (1805). Sensing that this was the time to strike, France's Emperor Napoleon sent his armies to invade Spain. He promptly removed King Ferdinand VII, and placed his own brother, Joseph Bonaparte, on the throne as King of Spain. Although this arrangement did not last long, the news that the French had deposed and replaced Ferdinand VII spread quickly to Spain's American colonies, where anti-royalists then seized their opportunity and established local "juntas" to govern independently, without Spanish authority. In the 1810s came the decisive move to liberation, when anti-royalists in various parts of the viceroyalties refused to recognize authorities loyal to Spain and proceeded to form their own autonomous governments. Meanwhile, in 1813, King Ferdinand VII was restored to power, after which he was determined to support the royalist forces that were trying to put down such insurrections, which had continued to spread in America. In 1815, he sent an expeditionary force to Venezuela, to intercept pro-independence forces that had gained control of New Granada. But in 1820, a group of liberal Spanish military officers who had been assigned to put down the insurrection in Buenos Aires deposed Ferdinand VII instead. Afflicted by war, poverty, and political upheavals, Spain was too weak to sustain decisive war efforts to regain its lost territories in Latin America (Halperín-Donghi 1993: 59). By 1826, the insurgents could claim victory: Spain had lost its colonies in almost all Spanish-speaking America except Cuba, whose independence would have to wait until 1898. The bloody wars to shake off Spanish colonial rule in the Americas lasted almost a century on the whole. By contrast, Portugal ceded its vast South American territory in stages to Brazil, a country that earned its independence entirely by peaceful means. Beginning with a declaration of independence in 1822, the process culminated in 1889, when Brazil became an autonomous constitutional republic.

In Spanish America, the wars of independence brought a special urgency to the question of what kind of polity would best serve the new sovereign nations. The matter was eventually decided by leaders who had some familiarity with the social and political theories of the time through exposure to the views of Enlightenment thinkers such as Thomas Hobbes (1588–1679), John Locke (1632–1704), Montesquieu (1689–1755), Jean-Jacques Rousseau (1712–1778), and Thomas Jefferson (1743–1826) among others. The liberal and libertarian conceptions of social justice advanced by some of these thinkers strengthened the rebels' antipathy toward colonial rule – as did the notion of a social contract, since it was obvious to the rebels that their peoples had at no point consented to the sovereign authority of Spain. With a parallel line of reasoning, the rebels were generally inclined to reject colonialism of any stripe, whether Spanish, British, French, or something else. The reaction of the people of Buenos Aires to invasions by the British during the Napoleonic Wars illustrates such anti-colonialist sentiment. They took place in 1806 and 1807, resulting in each case in a surrender of the invading troops to a local militia that fought them independently of any Spanish authority. Having defeated the British on their own, within three years the anti-royalists of Argentina established a sovereign government, and officially declared its independence from Spain six years later in 1816.

But the anti-colonialist sentiment of the 1810s was not enough for the leaders of the independence movements to reach an agreement on a unified vision concerning the type of polity that would best serve the new nations. Those favoring a liberal democracy faced the issue of whether it should take the form of a representative democracy with elected head of state and legislators, or a constitutional monarchy with elected legislature and executive but a symbolic, royal head of state. Yet in the era of Bonaparte, there was a third option on the table: a non royal authoritarian ruler, to serve at least temporarily.

3.1.2   The Political Role of the Latin American Military

Since at the time that concerns us here there were some actual figures in Latin America who embodied these different options, it will perhaps make these options more vivid if we consider two paradigmatic cases of contrary opinions on the role of military officers after independence. One is the case of General Simón Bolívar (1783–1830), who led the forces engaging the Spanish armies in northern Spanish America and favored an authoritarian form of republicanism for at least a good number of Latin American nations.[2] For, as shown later in this chapter, not only did Bolívar defend that option in his writings, but he himself assumed temporary dictatorial powers in Peru as well as in Gran Colombia (a vast territory comprising approximately present-day Colombia, Venezuela, Ecuador, and Panama). The other is the case of General José de San Martín (1778–1850), the Argentine leader of the revolt in southern Spanish America, who seems to have had no personal ambitions for political roles after independence, least of all that of becoming an absolute ruler. He favored instead a constitutional monarchy and was quite plain in expressing his worries about the future of the new nations if they were to fall into the hands of military dictators. He apparently declared: "The presence of a successful soldier (no matter how disinterested) is dangerous to the States that have just been constituted."[3]

At the same time, there is little evidence that San Martín had either expertise outside the battlefield, or an inclination to debate questions of social and political philosophy of the sort that interested Bolívar. In the course of writing about those questions, Bolívar developed two influential doctrines concerning the legitimacy of various forms of polity and their relation to the collective ethnic and racial identity of a nation. Referred to here as "Bolivarism" and the "*mestizaje* model of Latin American identity," I will take up these doctrines in turn after discussing a few biographical facts concerning the man who developed them.

3.1.3   Life and Work

South America celebrates Simón Bolívar as "el Libertador" ("the Liberator") for his military leadership in the wars of independence. However, he was also a statesman and philosophical thinker concerned about the complex moral, social, and political issues faced by Latin America post-independence. He was born in Caracas in 1783 to an affluent *criollo* family of cacao-plantation owners. After becoming an orphan at the

---

[2] Bolívar left abundant evidence in his writings attesting that authoritarian republicanism was his preferred form of political system for many Latin American countries. I discuss this evidence later in this chapter. But see also Romero (1998) and Brading (1991).

[3] Letter cited in Bushnell and Metford (2019).

age of nine, he had to rely for several years on an uncle for decisions about his wealth and education. His uncle hired private tutors for him, salient among whom was Simón Rodríguez, a disciple of Jean-Jacques Rousseau who introduced the young Bolívar to the philosophers of the Enlightenment. In the course of his education, which included two journeys to Europe, Bolívar came to admire the liberal values of the French and American revolutions and developed a general doctrine of what legitimatizes a form of polity, which he took to be consistent with those values. We may call this doctrine "Bolivarism" and summarize it as follows:

> Bolivarism – The doctrine that the best form of polity for a people is that which can promote three basic values: aggregate happiness, social safety, and political stability.

Bolivarism is a pluralistic, value-centered doctrine that Bolívar advanced without offering substantive reasons to support it. Nevertheless, such reasons can be derived from the principles of one or another of three political theories of his time with which he became familiar from his reading and European education: namely, the contractualism of Rousseau and Thomas Hobbes, the Lockean natural law theory of Thomas Jefferson, and the utilitarianism of Jeremy Bentham.

In due course, we'll discuss those reasons and consider whether they might in fact justify Bolívar's views on the best forms of polity for Latin America. For now, let's consider how the liberal values acquired during his education, together with his first-hand knowledge of the brutality of Spanish colonial rule in Latin America, led him to write a pledge to liberate the region, which he read in the presence of his teacher Simón Rodríguez during a visit to Monte Sacro in Rome. Bolívar's pledge has the force of an ambitious, solemn oath to dedicate his life to the liberation of Latin America. Contributing to his decision to make that pledge may also have been a sentiment of moral revulsion, shared by many Europeans at the time, toward Napoleon's coronation as Emperor of France in 1804 – an event that Bolívar personally witnessed, as he was in the audience. Historians speculate that Bonaparte's self-glorification by taking on the trappings of quasi-royalty aroused feelings of betrayal among many who had been ardent supporters of the values of the French Revolution, among whom we must count Bolívar. At the same time, in light of Bolívar's well-known political ambitions, we may infer that Napoleon's coronation might have prompted in him some feelings of admiration for the Emperor's glory and power. (In fact, as we shall see later, Karl Marx was very critical of Bolívar's "Bonapartist" program.)

In any case, when Bolívar returned to Caracas in 1809, he found that the anti-royalists there were gaining momentum. Within a year of his arrival, a sovereign junta had replaced the Spanish governor of the city. In the same year, Argentina followed suit, and a full-scale war of independence began to spread in Latin America. Bolívar played a leading role in it, not only during the revolutionary struggle but also during the political reorganization that followed the fall of Spanish dominions. Bolívar had several important roles in that national reorganization. He served as president and dictator of Gran Colombia, a vast South American country for which he also drafted a constitution. Furthermore, he held temporary authoritarian power in Peru, sanctioned the creation of a new country named after him (Bolivia), and even wrote a constitution for the latter. In addition, Bolívar pursued the pan-national unity of the new Latin American nations, and took the first steps toward attaining it by organizing a conference in Panama. Bolívar believed the entire subcontinent should become a federation coordinated by a central political authority, and invoked as a reason for this belief the shared culture and origins of the region.

At the same time, Bolívar, during this period of his life, produced a great deal of writing, mostly letters, newspaper articles, proclamations, speeches, decrees, and pieces of legislation – including two constitutions, one for Bolivia, the other for Gran Colombia. But the new ruling class, the *criollos* of Gran Colombia, Peru and Bolivia, forcefully rejected many of his policy decisions.[4] After 1826, he faced growing opposition in Gran Colombia and even a failed assassination attempt. Sent into exile by former comrades who were now the new political officials, Bolívar ended up, ironically, as a guest in the house of

---

[4] Here the word *criollos* should not be confused with the term "creole"; the former refers only to white Latin Americans of Spanish ancestry.

a Spaniard, the Quinta de San Pedro Alejandrino, Santa Marta, Colombia, where he died of tuberculosis in 1830, greatly disillusioned about Latin America's prospects.

3.2 Political and Moral Doctrines

3.2.1 Bolivarism

Bolívar's writings advance two doctrines of applied moral and political philosophy that are of interest for us here: Bolivarism, and the *mestizaje* view of Latin American identity. According to the doctrine of Bolivarism, the legitimacy of liberal democracy as a form of polity is not universal. To qualify as a liberal democracy, a political system must meet at least these requirements:

1. It must allow that citizens who meet certain commonly agreed conditions have a say on their nation's policies by participating in periodic, free elections of their leaders and representatives in the government; and
2. It must respect basic human rights and liberties for individuals and groups.

Bolivarism is a consequentialist normative theory of moral and political philosophy. As such, it is a value-based theory according to which the promotion of a certain set of values justifies preferring one kind of political arrangement over another. On this view, democracy is not an adequate system when it fails to maximize one or more of these three values: aggregate happiness, political stability, and safety for most people involved.[5] Since liberal democracy sometimes fails to do so, it follows that it is not the best form of polity across the board (i.e., universally). In fact, Bolívar's numerous praises for absolute monarchies of the past suggest that he took the legitimacy of *any* political arrangement to depend on its ability to promote those basic values. Since promoting them in turn depends on factors concerning the history and racial and ethnic background of each nation, the legitimacy of a political arrangement ultimately

---

[5] Bolívar uses the expression 'aggregate happiness' to mean, roughly, the classical utilitarian notion of *total balance of happiness over pain for most of the people concerned.*

depends on such historical, racial, and ethnic factors – a determinist thesis not at all new at the time of Bolívar.[6]

The best form of polity in the case of the Latin American nations, Bolívar believed, would depend partly on the characters of their people, which vary from nation to nation. But in most cases, liberal democracy would fail because most Latin Americans lack the "talents and virtues" that would render this system effective in maximizing the values of happiness, political stability, and safety of most people involved. Since the consequence that matters is the set of these three values, Bolivarism is a pluralistic form of consequentialism for which democracy might be valuable as means but not as an end.

As a result, Bolivarism entails a relativistic view of liberal democracy, plainly endorsed in the writings of the Libertador. For example, in his 1819 inaugural address to Congress in Angostura, he said, "regardless of the effectiveness" of democracy in the United States,

> ... It has never for a moment entered my mind to compare the position and character of two states as dissimilar as the English-American and the Spanish-American. Would it not be most difficult to apply to Spain the English system of political, civil, and religious liberty? ... [L]aws must take into account the physical conditions of the country, climate, character of the land, location, size, and mode of living of the people ... (Bolívar 1951a: 179–180)

He had already made similar claims in the "Jamaica Letter" of 1815 (Bolívar 2004) and the "Manifesto of Cartagena" of 1812. The civic (and moral) virtues he ascribes to the people of the United States and Britain involve traits that predispose them to freedom. Since the people of South America generally lack those traits, a centralized, non-democratic government might for them be the type of polity that could promote the best aggregate happiness, security for all, and political stability. Here in incipient form is an idea that will prove very dangerous in the history of Latin America:

---

[6] Such deterministic relativism about forms of polity is not new today, as shown by the twentieth-century "Asian-values" debate (Mahbubani 1998). But in Bolívar's century, a glaring illustration of it comes from one of his fierce critics, Karl Marx, whose own views on the matter of liberal democracy influenced a strand of Latin American thought in the twentieth century (see discussion in Chapter 8).

namely, that the region is not ready for democracy. First, it must achieve order, a condition for people to have freedom, and this must be achieved by whichever means necessary, including dictatorship.

Bolívar offers just one reason for his skepticism about the effectiveness of democracy in Latin America, which relies on a comparative assessment of the character of the peoples of the Americas. His whole argument rests on some empirical assumptions about two relations: one between the unique ethnic and racial makeup of South America and the character of its peoples; the other between democracy and his three basic values. The latter assumption is clear in some of his writings, where he explicitly blames the fall of the first independent government of Venezuela on the rebels' choice of a federal republic for the nation. He recommends that, once they regain control, the new government be a centralized republic – the only system that can work because of the diverse historical origins and ethnic and racial character of Venezuelans. On his view, those who admired the first Federal Constitution of Venezuela should bear in mind that it led to a disastrous result. Consistent with this line of thinking, he often praises the authoritarian regime of Ancient Rome and many absolute monarchies worldwide. Similar remarks appeared in the letter sent on September 28, 1815 to the editor of the newspaper *Gaceta Real de Jamaica* and his "Angostura Address" of February 15, 1819.[7]

Bolívar's constitutions for Bolivia and Gran Colombia offer similar authoritarian pictures of his preferred system of government for these new nations. In each of these countries, Bolívar envisions a government along the lines of what is sometimes called an "authoritarian republic" (Halperín-Donghi 1993: 64–68). It consists of a judiciary power, an executive power headed by an elected president *serving for life*, and a legislative power featuring a *hereditary senate*. In the "Angostura Address," he adds to these three branches of government a fourth branch: a moral power dedicated solely to the restriction of individual liberties by means of "moral" censorship. He claims to have "invented" the moral power while reflecting

---

[7] The "Angostura Address" (Bolívar 1851a) is a good source for Bolívar's positive views about government, while the "Jamaica Letter" (Bolívar 2004) sets out his objections to liberal democracy as a form of polity for Latin America. In the latter, after linking the fall of the first autonomous government of Venezuela to its federative form, he engages in lengthy reflections about the best polity for the future free nations.

on the virtues of the political systems of Ancient Greece and Rome. In the end, his authoritarian ideas were too extreme, even for the upper-class *criollos* who would after all have benefited from their application, since only these people would have been eligible for positions in Bolívar's hereditary senate and presidency for life.

To his credit, however, Bolívar championed the unity of Latin America, often referred to as 'pan-Americanism.' In fact, he prescribed the establishment of an overarching federation with political jurisdiction over all the new nations of Latin America. As a reason for this proposal he invoked the historical and cultural unity of the region, which he traced to the Spanish conquest, emphasizing that the conquerors knew no borders. He took steps toward making pan-Americanism a reality by convening all Spanish American nations in Panama in 1826. Most of them attended. But the project of constituting the biggest nation to exist on earth failed to take off. The civil wars and national partitions that followed the wars of independence should have signaled to Bolívar the impossibility of pan-Americanism. Moreover, the very idea of a super-federation of Latin American nations made critics of his authoritarian tendencies suspicious about the real motive behind his project.

3.2.2   The *Mestizaje* Model of Latin American Identity

Bolívar's *mestizaje* model of Latin American identity consists in a negative claim about the collective identity of Latin Americans: namely, that it is not exclusively European, or African, or Amerindian, but a mix of these. This identity is the unique product of historical events triggered by the Spanish conquest. Bolívar was the first thinker of the region to fully articulate a *mestizaje* model of Latin American racial and ethnic identity, which would later be revisited by other thinkers.[8] Arguably, in developing the *mestizaje* model Bolívar was partly influenced by the sixteenth-century tradition of Bartolomé de las Casas, especially his defense of the full 'humanity' of Amerindians. That Bolívar was familiar with Las Casas's

---

[8] Bolívar's *mestizaje* model started a tradition of notable people embracing the racial and ethnic diversity of Latin America. Among them were literary figures, philosophers, and public officials at the highest levels. I will have more to say about later developments of the model in Chapter 7.

thought is evident in some references in his writings, as well as in his declared intention to name a new capital he envisioned for Gran Colombia after the bishop.

In any case, Bolívar was the first to fully articulate the model and thus, he advocated an inclusive conception of Latin American identity far more progressive than the alternatives available at his time, about which I will have more to say in Chapter 4. Aware that he was breaking new ground, Bolívar notes in the "Jamaica Letter" that, unlike others, he does not think that caste or class can properly answer the question of the region's collective identity. On his model, Latin Americans' character hinges on their unique history, environment, and racially and culturally mixed origins. Moreover, they are the product of Spain, which due to its history and proximity to Africa, itself has a mixed identity.[9]

Many of his writings provide proof that Bolívar consistently vindicated the *mestizaje* model of Spanish American identity. In the "Jamaica Letter" and the "Angostura Address," a number of references to that model enter into statements of his vision for national organization, as well as his oracular predictions about the forms of polity more likely be adopted by the new nations.[10] For example,

> We must keep in mind that our people are neither European nor North American; rather, they are a mixture of African and the Americans who originated in Europe. Even Spain herself has ceased to be European because of her African blood, her institutions, and her character. It is impossible to determine with any degree of accuracy where we belong in the human

[9] In the nineteenth century, references to Spain's proximity to Africa had an unsavory pedigree, rooted in bigotry against Spain of the sort evident in the dictum that Europe ends at the French Pyrenees. In the following century, however, many Latin American intellectuals adopted the opposite value judgment, one that vindicated the mixed African-European identity of Spaniards and its positive contribution to Latin American racial and ethnic identity (Fernández Retamar 1976; Fuentes 1992).

[10] In the "Jamaica Letter" Bolívar predicts, for example, that democracy will flourish in Chile but not in Mexico. "The Kingdom of Chile is destined, by the nature of its location, by the simple and virtuous character of its people, and by the example of its neighbors, the proud republicans of Arauco, to enjoy the blessings that flow from the just and gentle laws of a republic" (2004: 117). On the other hand, "By nature of their geographic location, wealth, population, and character, I expect that the Mexicans, at the outset, intend to establish a representative republic in which *the executive will have great power*" (2004: 119, my emphasis).

family. The greater portion of the native Indians have been annihilated; Spaniards have mixed with Americans and Africans, and Africans with Indians and Spaniards. While we have all been born of the same mother, our fathers, different in origins and in blood, are foreigners, and all differ visibly as to the color of their skin: a dissimilarity which places upon us an obligation of the greatest importance . . . . (Bolívar 1951a: 181)[11]

Note that passages of this sort *never* take center stage in Bolívar's writings. Rather, they occur as premises, sometimes of an oracular tone, aimed at supporting some other point. He appeals to them to justify his choice of an authoritarian form of polity for some of the new nations. If their peoples differ greatly from North Americans, then it might be a good idea for those peoples to refrain from imitating the democratic political organization of North America. But Bolívar never offers any empirical evidence to support this conditional and instead invokes examples of unruly peoples who have lived under durable despotic regimes around the world or in Ancient Rome. If he intends to argue by analogy, then he needed to say more about the relevant features the Turks of the Ottoman Empire or the Romans of antiquity shared with, say, the post-independence Mexicans or Venezuelans. Without such support, his political opponents had no reason to accept his proposals.[12]

---

[11] This passage is one of his longest statements of the *mestizaje* model. It comes after he has told his Angostura audience: "We are not Europeans; we are not Indians; we are but a mixed species of aborigines and Spaniards. Americans by birth and Europeans by law, we find ourselves engaged in a dual conflict: we are disputing with the natives for titles of ownership, and at the same time we are struggling to maintain ourselves in the country that gave birth against the opposition of the invaders . . . " (1951a: 175–176).

[12] Note also that in the past century, the socialist revolution initiated by Hugo Chávez, sometimes called a 'Bolivarian revolution,' embraced some of the most authoritarian aspects of Bolivarism. Under his rule, in 1999 Venezuela adopted the "Constitution of the Bolivarian Republic of Venezuela," which sanctioned the creation of a moral power under the label 'Republican Moral Council.' Its role, according to Andrade and Lugo-Ocando (2018), has been to limit freedom of expression – in particular, freedom of the press. These authors report that by 2018, Venezuela was among the countries of the world with the poorest record in respect of basic freedoms. Although Bolívar's vision for the government of the nations of this region would render him unable to object to such developments, his social and political philosophy would commit him to rejecting the *socialist* Bolivarian revolution of Venezuela. See on this topic Keating (2013) and von Vacano (2012).

Most likely, underlying Bolívar's reasoning is a social determinism popular in positivist European circles at his time, which I discuss in Chapter 5. Bolívar gave it his own twist by postulating race, history, culture, and environmental conditions as factors that determined which political arrangements were best for the new Latin American nations. Since many of them, owing to the diverse character of their peoples, could not be effectively governed by democracy, some authoritarian form of government might be the most effective form of polity for them. Although some of these views were not innovations in Bolívar's time (but cf. von Vacano 2012), his appeal to the relevance of the *mestizo* identity of Latin Americans was unique and important.

Yet for some contemporary intellectuals in the region, what fueled the reaction by *criollos* against Bolívar that culminated in his exile and premature death was not his sympathies for authoritarian republicanism. It was instead the radicalism of his *mestizaje* model, which amounted to empowering traditionally marginalized racial and ethnic groups (Fuentes 1992a: 273). The local *criollos* were simply unwilling to share power and wealth with the lower classes. But it is disputable whether Bolívar invoked the *mestizaje* model of identity in an attempt to empower the lower classes. True, the historical record shows that he proclaimed the emancipation of the slaves in Venezuela during the early stages of the War of Independence, on July 7, 1816. He also wrote about the indignity of slavery. But the record also shows that Bolívar feared political power in the hands of Afro-Latin Americans, a group that includes the so-called *pardos* or mulattos. About them, he famously warned that a *pardocracia* (i.e., a government in the hands of the mulattos) would result in chaos and racial violence of the sort he had observed in Haiti (Helg 2003; Andrade and Lugo-Ocando 2018). However, his dealings with issues of race, ethnicity, and political power are plagued with so much ambiguity that I have to agree with Carlos Fuentes: there are several 'Bolívars,' depending on which of his writings are read and how they are read.

3.3 Marx's Critique of Bolívar

3.3.1 What Marx Said

Some reactions to Bolívar's social and political philosophy have focused on aspects of his moral character. A prominent critic of this sort is Karl Marx, who in 1858 published a biographical note about El Libertador in *The New American Cyclopedia*. After declaring that Bolívar had some traits of moral character that were unworthy of someone known as "The Liberator," Marx goes on to ascribe to Bolívar moral vices such as cowardice, envy, brutality, disloyalty, boastfulness, despotism, and frivolity. Surely, these are bad character traits for anyone to have, and especially for a military commander. But Marx here is engaging in a series of ad hominem arguments (i.e., arguments against the person) that may be fallacious, depending on the facts of Bolívar's actions and attitudes during the wars of independence. Evidently, criticism of this sort can only have any force if it is based on accurate, relevant evidence concerning those facts. And even if it does have force, it may leave Bolívar's philosophical thoughts untouched. On my view, we should be suspicious about Marx's arguments against Bolívar's moral character because of their exceedingly weak evidential support: Marx's sources were narratives by a few European historians of the time, who probably had no first-hand knowledge of the facts of the war. Without further support, we have no reason to accept, for example, the charge that "the few successes of the corps [of Bolívar] were entirely owed to British officers, such as Col. Sands." Or that once the Spanish threat was reduced, Bolívar "no longer thought it necessary to keep up the appearance of generalship, but leaving the whole military task to Gen. Sucre, limited himself to triumphal entries, manifestos, and the proclamation of constitutions."

On the other hand, the unreliability of Marx's sources is by no means established. He has supporters (e.g., Draper 1968) who argue that, charitably construed, Marx was objecting to Bolívar's propensity to favor authoritarian power, something amply illustrated in the constitutions he wrote for Bolivia and Gran Colombia. True, Marx wrote that one of those documents qualifies only as a "Bolivian Code, an imitation of the *Code Napoleon*." Marx, of course, was not inclined to endorse the universal value of democracy, a form of polity that he predicted would become obsolete after the decline of capitalism, when society would become ripe to enter the next historical phase – namely, that of a proletarian revolution leading to socialism. But according to Marx, democracy is a progressive polity during the phase of capitalism. On the other hand, the phenomenon of the restoration of empires during capitalism, to which he referred as 'Bonapartism,' is reactionary during that phase, for it signifies a regression to the system of absolute monarchies which belongs to a previous historical era, even if it does not involve a return of power to a king.

Could Bolívar respond to the charge of Bonapartism? It is true that he declined the offer of the throne of Gran Colombia. But although he was not interested in becoming its king, he did entertain the possibility of being its president for life, and also exerted dictatorial powers more than once. Furthermore, during the wars of independence he tried to recruit the help of Spain's colonial rival, the British Empire. Marx must have looked at that with suspicion, just as he must have looked with suspicion at Bolívar's enthusiastic praise for absolute monarchies. In addition, as we have noted, numerous writings strongly suggest that Bolívar did not endorse democracy across the board for the new Latin American nations. If this is what Marx really meant to criticize, I might agree. However, at no point did Marx provide textual evidence that he had read Bolívar. And at no point did he address Bolívar's arguments. As a result, although Marx's is an interesting critique of Bolívar's authoritarian tendencies, his critique does not go beyond a personal attack.

3.3.2   What Marx Should Have Said

In my view, Marx should have aimed his critique at the textual evidence of Bolívar's sympathies for instituting authoritarian republics in most of the new nations of Latin America. The evidence supporting this objection is abundant and includes classic texts such as the *Cartagena Manifesto*, the "Jamaica Letter," and the "Angostura Address" – together with the constitutions that Bolívar wrote for Bolivia and Great Colombia. Bolívar repeatedly offered, as a reason for preferring centralized governments in many Latin American nations, his hypothesis that unlike liberal democracies, centralized republics can more effectively promote the aggregate happiness, safety for all, and political stability of those nations. To support this claim, he invoked his assumption that Latin Americans cannot have democracy because of their unique history – and, most importantly, their unique mixed racial and ethnic backgrounds. On his view, these nations should be under the leadership of a centralized government run by people of his own social and economic class: the privileged *criollos*, who were the only people who were electable, given the form of polity outlined for these nations. Think of the vast nation of Gran Colombia: had it kept Bolívar's constitution, it would have had a government with an elected president for life and an elected but hereditary senate dictating all its laws and regulations. Likely the same president would have been in office for a considerable length of time. In addition, its government would have had a fourth power, the 'moral power,' in charge of monitoring the people's actions and attitudes, ready to censor them when it considered anything to be 'immoral.' In fact, after 1823 during a brief period as dictator of Gran Colombia, Bolívar himself created a moral branch of government, which notoriously declared the teaching of Bentham illegal in the country.[13]

3.4   The Upshot

Bolivarism makes the legitimacy of a form of polity contingent on its capacity to maximize Enlightenment values such as aggregate happiness, safety for all, and the political stability of a nation. But its relativization of democracy rests on shaky grounds, since this doctrine fails to provide arguments against the political-philosophical principles justifying liberal democracy that were available at the time of Bolívar. Prominent among these are:

1. A classical utilitarian justification – Liberal democracy is the right political arrangement because it maximizes aggregate happiness.
2. A natural law theory justification – Liberal democracy is the right political arrangement because it is the most conducive to respect for the inviolable rights that humans possess just because they are human.
3. A contractualist justification – Liberal democracy is the right political arrangement because it is the form of polity that qualifying members of society would prefer for themselves under ideal circumstances.

Although Bolívar seems to have been familiar with them from his education and reading, he failed to distinguish them, or realize their incompatibility with his own political philosophy. After all, his writings appeal to the

---

[13] Andrade and Lugo-Ocando (2018) plausibly attribute the proscription of Bentham during Bolívar's government to pressure from the Catholic Church – something that of course might explain the action, but cannot justify it.

authority of Rousseau, Montesquieu, Jefferson, and other thinkers of the period. We must conclude that such appeals were merely rhetorical devices.

If I am right, Bolívar failed to appreciate that compared with authoritarian systems of government, democracy accords people a higher degree of freedom and is therefore more conducive to the promotion of:

i. Aggregate happiness,
ii. Respect for human rights, and
iii. A degree of personal security proportionate to the degree of liberty self-interested individuals would choose to give up in exchange.

A number of different normative theories of political philosophy in fact argue for the value of liberal democracy on the grounds that it is more conducive to maximizing the production of one or another of these consequences.[14]

At the same time, Bolívar's moral and political philosophy has a progressive element, stemming from its *mestizaje* model of Latin American identity. True, his "neighbors to the North" deserved praise for their love of freedom and democracy, as he acknowledged. But in contrast to Latin Americans, at the time there had been no comparable vindication of North Americans' own racial and ethnic diversity by any intellectual and public official of the stature of Bolívar. Whether or not this difference has had any lasting effects in the differential character of race relations in each of the Americas is a complex empirical matter better left to the social sciences. Yet to understand the progressive aspect of Bolivarism, there is no better option than to compare it with the racist, civilization-versus-barbarism dichotomy of the generation that followed Bolívar's – and which I take up in the next chapter.

3.5 Suggested Readings

Andrade, G. and J. Lugo-Ocando. 2018. "The Angostura Address 200 Years Later: A Critical Reading," *Iberoamericana – Nordic Journal of Latin American and*

---

[14] For example, the legitimacy of democracy over alternatives can be defended by classical utilitarians on the grounds that it maximizes (i); by natural law theorists on the grounds that it maximizes (ii); and by social-contract theorists on the grounds that it maximizes (iii).

Caribbean Studies 47(1): 74–82. DOI:http://doi.org/10.16993/iberoamericana
.427

Close reading of Bolívar's "Angostura Address," with an eye to showing some ambiguities in his political philosophy. Takes those ambiguities to explain why the figure of Bolívar has been vindicated by representatives of the Latin American left, such as the "Bolivarian revolutionaries" of Venezuela and the FARC guerrilla group in Colombia, as well as representatives of the right, such as some Latin American dictators of the twentieth century, and Benito Mussolini.

Bolívar, Simón. 1812. *The Cartagena Manifesto. Manifesto Portal* (website).
    1951a. "Angostura Address," 1819, pp. 103–122 in *Selected Writings of Bolivar*, ed. Harold A. Bierck, Jr. New York: The Colonial Press (Reprint pp. 1–21 in Janet Burke and Ted Humphrey. 2007. *Nineteenth-Century Nation Building and the Latin American Tradition.* Indianapolis/Cambridge: Hackett) http://mani festoindex.blogspot.com/192011/04/cartagena-manifesto-1812-by-simon.html
    2004. "Jamaica Letter," 1815, pp. 105–119 in Susana and Gary Seay, eds., *Latin American Philosophy: An Introduction with Readings.* Upper Saddle Brook, NJ: Prentice Hall (also available online at http://faculty.smu.edu/bakewell/BAKEWELL/texts/jamaica-letter.html).

Classic sources for the views of the author discussed in this chapter.

Bushnell, David and John Callan James Metford. n.d. "José de San Martín: Argentine Revolutionary," *Encyclopaedia Britannica.* www.britannica.com /biography/Jose-de-San-Martin

Brief but informative account of the early years of the wars of independence.

Draper, Hal. 1968. "Karl Marx and Simón Bolívar: A Note on Authoritarian Leadership in a National-Liberation Movement," *New Politics* 7(1): 64–77. www.marxists.org/archive/draper/1968/winter/bolivar.htm

Rejects the view that Marx was misinformed about Bolívar, holding that he was reacting instead to Bolívar's authoritarian political philosophy, which Marx considered an instance of Bonapartism. On this interpretation, Marx thought that authoritarian republicanism was a regressive ideology for post-independence Latin America.

Fuentes, Carlos. 1992a. *El espejo enterrado.* Mexico: Fondo de Cultura Económica
    1992b. *The Buried Mirror.* Boston, MA: Houghton Mifflin.

A fascinating account of the contrasting political thought of Bolívar and San Martín. Emphasizes the progressive role of Bolívar's *mestizaje* model of Latin American identity but falls short of offering a critical analysis of his authoritarian republicanism.

Helg, Aline. 2003. "Simón Bolívar and the Spectre of Pardocracia: José Padilla in Post-Independence Cartagena," *Journal of Latin American Studies* 35: 447–471.

Although not focused strictly on Bolívar, this scholarly article offers helpful data about his political elitism and racism, which is especially evident in his doctrine concerning who should be eligible for public office in the new nations of Latin America – namely, only *criollos* from wealthy families. Offers evidence that Bolívar was particularly worry about granting too much power to emancipated slaves and people of mixed races.

Keating, Joshua. 2013. "Was Bolívar a 'Bolivarian'?" *Foreign Policy*, March 6. https://foreignpolicy.com/2013/03/06/was-bolivar-a-bolivarian/. Brief article arguing that Bolívar would have opposed the Bolivarian revolution of Hugo Chávez and Nicolás Maduro in Venezuela. Given my analysis of Bolívar's political philosophy in this chapter, I think that although he would have had no problem with the authoritarian element of this revolution, he would have rejected its socialist element.

Marx, Karl. 1858. "Bolívar y Ponte." *The New American Cyclopedia*, Vol. III. References here are made to the edition in the *Marxists Internet Archive*. www.marxists.org/archive/marx/works/1858/01/bolivar.htm

Polemic piece very critical of Bolívar, commonly ignored by the Latin American left.

Nuccetelli, Susana. 2017. "What the 'Nina'-Film Controversy Shows about African Heritage in the Americas," *The APA Newsletter on Hispanic/Latino Issues in Philosophy* (October): 4–7. http://c.ymcdn.com/sites/www.apaonline.org/resource/collection/60044C96-F3E0-4049-BC5A-271C673FA1E5/HispanicV17n1.pdf

Places Bolívar's model of Latin American identity in a historical context, which has Las Casas's vindication of the humanity of the Amerindians as an antecedent, and Vasconcelos's utopian cosmic race as a continuation. Argues that the influence of that model in the region is responsible for some differences in the character of race relations between Latin America and North America. Appeals to some differential reactions to the 2012 film *Nina* in each of the Americas to illustrate those differences.

Simon, Joshua. 2017. *The Ideology of Creole Revolution: Imperialism and Independence in American and Latin American Political Thought*. Cambridge, UK: Cambridge University Press.

Close examination of the philosophical ideas underlying proposals for the national organization of post-independence Latin America and the United States. Simon is interested in establishing some major commonalities and differences between the conceptions of nation building in Alexander Hamilton and Simón Bolívar among others.

Vinson III, Ben. 2018. *Before Mestizaje: The Frontiers of Race and Caste in Colonial Mexico*. New York: Cambridge University Press.

Monograph addressing issues of race in Mexico, and more broadly, in Spanish America during the colonial and the national-organization periods. Produces evidence of the racial discrimination that was characteristic of the colonial period, and which rested on an exceedingly complex system of racial and ethnic categorizations. Also analyzes the reactions to racism of some positivist nineteenth-century Mexican thinkers.

von Vacano, Diego A. 2012. *The Color of Citizenship: Race, Modernity and Latin American/Hispanic Political Thought*. Oxford: Oxford University Press.

Argues that Bolívar favored a Machiavellian type of republicanism, defined roughly along the lines of what I call 'Bolivarism.' But while I contend that Bolívar's inconsistencies amount to a ground for rejecting Bolivarism, von Vacano argues that they are a strength of the doctrine.

4   The Liberal Republicanism of Sarmiento and Alberdi

In this chapter, I consider a controversy between two political thinkers of the period of national organization that followed the end of the wars of independence in Latin America: Domingo Faustino Sarmiento (Argentine, 1811–1888) and Juan Bautista Alberdi (Argentine, 1810–1884). Each of them endorsed liberal republicanism, a family of doctrines of applied moral and political philosophy that was widely popular in the region during that period. As a result, Sarmiento and Alberdi had in common a general philosophical framework, even when each perceived his views as incompatible with the other. Nevertheless, I show here that they had in common much more than the general philosophical framework often ascribed to them.

4.1   Sarmiento's Liberal Republicanism

4.1.1   Life and Work

Argentinian educator, philosopher, and statesman Domingo Faustino Sarmiento championed the idea that geography, race, and education are factors that completely determine the Argentines' character in ways that determine the political and social arrangements that would be best for them. From the 1840s to approximately the 1860s, Sarmiento was an indefatigable liberal writer and political activist who won himself great influence both inside and outside Argentina. He is still celebrated there with a national anthem that praises his mastery of "sword, pen, and speech." Sarmiento wrote numerous essays, letters, and books in which he often combined literary narrative, history, biography, social commentary, and political pamphleteering. A classic among his books is a hybrid of these genres titled *Facundo, or Civilization and Barbarism*. First published in the Santiago de Chile newspaper *El Progreso* of under the title *Vida de Quiroga (The Life of Quiroga)*, it appeared in installments in May and June 1845. As in many of his other early writings, here too Sarmiento aimed at revealing the causes of Argentina's collapse into a state of lawlessness shortly after its independence from Spain. However he was not tempted to engage in any nostalgic vindication of colonial rule, because he was confident that democracy could prevail in his nation (and by extension, in other Latin American nations similarly affected by partition and civil strife). He believed that Argentina would adopt a liberal democratic order once it got rid of the causes of lawlessness, which on this view could be entirely attributed to the rise to power of the *caudillos* of the provinces. These were rural chieftains who had managed to gain their power by exploiting their popularity, especially among the temporary labor force of Argentina's *estancias* (large ranches). They began to acquire power during the wars of independence, and once these ended, they had enough power to defeat the more liberal leaders of the urban regions, who formed the first juntas and later declared the nation's independence from Spain.

One such *caudillo* of the province of Buenos Aires was landowner Juan Manuel de Rosas (1793–1877), who became governor of Buenos Aires by forcible means, and reigned with dictatorial powers from 1835 to 1852. To Sarmiento, Rosas was a symbol of lawlessness and therefore barbarism. Paradoxically, to Rosas's supporters he was "the Restorator of Laws," since he had after all restored a state of public order during his period of government.

Although Rosas did impose obedience of the laws of Buenos Aires with a firm hand, they were in fact his own laws. As the story is told by Sarmiento and other *unitarios* (i.e., opponents of Rosas), hordes of *federales* (i.e., supporters of Rosas) terrorized anyone who opposed his rule, not only in Buenos Aires but also in the country's interior, where he could count on the support of local *caudillos* (i.e., chieftains). Prominent among them was Facundo Quiroga (1788–1835), a populist leader of the La Rioja to whom Sarmiento in his book of 1845 sometimes refers as "tigre de los llanos" (tiger of the plains) and "espíritu de las pampas" (the spirit of the Pampas). Although Quiroga was assassinated shortly before Rosas seized control of the government of Buenos Aires, both are central characters in *Facundo*. The masses who led the *federales* to power also play a crucial role in this book.

Being an outspoken *unitario* and critic of Rosas, Sarmiento's life was in danger, and so he went into exile in neighboring Chile, from where he vigorously campaigned against Rosas for years until the tyrant was deposed in 1852. Upon Sarmiento's return to Argentina that year, he joined the forces working to establish a liberal democracy. From then until his death in 1888, he served in various official capacities, including as President of the Republic, an office he held from 1868 to 1874.

4.1.2   Civilization versus Barbarism in *Facundo*

In *Facundo* Sarmiento set out to explain the roots of Argentina's lawlessness and stagnation, betraying a deterministic doctrine whose similarities and differences with what I have called 'Bolivarism' in Chapter 3 will become obvious upon analysis. Sarmiento offered as an explanation a deterministic doctrine based on a dichotomy that can be summarized as follows:

> **The Civilization-versus-Barbarism Dichotomy**
> Some factors determine whether members of any ethnic and racial groups have a psychological character that predisposes them to be either civilized people or barbarians. Crucial among those factors are (i) the physical environment; (ii) race and ethnicity; and (iii) level of education.

Various deterministic doctrines that result from invoking one or more of these factors were widely popular among Latin American intellectuals of the time.[1] But here we need to take a closer look at Sarmiento's own deterministic doctrine, which takes into account factors (i) through (iii).

4.1.2.1   *The Physical Environment as a Determinant*

Given factor (i) in Sarmiento's casting of the civilization-versus-barbarism dichotomy, a people's physical environment is a determinant of their

---

[1] As we saw in Chapter 3, Bolívar himself was among the proponents of a determinist doctrine that counted history, race, and ethnicity as factors relevant to the form of polity suitable for a people. Although there is no explicit defense of the civilization-versus-barbarism dichotomy in his classic writings, his applied political philosophy might commit him to a weak version of that dichotomy, holding that some Latin American nations are not suited for liberal democracy.

tendency toward either civilization or barbarism. Sarmiento's defense of this thesis occurs not only in *Facundo*. For example, in his 1850 autobiographical *Recuerdos de Provincia* (*Memoirs from the Province*), he invokes anecdotal evidence about his own life to back it up. He argues for it with a narrative about the difficulties he himself faced in obtaining an education, owing to the fact that he grew up in San Juan, a remote western province of Argentina near the Andes, in a rural house far from the nearest school. Unable to participate in formal education, he read and studied on his own, ending up self-educated. This experience contributed to his belief that geographical factors play a role in the formation of a people's character. Although this anecdote alone hardly supports the thesis, scientific research in evolutionary psychology might support it if it were to discover that people's attitudes and conduct have been shaped by environmental pressures. In addition, we can note on behalf of Sarmiento that while distance is not an impediment to education today, in the Argentina of the nineteenth century it was. These facts suggest that Sarmiento might have a point in noting that people living in remote rural areas in his time grew up with environmental pressures that might have helped shape their attitudes and behavior.

However, this charitable interpretation of his thesis (i) fails to capture what Sarmiento had in mind with it. Consider *Facundo*, where his concern is to draw a sharp line between the civilized cities and the barbarian countryside of Argentina – and by extension, a similar line could be drawn among peoples of other Latin American nations. Sarmiento hypothesized that barbarism is the inevitable result of inhabiting vast prairie lands in general, and in particular, the vast plain that makes up much of central and southern Argentina, the so-called *pampas*. In chapter 1 of the book, suggestively titled "Physical Aspects of the Argentine Republic, and the Forms of Character, Habits, and Ideas Induced by It," he rhetorically contends that "[i]ts own extent is the evil from which the Argentine Republic suffers ... " (1998/1845: 9). True, as he says, at the time in the interior of the country one could travel great distances without seeing a village or a mountain. But Sarmiento's determinism goes a step further to claim a causal connection between topography/geography and psychological character: simply put, a plain "prepares the way for despotism," and since despotism grows in barbarism, a plain has a tendency to produce barbarism.

But why hold that there is a causal connection between inhabiting a region where one can only see the flat horizon, and a predisposition toward despotism and barbarism? Perhaps we can begin to answer that question by noting that during the nineteenth century, civilized people lived and traveled in the *pampas* at their peril. From here one may claim, with Sarmiento, "[t]his constant insecurity of life outside towns … stamps upon the Argentine character a certain stoical resignation to death by violence … Perhaps this is the reason why they inflict death or submit to it with so much indifference, and why such events make no deep or lasting impression upon the survivors."[2] Sarmiento thinks he has now established the causal link between geography and character. Cognizant of the empirical nature of that link (which, again, involves establishing a relation of determination), he seeks further support by drawing an analogy between relevant features of the *pampas* and of the endless steppes of Asia and Africa, where only Bedouins and other nomad people dwell. These he compared with *gauchos*, the nomads of the *pampas*. In either of the compared environments, caravans of nomads traverse the vastness with great hardship and in mortal danger.

Be that as it may, perhaps the analogy aims at supporting an argument that goes something like this: similarly to the leaders of African or Asian nomad tribes, the leaders of Argentinian provinces must often resort to violence to maintain order, thwart mutinies, or repel bandits and hostile native people. Therefore, people accustomed to living in this way become politically and morally coarsened, a state that involves tolerance of violence, treason, despotism, and other ills. Note that the argument now rests not only on moral but also on empirical beliefs that, as such, must be supported with evidence from the social sciences: we need data to establish any such correlation between life in vast plains or deserts and the tendency toward despotism, violence, and so on. Since Sarmiento produced no such evidence, we may conclude that he failed to establish thesis (i) above: there is no reason to see a causal link between people's geographical environment and a tendency to have authoritarian leaders or a proclivity to barbarism.

---

[2] Sarmiento (1998/1845: 10). He also refers to the *pampas* with clichés such as "the reign of brute force" and "the supremacy of the strongest."

4.1.2.2   Race and Ethnicity as Determinants

Let us now consider Sarmiento's deterministic thesis (ii), that a people's race and ethnicity determine their propensities to civilization or barbarism. In *Facundo* Sarmiento notes that the only common dwellers of the *pampas* are Amerindians and *gauchos*. The term *gauchos* in Argentina denotes people of mixed ancestry, usually Amerindian and Spanish. In the nineteenth century, they inhabited the *pampas*, occasionally working in *estancias* or hiding among the Amerindians when they ran into trouble with the law. Similar ethnic groups existed in other parts of South America, for example, the *Rotos* of Chile and the *Llaneros* of Venezuela. For Sarmiento, since the mores of Amerindians and *gauchos* were those of the distant plains, living in such an environment made them indolent, crude, and accustomed to squalor and violence. To emphasize the barbaric tendencies he saw in these groups, Sarmiento declared: "The Argentine Republic ends at the Arroyo del Medio" (1998/1845: 12). Here he is referring to a stream of water in the southern part of Buenos Aires province, which at the time marked the border with Amerindian controlled territory.

To draw this sharp line between the "barbaric" Amerindians and the *gauchos* of the *pampas* and the "civilized" inhabitants of the cities, Sarmiento invokes race and ethnicity. While the Amerindians and *gauchos* both roam over the *pampas*, it is only the Amerindians who are doomed to be barbarians, since the *gauchos* might be domesticated eventually and become civilized (provided the state implements this through laws penalizing vagrancy, something that Argentina did later that century).[3]

Accordingly, for the Amerindians Sarmiento had only terms of blame, while for the *gauchos* he combined general blame with qualified praise concerning their skills at horsemanship, shrewdness in relations to others, and knowledge of their physical environment. Even so, on Sarmiento's view, the *gauchos* come out as having a diminished moral standing (i.e., importance) in comparison to white people of any national origin. *Gauchos* even lack the moral standing of "noble savages" that James Fenimore Cooper gave to the Mohicans in his 1826 novel, which Sarmiento cites in

---

[3] Chapter 1 of *Facundo* contains one of Sarmiento's most explicit formulations of his social and racial biases. See Sarmiento (1998/1845, pp. 9–27), or reprint pp. 120–131 in Nuccetelli and Seay (2004).

connection with his enumeration of the practical virtues he ascribed to these dwellers of the *pampas*.[4] On his account, however, the Amerindians come out as having no virtues at all and thus, as being ineligible for moral standing. Accordingly, Sarmiento was committed to accepting the moral permissibility, or even obligation, of eliminating the Amerindians.

By bringing race and ethnicity factors to bear on his civilization-versus-barbarism dichotomy, Sarmiento made himself vulnerable to the grave charge of racism, although once again, he offered no concrete evidence for his views, which were partly empirical and partly evaluative. If we construe racism as the bias that race or ethnicity determines moral standing,[5] and the civilization-versus-barbarism dichotomy as ascribing various degrees of moral standing to the different ethnic groups of Latin America, Sarmiento's racist social stereotypes are as outlined in Table 1.

Given the taxonomy in this table, all Argentina's racial and ethnic groups fall more or less neatly on one side or the other of the civilization-versus-barbarism dichotomy. Sarmiento held that "[t]he people composing these two distinct forms of society do not seem to belong to the same nation …" (1998/1845: 19). Moreover, he appealed to some unidentified authorities to support his view that the physical environment is in part responsible for whether a people fall on one or the other side of that dichotomy. "Many philosophers have also thought," wrote Sarmiento, "that plains prepare the way for despotism, just as mountains furnish strongholds for the struggles of liberty …" (1998/1845: 14). He probably had in mind his two preferred Enlightenment thinkers, Montesquieu and Thomas Jefferson. However, as noted by Ilan Stavans (1998), Sarmiento typically made either unverifiable references like this one, or gave inaccurate information about the sources of his quotations. Left with no credible reason to support the racialist picture outlined in the above chart, Sarmiento's explanation of the lawlessness in post-independence Argentina collapses.

---

[4] Although Sarmiento mentions *The Last of the Mohicans* in *Facundo*, according to historian D. A. Brading (1991), it is James Fenimore Cooper's novel *The Prairie* that influenced him most.

[5] Adapting Peter Singer's definition of speciesism in *Practical Ethics*, I define racism as the bias that race determines moral standing. See also my discussion of the bias of sexism in Chapter 2.

Table 1 *Sarmiento's racial and ethnic stereotypes*

Europeans and North Americans of white, non-Spanish descent, plus the *criollos* of Argentina's major cities (at the time, Buenos Aires and Córdoba)	Sarmiento unambiguously counted these groups as qualifying as civilized and thus awarded them full moral standing.
White Spaniards	In Facundo (1998/1845) page 19, Sarmiento leaves it undecided whether these people are akin to other white Europeans, and thus eligible for civilization and to have full moral standing.
Afro-Latin Americans	This group qualifies as having some degree of civilization and therefore, some degree of moral standing. Of this group, he writes, "[t]his race mostly inhabiting cities, has a tendency to become civilized, and possesses talent and the finest instincts of progress" (1998/1845: 16).
Gauchos	In *Facundo*, Sarmiento is somewhat ambiguous about this group. On the one hand, he says that this group is "characterized by love of idleness and incapacity for industry" and "has not shown itself more energetic than the aborigines, when it has been left to its instincts in the wilds of America" (1998/1845: 17). So it seems the group qualifies neither for civilization nor for moral standing. On the other hand, Sarmiento leaves open the possibility that, if not "left to its instincts" (i.e., if monitored and trained), the group might actually qualify.
Amerindians	Sarmiento unambiguously counted these peoples as qualifying only for *barbarism* and thus as having no moral standing at all.

Janet Hooker (2017a: 68 ff.) has argued recently that a reading along these lines misses Sarmiento's real understanding of Latin American identity. Its error arises from focusing on *Facundo* and Sarmiento's other early writings, while his later works such as *Vida de Abraham Lincoln* (*The Life of Abraham Lincoln*) of 1866 are instead best at revealing what Hooker regards as a *mestizaje* model of Latin American identity. On her view, Sarmiento was in fact a "hemispheric writer" concerned about the "subaltern" status of his America (i.e., its underdevelopment), which he attempted to remedy by means of education first and immigration later. In addition, Hooker contends, Sarmiento is eager to bring the indigenous people of his country into civilized society by means of promoting their education. But I have found no textual evidence confirming her idiosyncratic claims about Sarmiento's views on identity, which amounts to denying the widely held thesis that he was a neocolonial liberal thinker who accounted for Latin American identity in terms of the European-transplantation theory. If his later writings are the best source, consider *Conflicto y armonía de las razas en América* (*Conflicts and Harmony of Races in America*), which certainly qualifies as late, since it was Sarmiento's next-to-last published book, appearing in 1883. A quick look at the book leaves no doubt that he upholds the racial stereotypes of *Facundo* until the end.[6]

4.1.2.3   Education as a Determinant

Finally, let us consider thesis (iii): that education determines whether people can be civilized or barbarian. If we assume that genocidal acts are barbaric, there are clear counterexamples to this claim in the history of the West. Hernán Cortés, the Spanish conqueror of Mexico, is a case in point. Having studied law before joining the conquest, Cortés counted as an educated man of his time. Yet he waged a savage war to dispossess the Aztecs of their lands and freedoms. Or consider the practice of scientific research on human subjects of the recent past. Some of these examples involved what may be considered barbaric abuse of experimental subjects,

---

[6] Consistent with the remarks on identity in *Facundo* (1998/1845: 14–19), in his later book *Armonía* not only does Sarmiento reassert his earlier racist view, but he also praises the United States for its policies toward Native Americans. That could not be more antithetical to the *mestizaje* model, which recognizes the Amerindians' contribution to the ethnic diversity of the region.

and not only were these performed by educated medical doctors: they were performed under the supervision of educated health officials.[7]

In light of such counterexamples, there is no straightforward interpretation under which thesis (iii) turns out to be plausible: it seems to be just plain false that a person's degree of education correlates with that person's degree of moral and civic virtues and vices. But perhaps what Sarmiento really means by thesis (iii) is his claim in *Recuerdos de Provincia* that there is a correlation between growing up in the remote countryside and having restricted opportunities for getting an education. Argentina's *estancias* at the time constituted an environment that encouraged feudal seclusion, while discouraging a sense of living according to commonly agreed rights and duties. In that environment, there is little room for acquiring the values of a cohesive society, and a lot of room for acquiring abilities in horsemanship, hunting, fighting, and the like, which become the most important values in people's lives.

Sarmiento of course deplored the fact that such are the "values" of the *caudillos* and the *gauchos*. Whether wealthy or poor, this means that people become barbarians as a result of their environment, which also cuts them off from education, culture, and all contact with the wider world. For them, the province mimics the *estancia*, since in both, proper government equally requires the firm hand of the *estanciero/caudillo*. By contrast, on Sarmiento's view not only do cities facilitate access to an education; they are also the vessels of civilization and of all human progress owing to their orderly and rational conventions of common life, conducive to commerce, industry, and the arts and sciences. Stamped with this kind of civilization, the psychological character of city dwellers exhibits a clear cultural superiority. But since under the Rosas regime Buenos Aires had been assailed by the barbarism of the countryside, Rosas becomes the main target of *Facundo*.

While Sarmiento was serving in public office, notably as Governor of San Juan and later as President of Argentina, he tried to spread this creed about the correlation between education and social progress. For example, while President he undertook a deep reform and expansion of the educational

---

[7] Think, for example, of the ghastly "experiments" on Jewish children in the Nazi concentration camp at Auschwitz conducted by the German doctor Josef Mengele. Or consider the syphilis study in Tuskegee, Alabama, carried out from 1932 to 1972 by doctors working for the US government's Public Health Service.

system in his country along positivist lines that he had learned about on diplomatic missions and journeys through Europe and to the United States, a country he greatly admired. But not all of his contemporaries shared his enthusiasm for trying to move his country forward by means of improving education. His main political rival among the liberals of Argentina, Juan Bautista Alberdi, argued that the engine of progress was to be found elsewhere.

4.2 Alberdi's Liberal Republicanism

4.2.1   Life and Work

Juan Bautista Alberdi was born in the northern Argentinian province of Tucumán, in 1810, the year the anti-royalists of Buenos Aires deposed its Spanish authorities and installed its first autonomous junta. A few months after his birth, his mother died, leaving him an orphan. It was in Buenos Aires that he later received a formal education in the institutions commonly attended by the offspring of upper-class *criollo* residents of the city. Like some of his classmates, he grew up to become a notable member of the country's mid-1800s intellectual and political elite. During his years in high school, at the Colegio de Ciencias Morales, as well as during the studies of jurisprudence that followed, he developed an interest in a wide range of disciplines, from literature and music to philosophy and politics. He also forged close friendships with other students, many of whom went on to become well-known public figures.

In fact, Alberdi's connections with renowned offspring of the *criollo* ruling class began early in life. The record shows that as early as 1830, while still a student in high school, he accepted an offer of lodging at the house of the grandfather of future literary figure Miguel Cané (1851–1905). And while still in law school, he developed close friendships with two other Argentine intellectuals, José María Gutiérrez (1809–1878) and Esteban Echeverría (1805–1851), both of whom were soon to have a place among the most important literary figures of Argentina's romantic movement. Alberdi's own works of literary fiction positions him as among the leading lights of the romantic group known as the 'generación del 37' (generation of 1837). Young Alberdi also became active in some of the most selective intellectual, artistic and social circles first in Buenos Aires, and later in neighboring Montevideo, where he sought exile from 1838 to 1852 during part of the period of Rosas's dictatorship.[8] Although he later returned to Argentina, being in exile became a familiar condition of life for him, owing to the number of enemies he made through his political convictions. Chief among them was Sarmiento, who at one point wielded great power in Argentine politics. In light of their fierce disputes, Alberdi appears to have thought of Sarmiento as someone who was even capable of plotting his assassination (Feinmann 1996: 167). Be that as it may, their differences on key issues were far from substantive – or so I argue in the next section.

But for now what matters is Alberdi's liberal doctrine for Latin America, which he began seriously developing after 1852, the year Rosas was defeated in the Battle of Caseros. That year Alberdi returned to Argentina and published the *Bases y puntos de partida para la organización política de la República Argentina* (*Bases and Starting Points for the Political Organization of the Argentine Republic*).[9] Consistent with the major liberal ideas of his time (in particular, Alexander Hamilton's), this book materially influenced the 1853 Constitution of Argentina. Unsurprisingly, it won Alberdi the nickname 'Father of the Argentinian Constitution.' We will now take a close look at two of its pillars. One is a recasting of Sarmiento's civilization-versus-barbarism dichotomy on Alberdi's own terms. The other is a program of selective immigration based on racial stereotypes as objectionable as Sarmiento's, such as the belief that northern Europeans had a greater

---

[8] By the late 1830s, Alberdi was an active member of the Salón Literario and the Asociación de la Joven Argentina, among other organizations. The latter soon became a political group of opposition to Rosas when transplanted to Montevideo by the Argentine exiles, who then called it 'Asociación de Mayo' as way to vindicate the Argentinians' rebellion against Spanish rule in May 1810. For a detailed biography of Alberdi, see Oscar Terán (2004: 123–132).

[9] Alberdi's *Bases*, the direct source of his native country's constitution of 1853, represents a classic exposition of his liberal political thought. In its introduction, he swiftly dismisses the Bolivarian *mestizaje* model of Latin American identity and proposes instead what I have called 'the European-transplantation model.' He also recasts Sarmiento's civilization-versus-barbarism dichotomy in terms of coast versus inland. For some excerpts in English from *Bases*, see Nuccetelli and Seay (2004).

tendency to value freedom, compared with the Spaniards, the French, and the Italians.[10]

4.2.2   Civilization versus Barbarism Revisited

Although Alberdi agrees with Sarmiento that postrevolutionary Latin America must choose between civilization and barbarism, he gives this dichotomy his own twist. For one thing, he takes Sarmiento to understand the dichotomy in terms of *knowledge versus ignorance* and proposes instead an interpretation in terms of *prosperity versus stagnation*. Accordingly, he rejects Sarmiento's claim that education is the key for the region's progress, contending that Sarmiento relies without evidence on the power of "ideas." Sarmiento, says Alberdi, missed the point, which is the economy. Once the focus is in the right place, the key to civilization is not expanding education but population growth, a precondition in Latin America for economic development. Commonly two slogans are offered in the literature to capture this disagreement: for Sarmiento 'to govern is to educate,' while for Alberdi 'to govern is to populate.' Alberdi thought that in the mid-nineteenth century, civilization in Latin America was inseparable from economic progress. From this premise, his line of reasoning for making immigration the key to such progress runs straightforwardly like this:

1. Civilization amounts to, or at least necessarily depends on, economic progress.
2. Economic progress requires the sort of disciplined, self-motivated, and skillful labor force that's available in, for example, Britain or the United States.
3. Latin America does not have, and cannot produce on its own, a labor force of that kind.
4. *Therefore,* the key to civilization in Latin America is to build such a labor force.
5. *Therefore,* the key to civilization in Latin America is selective immigration.

[10] See for instance volume vii of Alberdi's *Escritos Postumos* (Alberdi 1997).

Alberdi subscribed to the widely known tenet of capitalist economics according to which a successful economy ordinarily requires a sizable labor force, which in turn may contribute to the growth of markets. But as described by Sarmiento, nineteenth-century Latin America appeared abundant in vast, empty spaces sorely in need of industrious people to inhabit them and reap the benefits of their exploitable natural resources. If achieving civilization equates with achieving economic prosperity, and population growth is a necessary and sufficient condition of economic prosperity, then Alberdi's view that the flourishing of Argentine society depended upon solving the labor-force problem follows apodictically. Of course, a solution might be within grasp by means of *either* promoting inner population growth, fostering immigration from anywhere (i.e., nonselective immigration), *or* both. But for Alberdi there was only one possible solution to the problem: bring skillful workers *from northern Europe*. Why? The answers rest on his theory of Latin America identity.

4.2.3   The European-Transplantation Theory

Alberdi's program of selective immigration is closely connected to what Matías Farías (2017) calls 'the transplantation theory' of Latin American identity, also ascribable to Sarmiento. Given this theory, Latin America is simply an outgrowth of European civilization, it amounts to nothing more than a part of Europe transplanted to another continent. "What we call independent [Latin] America," writes Alberdi, "is nothing more than Europe established in America, and our revolution is nothing more than the separation of a European power in two parts . . . All in our civilization is European . . . " (2017/1853: 91, my translation). This passage appears in section XIV of his *Bases* under the suggestive subtitle, "The Civilizing Action of Europe in the Republics of South-America." The section runs for about five pages, in which Alberdi exalts the virtues of European civilization together with Latin Americans' historical, racial, and cultural connections to it. We are told that these peoples are the exclusive product of the European discovery: Europeans created and named all the major cities of Spanish America. They also gave their inhabitants a language and their ways of life, from clothes to books. The indigenous peoples, he thinks, have contributed nothing at all to the culture of this region: "the Amerindian neither figures in nor composes our political and civil society" (ibid.). About the contribution of Afro-Latin Americans, he has nothing at all to say. He simply ignores it.

But about the prospect of people of mixed races like the *gaucho*, he appears more pessimistic even than Sarmiento, who as you may recall leaves open the possibility that, if *not* "left to their instincts," the *gauchos* could be part of civil society. By contrast, Alberdi thinks that, when it comes to this group of marginalized people, there is little room for any *perfectibilidad* (literally, 'perfectibility,' by which he means 'capability to improve'). He declares unambiguously that, as far as the *gaucho* is concerned, even if one makes available "all the transformations of the best educative system, not even then could one render him similar to an English worker who works, consumes, lives with dignity and comfort."[11]

But such differences between Alberdi and Sarmiento on Latin American identity are, of course, very irrelevant. For the most part, they are in agreement about how to place the various racial and ethnic groups of Latin America in terms of the civilization-versus-barbarism distinction: the "savage" Amerindian and the *gaucho* on the one extreme, and the "civilized" Europeans and their *criollo* descendants on the other.

At the same time, although they generally agreed with this socially insensitive (indeed racist) picture, since Alberdi rejected Sarmiento's cities-versus-plains casting of the dichotomy, their views on this are not entirely the same. For Alberdi, what predisposes a people to be civilized or barbarian (and thus, to have or lack moral standing) is not whether they live in a city or on the plains, or whether they are educated or ignorant. Rather, it is what I have called above 'the race/ethnicity factor': namely, whether or not they are of European descent. Thus Alberdi's view amounts to a reductionism of Sarmiento's position, where the only factors that matter for being civilized – and therefore, for having moral standing – are race and ethnicity. He holds a kind of essentialism on this issue, whereby Europeans

---

[11] Alberdi (2017/1852: 98). Regarding the Amerindians, there is abundant textual evidence in this section of Alberdi's *Bases* that he made no room for them in civil society. To support his claims, he offers some beside-the-point arguments invoking, for example, the clothes the *criollos* wear (which were all of European style), or their negative reactive attitudes if a daughter were to want to marry an Amerindian.

qualify for civilization *by nature*: they could not become barbarians even if left to dwell in the *pampas*, to which he refers as "the desert" (2017/1852).

Yet Alberdi does concede that there is *one* geographical factor that plays a relevant role in the civilization-versus-barbarism dichotomy, though it is not the factor identified by Sarmiento. Rather, it is whether a people inhabits a region on the coast or one inland. Here is how he explains this coastal/inland factor:

> The only subdivision in the case of Latin American men is man from the coast or man from the inland. This division is real and profound. The man in the first group is the result of the civilizing action of the Europe of this century. The man in the other group is the result of the Europe of the 16th century, the time of the Conquest. He remains intact, as if preserved in a vessel, in the people of the interior of our continent, where Spain put him with the intention that he remain that way. (Alberdi 2017/1852: 93, my translation)

But why would it be that coastal regions fall on the 'civilization' side of the divide while interior regions do not? Given Alberdi's Eurocentric bias, the claim in this passage makes a lot of sense because it is through the coastal cities that Latin America has direct contact with Europe. He actually says that inland cities are perforce culturally backward, even cities with universities (he may have been thinking of inland Córdoba, Argentina, with its sixteenth-century university). For him, the life of universities is not crucial to the spread of civilized culture in the modern world because only the life of commerce and free trade can play such a civilizing role. On Alberdi's view, that life, with all it had to teach Latin Americans about modernity and progress, can thrive only in the cosmopolitan coastal cities. What they need to learn, Alberdi thinks, is to be learned there, and not in the hoary, classical studies promoted by the academy. Since it is easy to imagine that Latin American universities in Alberdi's day, still dominated by Scholasticism, were in fact not very exciting places, his view, charitably construed, is a kind of pragmatism far from any sort of philistine rejection of scholarship and high culture. In the company of other nineteenth-century liberals, Alberdi believed that a more open society based on commerce and free enterprise within a democratic polity was the key to progress and human flourishing in Latin America.

4.3   The Upshot

I have argued that, in matters concerning the aspects of their political thought relevant to the present discussion, the differences between Sarmiento and Alberdi are almost trivial. For one thing, each of these thinkers had a strong faith in market capitalism, which at the time was a progressive view firmly opposed to autocratic rule. By contrast with Bolívar, who believed in the effectiveness of dictators, Sarmiento and Alberdi thought that dictatorial regimes were a great evil to be resisted. Their vision for the future of Latin America favored elitist representative democracies in which "qualifying" people could choose their leaders in regular elections. It combined a liberal defense of democracy based on values such as freedom, order, and economic development, with a backward view in terms of who, among Latin Americans, in fact qualified for the exercise of democracy.

On the issue of the racial and ethnic identity of Latin America, Alberdi was in profound agreement with Sarmiento, regardless of the numerous small issues that found them in different camps.[12] Their European-transplantation view of Latin American identity praises the "civilizing" effects of Europe on Latin America, to which Sarmiento added those of the United States. It is not only antithetical to the view of Latin America's identity as a mixture of races and ethnicities. It conflicts also with the recognition of the region's Iberian legacy that came at the turn of the century, which I revisit in Chapter 7. That recognition was implicit in Bolívar's acknowledgment that the Spaniards were already a mixture of African and European races when they invaded the Americas, where their hybrid blood combined further with that of the Amerindians. In light of these views, there is no doubt that both Alberdi and Sarmiento were neocolonial thinkers for whom Latin American culture was, and must remain, entirely Western. There is no trace of non-Western cultures in Latin America's collective identity. According to both of them, whatever is "civilized" and therefore worth keeping in Latin America has roots in France, Britain, or the United States.

[12] The numerous disputes on matters of public policy between Sarmiento and Alberdi are well documented in letters attacking each other that they published in newspapers and magazines during the second half of the nineteenth century. Sarmiento published 101 letters that were collected later in a volume titled *Las ciento y una* (*The Hundred and One*). A reprint of Alberdi's letters attacking Sarmiento appeared in his book *Cartas Quillotanas* (*Quillotanas Letters*).

But at the end of the day, neither Sarmiento nor Alberdi could provide any plausible reason for the civilization-versus-barbarism dichotomy. Apart from some superficial observations about the ways of life of people they considered barbarians, they had no credible evidence for claims such as that which suggested that the Amerindians could not be industrious and live in a peaceful society. It goes without saying that their racist diagnoses of the problems facing post-independence Latin America must be rejected on moral grounds. It would, however, be a mistake to dismiss Sarmiento's and Alberdi's liberal programs, so full of bias, as unimportant since, for good or ill, they were most influential among the *criollos* political philosophers of the region at that crucial time. What shall we make of this unsettling conclusion? Perhaps only that assent by peers rewards wisdom less often than folly.

Note finally that both Sarmiento and Alberdi abandoned the *mestizaje* model of Latin American identity championed by some of the political thinkers of the previous generation, most notably Bolívar. Yet these three Latin American thinkers shared a basic commitment to social and political determinism, since the three of them independently regarded certain factors of Spanish America concerning the physical environment, history, and racial as well as ethnic background of its peoples as determinants of the social and political arrangement they could, and should, have. This agreement is not surprising since these Latin American thinkers were autochthonous proto-positivists. And the positivism of the nineteenth century was of course a deeply deterministic general philosophical outlook, about which I will have more to say in the next chapter.

4.4   Suggested Readings

Alberdi, Juan Bautista. 2017/1852. *Bases y puntos de partida para la organización política de la República Argentina*. Buenos Aires: Biblioteca del Congreso. https://bcn.gob.ar/uploads/BasesAlberdi.pdf

A classic source for Alberdi's views that are discussed in this chapter.

Farías, Matías. 2017. "Prólogo," pp. 7–54 in Alberdi 2017/1852.

Comprehensive study of the chief theses in Alberdi's "Bases," with a focus on his European-transplantation model of Latin American identity and his casting of the civilization-versus-barbarism dichotomy.

Feinmann, José Pablo. 1996. *Filosofía y Nación: Estudios sobre el pensamiento argentino*. Buenos Aires: Ariel.

Excellent source for the liberalism of Sarmiento and Alberdi's political philosophy (pp. 166–172). Since both thinkers pushed for legislation friendly to European investments in the region, Feinmann considers them neocolonial figures who aimed at promoting European interests in Latin America. Both of them supported economic protectionism in Europe but not in Spanish America. But Sarmiento was a hard liberal who advocated for a centralized power in Buenos Aires, while Alberdi was a soft liberal who had federalist convictions and favored assigning more representation in the government to the provinces.

Hooker, Juliet. 2017a. *Theorizing Race in the Americas: Douglass, Sarmiento, Du Bois, and Vasconcelos*. New York: Oxford.

Interesting for readers seeking a new, provocative interpretation of Sarmiento's views on race and identity. I have argued above that there is no sufficient textual evidence for agreeing with Hooker's claim that the Sarmiento of *Facundo* is not representative of his mature political philosophy.

Sarmiento, Domingo F. 1998/1845. *Facundo or, Civilization and Barbarism*. New York: Penguin,

A classic source for Sarmiento's views as discussed in this chapter.

Schulman, Sam. 1948. "Juan Bautista Alberdi and His Influence on Immigration Policy in the Argentine Constitution of 1853," *The Americas* 5(1): 3–17.

Favorable reading of Alberdi's program of selective immigration. Argues that when implemented in Argentina, the program triggered the country's development and accounts for the boom in trade that this country underwent during the early twentieth century.

Stavans, Ilan. 1998/1845. "Introduction," pp. vii–xiv in Sarmiento 1998/1845.

Brief but informative introduction to Sarmiento's *Facundo*, with an emphasis on the analysis of the hybrid literary forms represented in this book.

Swanson, Philip. 2003b. "Civilization and Barbarism," pp. 69–85 in Swanson 2003a.

Good as an introductory reading to the dichotomy of civilization versus barbarism. Contends that it was in fact triggered by the partisan belligerence of leaders in the wars of independence, some of whom where rural *caudillos*. The author also interprets that dichotomy in terms of the opposition between the *unitarios* who pursued a centralized form of government and the *federales* who fought for more political power in the hands of the provinces. While the intellectual leaders from the cities defended unitarianism, the landowners preferred federalism. Swanson offers a reductionist reading of Sarmiento's *Facundo* according to which its goal is "simply arguing that any system of government not based on fairness and consensus is akin to barbarism" (p. 72).

Terán, Oscar. 2004. *Las palabras ausentes: Para leer los escritos póstumos de Alberdi.* Buenos Aires: Fondo de Cultura Económica.

Somewhat speculative analysis of Alberdi's *Escritos Póstumos (Posthumous Writings)* which nonetheless provides a useful map of this monumental work consisting of sixteen volumes. First published in 1886–1887 within his *Obras Completas* and reprinted as an independent work in 1997, *Escritos* contains some explicit formulations of some of the ideas discussed in this chapter, such as the European-transplantation theory that underlined Alberdi's program of selective immigration. Guided by a map provided by Terán (p. 95), readers interested in that particular theory of Alberdi's should read volume vii of the *Escritos*.

5   Homegrown and Imported Positivism

In the first half of the nineteenth century, the prospects for the new Latin American nations appeared rather gloomy. The countries that had fought as one to free themselves from Spain's colonial rule were soon plunged into two decades of civil war and social unrest, approximately between the years 1810 and 1826. And Brazil, a nation that had achieved its independence from Portugal by diplomatic means, ended up being governed by a new monarchy with its seat in Rio de Janeiro. Widespread poverty and political stagnation afflicted both the Spanish- and the Portuguese-speaking nations of the American continent.

Unsurprisingly, then, the most interesting philosophical work of the region at the time turned to questions concerning the best ways to advance "civilization," "progress," "order," and the like. As peace and political stability at last took some hold throughout Latin America in the 1850s, social and political questions continued to be the chief focus of noteworthy work in Latin American philosophy. This philosophical inquiry was motivated, at least in part, by the stark contrast between the subcontinents, a prosperous north and a stagnated south. That undeniable reality presented a puzzle that major thinkers of Latin America wished to solve by developing deterministic theories of their own, broadly modeled on European doctrines of the time. Think, for example, of Sarmiento and Alberdi, who together with other early Latin American positivists, paved the way for a quick, full-blooded adoption of European positivism. Arturo Ardao (Uruguayan, 1912–2003), a historian of the movement, sets its high noon in Latin America between 1870 and 1911. He also notes the previous existence of an autochthonous positivism this side of the Atlantic, which facilitated a quick adoption and transformation of European varieties, such as Comtean positivism, classical utilitarianism, and social Darwinism.[1]

You may recall from the previous chapter on Sarmiento and Alberdi that a central question for those early positivists was "Who are we?" – to which they gave deterministic answers based on factors such as race, ethnicity, and geography. For later positivists, that question clearly had a normative force, since they recast it as asking instead "Who should we be?" These intellectual *criollos* of the ruling elite took themselves to have already figured out the collective identity of their nations and found problems with it. They were eager to change it in any ways that might be conducive to order, progress, and eventually freedom. True, their nations had won their political independence from Spain and Portugal. But cultural, religious, and philosophical independence was something else again. These kinds of independence required the elimination of persistent conservative values in society, which positivists associated with Iberian rule and the Catholic Church. Was it worth it to hold on to such values? Or were there other, better, role models that could help these fledgling societies on the way to prosperity? Positivists responded with a plain 'No' to the first question, and an equally plain 'Yes' to the second.

5.1 Positivism Characterized

5.1.1 Narrowly Construed Positivism

As Spanish and Portuguese influence declined throughout the Americas during the nineteenth century, that of France, Britain, and the United States grew proportionately, and Latin American thinkers increasingly looked to these nations for new paradigms in political and social philosophy. The local positivists interpreted those paradigms as offering practical directions for the prosperity and stability of their nations. On their view, if the people of these nations could reinvent themselves by adopting the distinctive mindset of the French or of the "Anglo-Saxon" cultures, perhaps they would evolve to enjoy similar achievements in commerce, politics,

---

[1] Ardao (1963) reconstructs the history of Latin American positivism along these lines. For other reconstructions of this doctrine consistent with Ardao's, see for example Cappelletti (1991), Miliani (1963), and Clark (2009).

and technology, which would lead them to prosperity and social progress. The desired mindset was made up of normative judgments about what sorts of things were valuable and which courses of action worth pursuing. It constituted a worldview shaped by the philosophy of positivism, which Latin Americans increasingly saw as fueling the success of European and North American industrial societies.

Positivism is in fact a family of philosophical and methodological doctrines. Narrowly construed, the term 'positivism' refers to the doctrine that Auguste Comte (French, 1798–1857) articulated as the scientific study of societies, which he called 'sociology.' This doctrine develops some ideas of the utopian socialists of an earlier generation, especially of Claude-Henri Saint-Simon (French, 1760–1825), a teacher of Comte, who influenced him through his pioneering *Nouveau Christianisme* of 1825. In this book, Saint-Simon hypothesized about the nature of mature societies and contended that political doctrines must be based on empirical data from history and the social sciences. Without a doubt, Comte was influenced also by evolutionary biology and the epistemology of empiricism (more on this shortly).

With these and other elements, Comte produced an original account of the evolution of thought and societies that was itself highly influential from the 1850s onward, especially in France and Latin America. He offered it in a series of volumes published under the titles *Cours de philosophie positive* (1830–1842) and *Système de politique positive* (1851–1854). Relevant to our discussion is the law of three stages that Comte offered in *Cours*, which he took to regulate the development of human thought (and by extension, human society). As this law goes, human thought inexorably transitions from one to the other of these three stages:

i. A magical or theological stage in which human thought aims at the explanation of natural phenomena, whether they be natural things, states, or events, by relying on the positing of gods, evil creatures, angels, or other supernatural agents.

ii. A metaphysical stage in which human thought aims at the explanation of natural phenomena by relying on the positing of supra-sensible but impersonal entities – these include the substances, qualities, vital forces, or other entities posited in metaphysics and any pseudo-

empirical thing, state, or event posited in science (e.g., ether, phlogis-
ton, Atlantis).

iii. A final, positivist stage in which human thought aims at the explanation of natural phenomena by relying on science. At this stage in the
development of thought, science has abandoned any reliance on metaphysics and proceeds only by empirical methods.

This brand of positivism, call it 'Comtism,' has some remarkable features
that, when transplanted to Latin America, were bound to annoy conserva-
tives. For one thing, Comtism seems incompatible with religious belief
since it is committed to considering it a product of the least developed
stage (i) above. Moreover, Comtism entails that traditional metaphysics –
say, Thomism, Cartesian dualism, or Kant's transcendental idealism –
counts only as the product of stage (ii) and must therefore be overcome
by mature thought, which is that of stage (iii). So both religious and metaphysical thinking must be overcome by scientific, empirical theories.

In addition, Comte recommended that, in a society where thought had
reached the third stage of development, government would take the form of
a sociocracy. On this proposal, scientists, whose beliefs rely exclusively on
observation and hypothesis, run the government. As eccentric as sociocracy
may seem, the idea that scientists should either advise or control the government was something familiar to the utopian socialists of the generation
previous to Comte's. And it was implemented with mixed consequences in
Latin America, especially in Mexico and Brazil. However, not all positivists
accepted these typically Comtean doctrines. The term 'positivism,' when
broadly construed, applies also to a number of other philosophical doctrines
of the nineteenth century and beyond.[2]

5.1.2   Broadly Construed Positivism

Positivism broadly construed (which hereafter is simply referred to as
'positivism') includes a family of theories incompatible with any idealist
philosophy but compatible with a naturalist ontology and an empiricist

---

[2] Other theories consistent with positivism, broadly construed, include logical positivism, empirio-criticism, and all varieties of evolutionary ethics.

epistemology. We may formulate these background assumptions of all positivist theories this way:

- Naturalism – The thesis that the natural world is all there is.
- Empiricism – The thesis that knowledge of what there is relies only on either observation or inference from observation.

To qualify as positivist, a theory must be consistent with these theses and any of their implications. For example, naturalism entails:

- Secularism – The thesis that there is no supernatural agency.

Given this implication of positivism, belief in supernatural agents or supernatural causes is groundless: there are no such things.[3] It follows that there are no good grounds for standard religion (i.e., religion in the Abrahamic traditions). Yet at least at some point Comte himself was in favor of a "religion of humanity," which amounts to no religion at all. Furthermore, it is well known that his followers around the world created institutions of the sort called 'Church of Humanity,' where secular people gathered to discuss, among other things, matters of life and death, but from a scientific rather than a religious perspective. However, the very idea of a Church of Humanity appears to make a creed or dogma out of secularism, a move that would render positivism antithetic to philosophy.[4]

Other theses commonly associated with positivist theories, even if not entailed by them, include:

- Physicalism – The thesis that all there *is* is the physical world.
- Scientism – The thesis that science is the *only* path to knowledge of what there is.

---

[3] Since, according to naturalism, the only real phenomena are those of the natural world, it follows that there are no supernatural beings, and therefore, that terms such as 'angel' and 'God' do not name any agents who actually exist – they are similar to 'Santa Claus' or 'Superman' in that they are merely names of fictional entities.

[4] Among those who would agree with this claim is Ludwig Wittgenstein, for whom having a creed, even an atheist creed, is incompatible with the open-mindedness needed to be a philosopher. In *Zettel* (Wittgenstein 1970: 81), he writes "455. (The philosopher is not a citizen of any community of ideas. That is what makes him into a philosopher)."

- Progressivism – The thesis that perfectibility (i.e., change for the better) is inevitable for certain entities such as biological organisms, human societies, or even celestial bodies.

Compared with naturalism, physicalism makes the stronger claim that everything in the natural world is physical. If so, there are no immaterial entities such as minds, meanings, numbers, or moral right and wrong. But a naturalist who is not a physicalist would deny that. She could say that the universe contains, besides material objects, properties of material objects such as minds (Moore 1953). The physicalist might reply that physics has demonstrated that only physical things can be causes of natural phenomena. But we now have an ongoing debate in metaphysics that goes beyond what can be undertaken here. For our purposes, let us simply note that many positivists have endorsed physicalism even when they were committed only to naturalism. Their physicalism was fueled by their conviction that only science can reveal what exists in the universe. That is, it was fueled by scientism, a thesis that is consistent with, but not entailed by, the empiricism required to qualify as a positivist.

For different but related reasons positivists have been attracted to progressivism, which vindicates the inevitability of progress among societies, species, and so on. Latin American positivists had great confidence in social progress, accounting for it along either Comtean or Spencerian lines. They showed these tendencies largely in two ways. The Comtean notion of progress cropped up in theories about how to bring political stability, economic prosperity, and technological advancement to their new nations, commonly embracing the motto "order and progress." The Spencerian notion underwrote some racialist speculations about groups of people it perceived as better or worse fitted for survival. The Latin American positivists of the next century would also embrace progress, but with different twists, among which the Marxist account was salient. This account invoked the metaphor of the "wheel of history" to refer to the view that societies' economic and social conditions constantly move forward toward better stages. I will have more to say about all these perspectives on progress as they become relevant to the topics considered next.

5.2 Positivism in Chile: The Lastarria/Bello Controversy

Since positivism can be shown to have had considerable influence in Latin American thought, let us first take a close look at its role in a controversy between two of Chile's most prominent positivists of the mid-nineteenth century, Andrés Bello (Venezuelan-born, 1781–1865) and José Victorino Lastarria (Chilean, 1817–1888). They were both influential in the post-independence period, though Bello, being from a previous generation, also played a role during the wars of independence. The controversy of interest to us here concerns chiefly whether philosophical reflection on the true nature of Spanish colonial rule in America might promote progress in Chile, and by extension, other Latin American countries. Lastarria and Bello agree that progress is necessary but disagree about how to achieve it. While Bello comes out of this controversy as linking progress with order and fearing that radical changes might undermine that order, Lastarria associates progress with a radical departure from what he regards as a conservative worldview inherited from Spain and the Catholic Church. In the course of challenging what seems to him the conservative worldview of Bello, Lastarria proposes a philosophical approach to historical research that also clashes with Bello's position on the methodology of history.

Now, since the question of which is the best historiographical method is an issue that falls beyond my expertise, in what follows I outline Lastarria's position but focus mostly on what he wrote about the value for post-independence Latin America of engaging in a moral assessment of the ills of the Spanish conquest. I believe that Bello's views on this topic fall short of meeting Lastarria's challenge because they founder on the so-called *problem of justice*, the classical utilitarianism that Bello defended in some of his writings. He came to accept that moral theory during his nearly two decades of residence in Great Britain, perhaps as result of conversations with his friend, James Mill (1773–1836), who contributed, along with his son John Stuart Mill (1806–1873) and Jeremy Bentham (1748–1832) to the establishment of classical utilitarianism. Bentham and John Stuart Mill offered an account of right conduct that grounds it entirely on two psychological and therefore natural properties, happiness and pain. These psychological properties are to be studied with the empirical method of scientific psychology. Since classical utilitarianism does not make the moral rightness (or wrongness) of actions contingent on any supra-empirical properties whose study would fall within the provinces of theology or metaphysics, classical utilitarianism turns out to be a form of positivism broadly construed.[5] Its sole principle of right conduct, known as the 'principle of utility,' holds that whether an action is right or wrong in a circumstance depends on its tendency to maximize or minimize the total balance of happiness over pain for most people concerned.[6]

On the other hand, Lastarria too took the consequences of some actions to matter morally, but for reasons that need not consist in this utilitarian principle. His positivist challenge to Bello, and therefore, to the ruling elite of Chile at the time, emphasized the value of justice and freedom alongside the value of prosperity and progress. As I read Lastarria, justice and freedom are worth pursuing for their own sake, not merely as means to happiness.

5.2.1   Lastarria on the Legacy of the Conquest

As we have seen, the Latin American positivists generally rallied against values, institutions, and practices they associated with colonial Spain and the Catholic Church. They regarded them as impediments to social and economic progress, the highest social value on their agenda. Both Bello and Lastarria accepted this premise. But for the latter, a necessary condition for progress in Latin America was freedom, broadly construed to include the typical freedoms of liberal democracies, from free trade to freedom of the press, freedom of expression, and freedom of religious belief, including secularism. Some of Lastarria's writings explore historical issues to support

[5] Classical utilitarianism meets all three conditions outlined above for being a positivist ethical theory: namely, it qualifies for a type of secularism, naturalism, and empiricism. The two standard sources for classical utilitarianism are Jeremy Bentham's *Principles of Morals and Legislation* (Amherst, NY: Prometheus, 1988/1789) and John Stuart Mill's *Utilitarianism* (Indianapolis: Hackett, 1978/1861).

[6] Jorrín and Martz (1970: 99) also ascribe to Bello the moral and political philosophy of classical utilitarianism. In fact, Bello was not the only Latin American thinker of the period attracted to classical utilitarianism, as shown by the philosophy of some of the Mexican positivists considered later in this chapter. According to Francisco Romero (1949), Bentham himself actively sought contact with, and provided recommendations to, political thinkers of the region. Romero's example of classical utilitarian in Argentina is Bernardino Rivadavia (1780–1845), member of the postrevolutionary governing elite and the country's first President (1826–1827).

his conviction that the remnants of a colonial worldview in post-independence Latin America precluded the materialization of freedom, justice, and prosperity. Notable among these writings is a speech delivered at the University of Chile at Santiago in 1842 under the title, "Investigaciones sobre la influencia social de la conquista i del sistema colonial de los españoles en Chile" ("Investigations on the Social Influence of the Spanish Conquest and Colonial Regime in Chile"). There are some facts about Lastarria's life that can help explain what might have prompted him to revisit Spanish colonialism at a time when most of Latin America had put it behind them – or so it seemed.

Lastarria belonged to the first generation of Chilean *criollos* born after independence. Highly educated, in 1839 he had already become a reputable educator himself at the Instituto Nacional of Santiago in the area of jurisprudence. But not only was the law among his interests and competences: like many other prominent intellectuals of his time (think of Alberdi, Sarmiento and, as we will see, Bello), he also tried his hand at literature, history, politics, and diplomacy. His performance in all these fields showed a commitment to a radical liberal agenda on how best to promote progress in the region. In the "Investigaciones," he aimed at advancing this agenda by persuading his educated audience at the University of Chile about (i) the advantages of "philosophy of history" over "narrative history" and (ii) the backwardness of Spain's colonial rule in Latin America in some domains he considered crucial to progress. The first issue concerns the methodology of historical inquiry; the second includes, but is not restricted to matters of morality and the law.

Lastarria's reason for preferring philosophical over narrative historiography concerns the practical implications of this discipline for the new Latin American nations. On his view, this methodology would allow the people to become aware of the backwardness of certain values, institutions, and practices, which in turn would motivate them to adopt values, institutions, and practices more consistent with liberal freedoms and prosperity. The Spanish conquest is the historical event that Lastarria selected in the "Investigaciones" to illustrate his conception of philosophical history. He was convinced that the philosophical interpretation of some relevant facts concerning the conquest may allow Chileans to draw some "lessons" for the present and future betterment of their country. For him, historical inquiry has only an instrumental, not an ultimate, value. In Latin America, the study of history is a means to something valuable.

That he takes historical inquiry to be a means for something else is clear in various passages of the "Investigaciones," for example when he recommends to "those who love their fatherland and truly desire its good fortune" that they should "regard the philosophy of history as an essential part of their knowledge in the social sciences ... " (2007/1842: 80). Three hundred years of colonial domination can provide Lastarria with a wealth of examples illustrating how philosophical history can be put at the service, not only of preventing some far-removed future errors, but of correcting present ones. After all, the events of that period "are not so isolated from nor so independent of our era that we can regard them as having no influence on the republic's present state" (2007/1842: 81). Among the events, institutions, and practices characteristic of three centuries of colonial rule he chooses to focus on those with implications for morality, legislation, and administration. Given historical data recorded by the Spaniards themselves, he argues, Spain's rule in America was characterized by pervasive crimes against the native people, abuses of power, corruption, legal incoherence, and administrative ineptness. It failed on every count, from the moral and the political, to the financial and the administrative. His account makes it clear that for him, descriptive language is not enough to convey the wrongs of the colonial period. As evident in the following passage, he in fact indulges in heavily evaluative language:

> [T]he Spaniards conquered [Central and South] America, soaking its soil in blood, not to settle it but rather to seize the precious metals that it so abundantly produced. Driven by the hope of gathering enormous riches at little cost, torrents of adventurers flooded the New World, and they directed their activity to this sole objective, using every possible expedient or outrage necessary to attain it. In the end reality made the illusion disappear, and the conquistadors, convinced by their own experience that the productivity of the American mines was not so great as they had imagined, began to abandon their reckless speculations and dedicate themselves little by little to agricultural and commercial enterprises. But this ... did not yield as much as it might have ... because they had neither the taste nor the intelligence to exploit this new source of wealth, and, in addition, their government, with

its absurd industrial system, brought to a standstill at the outset all the wealth that they could have expected. (Lastarria 2007/1842: 82)

In many other passages of this sort in the "Investigaciones," Lastarria explicitly mixes the factual with the evaluative, effectively painting a picture according to which Spain's colonial rule consisted mostly in the transplantation to America of a great number of Iberian vices. His argument endeavors to show that such vices continued to undermine the road to prosperity and freedom of post-independence Chile, since those values could not take root and flourish under conditions of pervasive administrative improvisation and legal incoherence, and of institutions run by public officials affected by arbitrariness, corruption, greed, and disregard for the value of human life and property. Lastarria held not only the conquistadors accountable for past injustices, but also those who protected them (i.e., the Spanish state and the "Curia").[7] This narrative seems consistent with the view of mainstream positivists in Latin America, who generally rallied against any remnants of institutions and values associated with Spain's colonialism and the Catholic Church.

But not all Chilean positivists agreed on the pace for such changes advocated by liberal reformers like Lastarria, since some feared that opposition by conservative forces could upset the relative stability that Chile enjoyed, which contrasted with the chaos and violence reigning in other nations of Latin America at the time. According to historian Iván Jaksić (2001: 135), the faculty members who attended Lastarria's reading of the "Investigaciones" in 1842 were among those Chileans who feared rapid change. Jaksić describes their reaction as that of being "stunned." One of those stunned participants, it appears, was Bello, the rector of the University of Chile, who had invited Lastarria to give the inaugural lecture for a new department of history.

---

[7] Note that Lastarria did offer very detailed historical data in support of his charges. These range from facts about the institutions of slavery known as the *mita* and the *repartimiento* (forms of *encomienda*) to some laws of the Indies prohibiting free trade and access to foreign books in Latin America. He took those laws to be deliberate attempts at promoting ignorance in the population (p. 85), which coincides with what other philosophers and historians have written on the topic. See for instance Francisco Romero (1949: 111) and Meri Clark (2012: 41, n. 3).

5.2.2   Bello's Cautious Response

Andrés Bello, another talented man of letters, was born during the period of Spain's colonial rule and actually worked for the local Spanish government of Caracas for a brief period before the wars of independence. He also had Simón Bolívar among his private students. In any case, with the revolt of 1810 he joined Bolívar on a diplomatic mission to obtain the support of Britain for the revolutionary cause and decided to remain there tutoring, writing, studying, and conducting occasional negotiations on behalf of Gran Colombia and Chile. During nineteen years of residence in Britain, he became more knowledgeable in a wide variety of disciplines and topics, including the ethical theory of classical utilitarianism, whose relevance to the present controversy will shortly become plain. In 1829, Bello accepted an invitation to help organize the education system of Chile, where he then moved and remained until his death.[8]

In 1842, Bello was among the faculty assembly at the University of Chile who attended Lastarria's reading of his "Investigaciones." In fact, as the rector of the university, he thought it appropriate to select his former student Lastarria for an inaugural lecture on the study of history, a discipline then forming a new department at the institution. He knew Lastarria quite well, but whether he could have anticipated the contents of his essay remains unclear. Bello later made his objections to those contents crystal clear in the two replies published in 1844 in the magazine *El Araucano*. He was skeptical of Lastarria's radical liberalism, favoring instead a gradualist agenda for enacting any changes in the institutions and laws of post-independence Chile.

Conversely, Lastarria was skeptical about Bello's gradualist liberalism. In fact, according to Jaksić (2001: 134), in his *Recuerdos literarios* (*Literary*

---

[8] Bello too was among the most accomplished "men of letters" in Latin American positivism. Besides poetry, he devoted himself to areas as diverse as jurisprudence (both national and international), history, politics, journalism, and Spanish grammar. In fact, his 1847 *Grammar of the Spanish Language* deserves a special mention since it achieved lasting success, quickly becoming one of the most authoritative sources for the rules of syntax of his native language, not only in Latin America but also in Spain. In addition to his success in literature and linguistics, he had many accomplishments in public office, serving in three administrations, including the senate. He was one of the founders of the University of Chile, of which he later became rector.

Memoirs) Lastarria depicts Bello as someone "personally and politically a conservative ... a left-over of the colonial regime ... ." If so, his "Investigaciones" might also have aimed at provoking Bello, who of course set about arguing against its two main claims.[9] First, on Lastarria's dichotomy of philosophical versus narrative history, Bello thought that the dichotomy was a false one, since historical inquiry is valuable (i) for the sake of getting an accurate narrative of the facts, and (ii) for drawing lessons about the present and the future *provided the historians gets their facts right first.*

Second, about Lastarria's position on the legacy of the Spanish conquest, Bello disputed in particular its interpretation of the facts, though he had some questions about the facts described by Lastarria – for example, when he writes:

> But let us be fair; it [Spain's colonial rule] was not a *ferocious* tyranny. It kept the arts in chains, clipped the wings of thought, even plugged the springs of agricultural fertility, but its policy was one of restrictions and privations, not torture and blood. Penal laws were administered loosely. In punishing acts of sedition it was not extraordinarily severe; it was what despotism has always been and no more, at least with respect to the Spanish race, up to the period of general uprising which ended with the emancipation of the American dominions. (Bello 1997b/1844: 162)

Bello then went on to emphasize the similarities between Spain's and Rome's conquests, praising some "civilizing" elements that conquered people acquired from the conquerors (language, buildings, etc.). Note also that in the above quote Bello explicitly avoids any reference to wrongs inflicted by the conquerors on Amerindians.[10] But putting these moral

---

[9] In his article "Race and National Political Culture," Jaksić (2011) also finds a conservative tendency in Bello in connection with some insensitive remarks this grammar expert made about the language of the Mapuche of Chile.

[10] In the cited passage of Bello's reply to Lastarria he avoids reference to the consequences of the conquest on Amerindians by explicitly narrowing his claim to "the Spanish race." But in another passage he refers to those consequences in purely descriptive terms, without drawing the necessary utilitarian conclusion from the vast suffering and death inflicted on those peoples. He may not have counted the Amerindians as peoples, for he merely noted:

> In America ... the sentence of destruction has been pronounced over the native people. The indigenous races are disappearing, and in the long run will be lost

matters provisionally aside, his reply to Lastarria appears to consist in nothing more than a companion-of-guilt argument based on the belief that Spain's colonial rule had not been worse than the colonial rule of other European powers during the modern expansion. On Bello's view, there was no reason in the post-independence period to steer historical inquiry toward the colonial past. Perhaps he thought that, in the 1840s, focusing inquiry on the backwardness of the Spanish conquest was unwise because it could release some destabilizing forces in society, which luckily had been kept under control in Chile after independence. In support of this argument he could have invoked evidence from neighboring countries pointing to the pernicious effects of pervasive lawlessness and partisan fighting.

But if we put that somewhat speculative line of reasoning aside, the obvious candidate for a reconstruction of Bello's argument runs:

1. We should engage in an evaluation of the legacy of the Spanish conquest only if Spain's colonial rule was more backward than the rule of other colonial powers during the modern European expansion.
2. Spain's colonial rule was not more backward than the rule of other colonial powers during the modern European expansion.
3. *Therefore,* we should not engage in an evaluation of the legacy of the Spanish conquest.

This reconstruction, however, produces a failed argument, one that founders on the beside-the-point fallacy. After all, the argument patently fails to address, not only Lastarria's analysis of the ills of the colonial system, but also the lessons he wished to draw from that analysis. Plausibly premise (2) is true, but why accept dubious premise (1)?[11] However, there is a more

among the colonies of transatlantic peoples, leaving no more traces than a few words that have crept into the newly brought languages, and scattered monuments where curious travelers will ask in vain the name and description of the civilizations that brought them into being. (Bello 1997/1844: 164)

In other writings, Bello made remarks consistent with this insensitive description of the moral wrongs of the Spanish conquest. See the discussion of Bello on this issue in Jaksić (2011).

[11] Moral philosophers who directly or indirectly address the social evil of the Spanish conquest are divided on the issue of whether its ethical backwardness was greater

charitable reconstruction of Bello's reply. It builds on the somewhat speculative line of reasoning outlined first, whose reliance on the principle of classical utilitarianism, the principle of utility, can easily become apparent. Recall that according to this principle, an action is right or wrong in a circumstance depending on its tendency to maximize or minimize the total balance of happiness over pain for most people concerned.

Bello could invoke this principle to argue that Lastarria's philosophical account of Spanish colonialism would have bad results, such as the awakening of Chile's most conservative forces and encouraging them to make war on the radical liberals. In the "Investigaciones," Lastarria is proposing a course of action that is not the best in terms of promoting the total balance of happiness over pain for all Chileans because it will have the opposite effect (widespread lawlessness, warfare, and so on). Now Bello has a stronger reply, one that runs along these lines:

1. In the Chile of the 1840s, the best approach to historical inquiry is one that minimizes the chances of creating social discord.
2. A philosophical approach to the history of Spain's colonial rule may create chaos and military strife.
3. Chaos and military strife are not the states of affairs that would maximize happiness for all concerned.
4. Any state of affairs that does not maximize happiness for all concerned is wrong.
5. *Therefore*, in the Chile of the 1840s, it is wrong to engage in a philosophical approach to the history of Spain's colonial rule.

The conclusion of this argument (5) would follow provided two things are true: the classical utilitarianism in premise (4) and the empirical claims in the other premises. Yet even if we grant all premises, the argument is unsound. For there may be considerations regarding past injustices that are strong enough to outweigh the utilitarian premise. It is not new that classical utilitarianism faces the so-called problem of justice, which is the problem of failing to accommodate powerful moral intuitions about the moral status of actions in order to increase overall happiness but at the cost

than, say, that of the US system of slavery or of the Holocaust. I will say more about this issue in the section "Concluding Remarks."

of permitting grave moral wrongs against individuals. Evil is evil independent of any "valuable" consequence it might on occasion have for most
concerned. Think for example of a simple scapegoat scenario in which
a person who is known (to the authorities) to be innocent receives a harsh
punishment, even death, in order to satisfy a large number of people who
believe them guilty. The scenario can be improved to make it resistant to
a wide range of classical utilitarian rejoinders.

By comparison, Lastarria's case looks stronger than Bello's. Even if it
does not exclusively focus on past injustices, its description of the conquest
contains enough ethical language to allow us to assume he was aware of the
primacy of justice. That is, with small adaptations, Lastarria can have his
own consequentialist argument where justice – or the lack of it during
colonial rule – figures prominently among the effects of actions to be
valued. The argument would go this way:

1. Spain's institutions, laws, and practices in colonial Latin America had
   bad consequences not only legally and institutionally, but also morally
   (prominent among which were serious breaches of justice).
2. If Chile hopes to achieve prosperity and freedom, it must rid itself of any
   remnants of colonial institutions, laws, and practices.
3. Chile hopes to achieve prosperity and freedom.
4. *Therefore,* Chile must rid itself of any remnants of colonial institutions,
   laws, and practices.

Premise 1 is well supported by the historical data provided in Lastarria's
"Investigaciones." Premise 2 expresses his beliefs that in post-
independence Chile (i) there were many remnants of colonial institutions,
laws, and practices; and (ii) such remnants are incompatible with progress
and freedom. Evidence for (i) is not difficult to find: even Jaksić (2001: 136),
who is broadly supportive of Bello's position in this controversy, provides
such evidence in the form of an illustrative story involving freedom of the
press in post-independence Chile. It appeared that a journalist, Francisco
Bilbao (1823–1865), dared to criticize the Catholic Church in "Sociabilidad
Chilena" (Chilean Sociability), an article published in the periodical *El
Crepúsculo.* As a result, Bilbao was brought to trial in 1844 for violations of
a press law, accused of blasphemy, immorality, libel, and sedition. He was
found guilty on two counts. Events of this sort must have been very

frustrating for Lastarria, who as a consistent positivist associated the Spanish colonial period with obsolete conservative values and religion. He must have thought that the values underwriting court decisions such as this were responsible at least in part for the slow pace of social, political, and economic progress in Latin America. He explicitly claimed that, in his native country, increasing degrees of conservatism and religion in society correlated to decreasing degrees of individual and "industrial" freedom, a claim for which he offered some statistical evidence (2000/1878: 219). At the same time, like any other positivist, he remained confident in the inevitability of progress. Since during the wars of independence Chile had reacted decisively against the conservatism of Spain and "the Curia," there was some reason for Lastarria to hope that his nation could do it again during the period of national organization. He strongly believed in Chileans' potential for social evolution (2000/1878: 225).

5.3   Positivism in Brazil: The Nonreligious Religion

Comtean positivism gained the status of mainstream social and political philosophy in Brazil during the last four decades of the nineteenth century. Although its transplantation to Brazil did not produce any significant, *direct* contribution to Comte's doctrines, as we will see here, it produced significant practical consequences from which some lessons about those doctrines should be drawn. There is evidence that by 1868, Tobias Barreto (Brazilian, 1839–1889), who had developed strong sympathies for Comtean positivism while studying in Paris, played an important role in spreading it in his native country. Fellow Brazilian Luís Pereira Barreto (1840–1923) continued the job in his *As Três Filosofias* (The Three Philosophies), a positivist work whose first volume appeared in 1874. Pereira Barreto adapted, among Comtean objections, those against mainstream metaphysics and religion, and directed them against Cartesian metaphysics and Christian values. He thereby antagonized both the Catholics and the Protestants of Brazil.

But it was mathematician and educator Benjamin Constant Botelho de Magalhaes (1767–1830) who most enthusiastically spread Comte's ideas about society and polity in his native Brazil. He fully embraced, for example, Comte's law of three stages, together with the theses that (i) a society's progress toward maturity was inevitable and (ii) any mature society would distribute wealth in ways such that unfair economic inequalities would cease to exist. Benjamin Constant rightly thought that, at the time, there were far too many inequalities in Brazilian society. Once a professor of mathematics at the elite Military School of Rio de Janeiro, in 1873 he began persuading future leaders of the country of the practical virtues of Comtean positivism for Brazil. At the same time, with the help of an inner circle of disciples, he also actively campaigned to promote Brazil's progress toward becoming a mature society. But not all the Comteans of Brazil were emphasizing the social progressivism of the doctrine. Others were more interested in giving up such progressivism to focus instead on developing the doctrine's secularism to some paradoxical extremes.

5.3.1 Religious Secularism

Led by Brazilian thinkers Miguel Lemos (1854–1917) and Raimundo Teixeira Mendes (1855–1927), other Comteans in Rio de Janeiro formed a group committed to an extreme secularism that is sometimes referred to as 'the Apostolate' and also 'the Positivist Nucleus.' These positivists reduced Comte's philosophy to a kind of anti-religious religion. In other words, they eliminated Comte's doctrine of social progressivism and focused instead on his secularism, understood as a creed that needs to be accepted and preached – rather than a philosophical doctrine to be argued for. Evidence of this paradoxical attitude toward religion is not difficult to find in the actions of the founders of the Positivist Nucleus. For example, in 1881 Lemos and Teixeira Mendes founded the Igreja Positivista do Brazil (Brazilian Positivist Church), thereby plainly illustrating how far they were willing to take their conception of secularism.[12] In 1897, they were behind the creation of a 'Temple of Humanity,' which was a chapel devoted to the preaching of Comte's 'Religion of Humanity.'[13] Yet by showing no

---

[12] These institutions are still around in some incarnation, as suggested in the blog *Positivism: Secular, Social, Scientific*, http://positivists.org/blog/brazil, which provides current addresses for a Brazilian Positivist Church and also a 'Clube Positivista' (Positivist Club). For a sympathetic view of such institutions see Gustavo Biscaia de Lacerda (n.d.), but also cf. Frederic Amory (1999).

[13] True, the members of the Apostolate were not the only Brazilian Comtean positivists who applied themselves to the creation of societies and other militant organization. Benjamin Constant himself, together with some scientists and students of the Military

progressive social and political agenda, the members of the Positivist Nucleus who ran the Brazilian Positivist Church isolated themselves from what others considered mainstream positivism. According to one of the most notable figures of Brazilian positivism, Euclides da Cunha, the Positivist Nucleus had no significant impact in Brazil because

> [it] withdrew itself around one philosopher [Comte], and stood aloof. No one saw it anymore, and it is hardly known whether it still exists, reduced to two admirable men [Lemos and Teixeira Mendes], who speak now and then, but who do not make themselves heard, from so far away come their voices, so long did they dwell in the ideal territory of a utopia, in the dualism of positivity and dream.[14]

By the turn of the century, da Cunha himself would abandon his Comtean positivism for a Spencerian social Darwinism, thus illustrating a typical transformation of European positivism in Latin America. Like other former cadets at the Military School influenced by Benjamin Constant, by the end of the nineteenth century, he too was disappointed by the failure of Comtean positivism to deliver social progress after the revolution of 1889, a *coup d'état* that proclaimed the Republic, thereby ending the rule of monarchies in Brazil.

But that transformation in theoretical framework does not affect the two consequences we need to draw from our brief survey of the history of Brazilian positivism: its secularism was in one respect a negative consequence and in another a positive one. For when secularism becomes a creed as it did for the Positivist Nucleus, it can have *no* philosophical foundations. After all, creeds are dogmas. The secularism of the Positivist Nucleus amounted to a self-contradictory position that preached against the

School, founded the Sociedade Positivista (Positivist Society) of Rio de Janeiro in 1871, from which they launched challenges to the religious and conservative values still prevalent in Brazilian society at the time. But by contrast with the Positivist Nucleus, the positivist Society did not limit its actions to undermining the influence of religious beliefs and institutions but tried to advance a number of social and political causes.

[14] From da Cunha's *Obra Completa*, cited in Amory (1999: 88). This passage is from a speech read at the Brazilian Academy of Letters in 1906. Euclides da Cunha (Portuguese, 1866–1909) was a disciple of Benjamin Constant who distinguished himself in journalism and literature. He is best known for his novel *Rebellion in the Backlands*, a hybrid of sociology and literature.

practice of preaching. On the other hand, we must take into account the fact that political independence from Iberian rule in Latin America did not bring about intellectual independence right away. Conservative Catholic values continued to dominate society even after the 1850s. Thomism, together with its Scholastic method, continued to dominate institutions of higher education, including those imparting "scientific" education. So, if we bracket the self-contradictory character of the secularism of the Positivist Nucleus, we can say that the real-life experiment of applying European positivism to Brazil (and many other Latin American countries) in general supports the argument that the secularism of the movement had some good results. We may conclude with Risieri Frondizi (Argentine, 1910–1985) that,

> It is unfair to judge the positivists' contribution to philosophy in terms of their written work or in terms of the new ideas developed. Positivistic theories arose as a protest against Scholasticism; their job was to free philosophical issues from the monopoly of the Catholic Church. And they did it very well. Since positivism, a free examination of any philosophical question is possible in Latin America, and even those who later on repudiated positivism took advantage of this definite and fundamental contribution of the positivists.[15]

5.3.2   Social and Political Progressivism

On the other hand, as one may expect given Comte's vindication of social progress, many of the Brazilian positivists worked tirelessly to produce it in Brazil. Among their practical achievements were legislation that materially ended slavery, separated religion from the state, and instituted monogamy as the sole institution of marriage. Some historians of the movement go as

---

[15] Frondizi (1943b: 181). Although in this passage Frondizi was referring to the practical consequences of positivism in Argentina, something analogous can be said of positivism in the Latin American countries where it had some influence. As discussed earlier in this chapter, in Chile for example Lastarria led the positivist opposition to the intellectual dominance of the Catholic Church. He illustrates well what Frondizi had in mind when praising the effects of the movement. For a similar evaluation of its practical consequences, see Jorrín and Martz (1970), Subercaseaux (1980), and Woll (1976).

far as crediting them with improvements in class and race relations, key advancements in democratic institutions, and the spread of awareness about the damaging effects of war and imperialism.[16] In addition, Benjamin Constant played a key role in the progressive revolution of 1889. But it is not clear what the Comtean Positivist Nucleus contributed to these events. In his *History of Ideas in Brazil*, philosopher João Cruz Costa contends that its members were not actually involved in the creation of the Republic. But there is some disagreement on this since others maintain that both Benjamin Constant and the Positivist Nucleus played a leading role in the events of November 1889. According to the latter, it was Benjamin Constant *together with* Lemos and Teixeira Mendes who wrote the constitution of the Republic (Amory 1999).

Whether one group of positivists or both groups should be credited, the Comtean positivists had much to do with the modernization of Brazil, including a host of social improvements. True, social and political concerns were not only to be found among Comtean positivists. After all, by the turn of the century many former Comteans were sympathetic to other positivist doctrines such as social Darwinism and the classical utilitarianism of J. S. Mill. In addition, some Brazilian intellectuals of a non-positivist philosophical persuasion might also have had a role in the national reorganization after the revolution. However, the influence of the Comteans in the creation of the Republic is undeniable: Comte's idea of a mature society characterized by stability and prosperity is in fact captured in the Brazilian flag, which bears the motto "Order and Progress."

Furthermore, although the government of Brazil never got to be a sociocracy at a national level, it appears that Comtean positivist Julio de Castilhos established one locally, in Rio Grande do Sul. A follower of Comte, he apparently regarded scientists as the most suitable candidates to govern a "mature" society (which for Comte is the type of society that corresponds to the third, positivist stage of development of human thought). Castilhos must have assumed that with the proclamation of the Republic Brazil had entered that final stage. However unrealistic his political ideas may have

---

[16] Brazilian positivists, who like most positivists of the region regarded the legacy of Iberian colonialism as an impediment to progress, were determined to undermine that legacy by means of public policies. For more on the their impact on public policies, see Biscaia de Lacerda (n.d.), Coutinho (1943), and Merquior (1982).

been on the grand scale, the literature provides abundant evidence of more down-to-earth social and political changes driven by Brazil's Comtean positivism.

In view of those changes, we can agree with most critics that positivism in Latin America was a unique phenomenon. A quick review of the historical data suggests that Comtean positivism appears to have had greater consequences in Brazil than in France, the country of its philosophical origin.[17] The case of Brazil in fact provides a test of the alleged scientific status of Comtean positivism as a sociological theory that makes testable predictions about the development of a society. If false, those predictions would falsify the theory and show that it is pseudoscientific. The positivist experiments of Benjamin Constant and other Brazilian positivists of the second half of the nineteenth century provided a crucial ground for testing that theory. And the results were mixed: on the one hand, there were some "positive" changes such as those mentioned in this section; but on the other, by the end of the century there were great social ills. The failure of the Republic of 1889 was inevitable in light of uncontrollable financial speculation, civil war in the south, and insurgency in the northeast (Amory 1999). All these led Brazilian positivists like Euclides da Cunha to look for alternatives to Comte's pseudoscientific sociology.

5.4 Positivism in Mexico: Porfirism and Anti-Ultramontanism

If positivism's record in Brazil was one of ambitious social and political programs often taken to have had only ambiguous results (some good, others bad), positivism's record in Mexico was one of even more ambitious aims and ended in unmitigated disaster. At least, that is the conclusion generally drawn in the work of Leopoldo Zea (1912–2004), perhaps the twentieth-century philosopher who has shown the most interest in examining the practical consequences of positivism in his native Mexico. In this section, I draw a conclusion about the practical consequences of positivism

---

[17] Historians of the movement would agree with this statement. See, for example, Afranio Coutinho's "Some Considerations on the Problem of Philosophy in Brazil" (especially pages 187–188), J. G. Merquior's "More Order than Progress?" (Merquior 1982), and João Cruz Costa's *A History of Ideas in Brazil* (Cruz Costa 1964).

in Mexico that is more moderate than Zea's. If I am right, then the Mexican thinkers who conducted the positivist experiment are open to objection because of their own philosophical eclecticism and the disastrous social and the practical consequences of their experiment. But they were on the right track in diagnosing that nineteenth-century Mexico, like other Latin American countries, suffered from 'Iberian ultramontanism,' an expression used by historians of post-independence Latin America to refer to the extreme conservativism of the Catholic Church and old colonial rule (Ardao 1963: 522–523). On my view, the Mexican positivists should get some credit for having challenged ultramontanism.

5.4.1   Three Generations of Mexican Positivists

Positivism in Mexico came largely in three waves, which correspond to three generations of thinkers. The first two waves were caused by single figures, the third by a group to whom I will refer generally as *los científicos* (the scientists) – although this label was initially designated to apply only to those members of the group who were active in the nation's politics. Roughly, the first wave of positivism was due to the work of autochthonous positivist José María Luis Mora (1794–1850). Mora – a priest, lawyer, writer, and newspaper editor – was also a liberal political thinker whose chief interest lay in post-independence reform in his native Mexico. The roots of his political thought were in Enlightenment traditions, especially the social contract theories of Hobbes and Locke. But on the issue of the goals of the state, he was sympathetic to Bentham's classical utilitarianism, since he favored a value-based normative theory consistent with the standard (somewhat inaccurate) understanding of Bentham's principle of utility as applied to the state: namely, that the proper goal of the state is to maximize happiness for the greatest number of people.

To Mora, the state did have the duty to pursue the aggregate happiness of individuals, and to that effect, he recommended that "the land, the basic resource of the country, must be in the hands of the state, which in turn will sell it to small owners who will be the basis for the creation of an extensive and solid productive class." Of course, the Catholic Church, an institution that owned vast tracts of land in Mexico, might not have welcomed Mora's recommendation. Indifferent to that, he was recommending a measure conducive to the creation of a substantial middle class, which he hoped would be the catalyst of social reform and economic progress, much as had the middle classes in Britain and the United States. This in turn required a change from the colonial, authoritarian worldview to a new outlook in which persons would come to think of themselves as producers of wealth, and therefore cultivate habits of industry and self-reliance that would enable Mexico to achieve economic independence. Government power, Mora maintained, ought to be merely the guarantor of fair terms of competition between self-interested strivers, not a source of wealth itself. But if this new way of thinking was to take hold in the minds of average Mexicans, Mora believed, a revolution in education was necessary. In this, he anticipated the second wave of positivism, which developed under the influence of Comte.

That second wave took root in Mexico thanks, in large part, to the work of Gabino Barreda (1818–1881), a Mexican lawyer and medical doctor who came to embrace Comtean theory while a student in France. Upon return to Mexico in 1867, he delivered a speech, the "Oración Cívica" (Civic Prayer), in which he applied Comte's law of three stages of development of human thought to the history of Mexico. In the "Oración," Barreda claimed that his country had already passed through these three stages. He equated Mexico's colonial period with the law's first, theological stage; the wars of independence with its second, metaphysical stage, and the post-independence period in which Barreda happened to be living, under the Presidency of Benito Juárez, with its third, positivist stage. Having acquired leverage in the Juárez administration, Barreda devoted his efforts to enacting positivist reforms, especially in education. As an educator, he had a profound impact on the first generation of Mexican positivists to act as a group. They were among his disciples at a newly created elite school under Barreda's direction, the Escuela National Preparatoria for men.

Barreda's disciples made up a third wave of positivism in Mexico that began as Comtean. These positivists thought of themselves as 'liberal-conservatives' because they were for social progress but thought it could be achieved only by conservative means. Accordingly, they favored evolution, rather than revolution. Later they became more attracted to Millian utilitarianism and Spencerian social Darwinism, though they never entirely abandoned Comtism. For this generation of positivists, the worldview of most Mexicans at the time was not that of a progressive, secular society. It belonged instead to the colonial period and the Catholic Church. Not surprisingly, these positivists were out to effect a change of worldview in Mexico, and to do that, they would of course need control of key offices in the government. Given their sympathies for the empirical methods of science, when they decided to form a political party in Mexico, opponents and the public began to refer to them as the *científicos* (*scientists*), a term I have already introduced to denote the Mexican positivists of the third wave.

5.4.2   The Incomplete-Independence Theory

The *científicos* shared with other positivists of Latin America, especially of Spanish America, at least the following characteristics:

- They endorsed one or another of the European doctrines that I have classified as forms of positivism, broadly construed.
- Equipped with that broad theoretical framework, they developed an applied theory of social and political philosophy of their own, which was in principle devised to promote three chief values, whenever possible, in Mexico: order, progress, and freedom.
- The changes they thought necessary to promote those values were at the time radical.
- To justify their reformist agenda, they invoked what we may call the 'incomplete-independence theory.'
- That theory rests on empirical assumptions about some causal connections between certain social ills of the post-independence period (e.g., widespread poverty, civil war, and authoritarian rule) on the one hand, and ultramontanism on the other (i.e., the extremely conservative worldview of the colonial period and the Catholic Church).
- Some of those empirical assumptions may have been true.

Let us consider how these features apply to the views of the *científicos*. Their theoretical framework was largely Comtean first, followed by a mix of Comtean, Spencerian, and Millian doctrines. They invoked those doctrines to account for their "liberal-conservative" social and political agenda, which aimed at promoting the three values in a sequence considered empirically possible: order first, progress second, and freedom last. On their view, the backwardness of the worldview of most Mexicans justified such a gradualist approach. But why would most Mexicans have a backward worldview? The *científicos* answered by means of the above mentioned incomplete independence theory, which was already available at the time, owing in large part to Lastarria among others, and consists of two claims:

1. The inbred values of Spanish culture and Catholicism remained in Latin America after its political emancipation in the early 1800s.
2. Those values amount to an obstacle to prosperity and freedom in post-independence Latin America.

That is, the wars of independence had not been able to rid Spanish America of the cultural, moral, and religious conservativism of the colonial period. Unlike Sarmiento, Alberdi, and some other post-independence thinkers of the region, the *científicos* did not emphasize causal connections between Mexico's social ills and the race/ethnicity factor, although there is evidence that at least some of them may have relied implicitly on such connections. What they offered instead was a narrative suggesting certain causal links from premises about a glaring value contrast distinguishing Mexicans from their neighbors to the north. According to that narrative, most Mexicans of the late nineteenth century lacked the independent-minded political spirit and work ethic that made prosperity and participatory democracy a success in the United States and Britain. Most Mexicans never acquired those traits of character because their worldview was still attached to a feudal system and a Catholic hierarchical conception of authority. They cared too much about religion, and complacently obeyed *caudillos* simply because they were used to obeying; they were used to thinking that political decisions were not for them to make and that a free and orderly "open society" was beyond their reach.

Here is how Zea described this comparative narrative of the positivists: "[to them] their own race appeared romantic, idealistic, given to utopias and to sacrificing reality to dreams .... Nations founded by this race, the argument went on, could not but be inferior to those with a practical sense, such as England and the United States" (Zea 1949: 169). In this passage, Zea relies on a racialist interpretation of the incomplete-independence theory. But when charitably construed, some evidence could be provided in support of the theory. In some important respects, the ultramontanism opposed by the Mexican positivists existed then and persists today in Latin America. To support the claim that ultramontanism existed in their time, it suffices to recall the case of journalist Francisco Bilbao mentioned earlier: he was indicted and convicted of criticizing the Curia of post-independence Chile. Or consider the case of Ecuador, where ultramontanist Gabriel García Moreno worked to vindicate the role of the Jesuits in colonial times and even managed to influence the constitution of the country to include the requirement that only Catholics could vote (Romero 1998: 242). Historical evidence of this sort may have been extensive in nineteenth-century Mexico, where the Catholic Church had great power. As for the claim that ultramontanism is still a force in Latin America today, it suffices to take a quick look at the impact of Catholic values on legislation concerning issues such as abortion and medically assisted death.[18]

But the desire on the part of reformers to change the Mexican mind did not sit well with many people. The admiration of the United States in the positivists' narrative conflicted with the popular distrust and hostility harbored as a result of the imperialistic war that the United States waged against Mexico, which had concluded in 1847 with the loss of disputed territory. Not surprisingly, public opinion in Mexico was not favorable to the United States, and the local positivist creed that they should acquire that nation's values. But their response was not immediate because, as Zea points out, under the influence of that narrative, they also began to foster feelings of inferiority in their "romantic, idealistic" Latin culture as compared to the "practical, down-to-earth" culture of the English-speaking world.

Now, for the *científicos*, it was not enough just to point out that Mexicans at the time were less suited to order, progress, and freedom than their neighbors to the north, and then offer the incomplete-independence theory to explain that empirical fact. They needed a plan to get Mexican society to establish order and then transition to progress, and whenever possible, to democracy. Although Barreda had declared Mexico a mature society for which order, progress, and freedom lay within reach, the Mexican positivists of the third wave were not that optimistic. Freedom could either wait or could be given out only partially until order was established. In this plan,

---

[18] In the case of medically assisted death, it is only legal in Colombia (since July 3, 2015). In the case of abortion, the Guttmacher Institute's factsheet "Abortion in Latin America and the Caribbean," reports that six countries ban abortion for any reason and that 97 per cent of women of reproductive age in the region live in countries with restrictive abortion laws. March 2018, www.guttmacher.org/sites/default/files/fact sheet/ib_aww-latin-america.pdf

the educational system had the most crucial ideological role to play: compelling Mexicans to value practicality and order over tradition and religion.

Luckily for the positivists, in this period of Mexican history there was a suitable person to lead this positivist program and convince many people to support it. Justo Sierra (1848–1912) – a man of letters, senator, minister of education, historian, educator, and editor of the newspaper *La Libertad* – stood out as the leader of the Mexican positivist creed who clearly articulated the plan. In *La evolución política del pueblo mexicano* (The Political Evolution of the Mexican People) he warned Mexico's ruling elite "What remains for us to accomplish today is entirely a task of emancipation: the riddance of superstitions. This task (which is the duty of the Church also) is the responsibility of science, of the schools, and of the teacher" (1969/1900–1902: 88). Sierra himself de facto determined Mexico's educational policies from 1880 to 1910 (Zea 1949: 171). On his view, Mexico needed to renovate its educational system in order to be capable of surviving as an independent nation that could compete alongside its powerful neighbor to the north. A progressive and scientific education that could contribute to the needs of industry and commerce were the key to this, he believed, and this could come about only through a complete separation of the educational system from the power of the Church.

Sierra's program had the backing of the Unión Liberal, a political party created in 1892 that supported the authoritarian general Porfirio Díaz in 1884.[19] Having ruled Mexico briefly from 1877 to 1880, Díaz seized power again from 1884 to 1911 (almost thirty years). During his regime, known as the 'Porfiriato,' the ideological leaders were in fact the positivists. On their view, if Mexico was to embark on the great social experiment of changing the people's worldview along the lines described above, the best way to enact that change was by means of an "honest tyranny." But for a number of reasons, to be considered next, their strategy ultimately did not work.[20]

---

[19] The party, also called the party of *los científicos*, played a prominent role in public policy in the 1880s, when Pablo Macedo, Rosendo Pineda, Francisco Bulnes, and Sierra served in the Chamber of Deputies.

[20] Here is Ardao's succinct description of their unfortunate choice:

> The party of the Scientists, from the very beginning stronger than the Conservative and Liberal parties, and inspired by the great intellectual Justo Sierra, adopted the positivist ideology as its political creed. Thus, resorting to Comte, they found a justification for the dictatorship as a means of maintaining order, based on scientific principles. They

5.4.3   Objections Facing Mexican Positivists of the Third Wave

5.4.3.1   *Shaky Eclecticism*

Mexican positivists mixed elements of Comtism, classical utilitarianism, and social Darwinism without fear of contradiction. Mora put forward a contractualist justification of the state that freely combined elements from the Hobbesian and Lockean accounts, even though those accounts are usually considered incompatible. To that contractualist justification, Mora added a conception of the goals of the state shaped by classical utilitarianism, a doctrine regarded as a competitor of Lockean natural-law theory. Barreda, on the other hand, vindicated Comtism together with a conception of society in which order, progress and liberty are the three ultimate, universal values. However, according to Comtism, when society reaches maturity there must be a redistribution of wealth – something incompatible with liberty as construed by the thinkers of Enlightenment.

Zea, however, appears to regard the eclecticism of the Mexican positivists as a strength. He recognizes *no* inconsistency in their combining Comtism, classical utilitarianism, and social Darwinism. True, these theories have in common that each holds that one or more natural characteristics should be promoted. But since. each regards different natural characteristics as valuable (respectively, fully developed rationality, happiness, and fitness for survival), they turn out to be incompatible. For example, the individualism of Mill is incompatible with Comtean positivism and social Darwinism. After all, while Mill allows the state to interfere with an individual's liberty only when their actions may harm others, Comteans and Spencerians do not make much room for individual liberty. Moreover, the *científicos* could not accept Mill's view on liberty since they thought that, at least temporarily, the only liberty that Mexicans should have was freedom of trade.

also invoked the ideal of liberty, borrowed from Mill and Spencer, but applied it only in economic matters. Porfirism and positivism became one. Political positivism was defeated by the Revolution of 1910, and at the same time the intellectual positivism of the 'Ateneo de la Juventud' also came to an end. (Ardao 1963: 520–521)

Support for other freedoms was contingent on the people's ability to learn how to live in an orderly society. As we saw, on these thinkers' view the masses would have to be educated before they could be trusted with common democratic liberties. It was the mission of the Porfiriato to govern paternalistically, deciding what was in the "best interests" of the Mexican people until they acquired the proper worldview. The *científicos* fully accepted Díaz's laws restricting personal liberties, considering them necessary steps to enforce public order while the educational transformation of society was underway. As Zea is quick to point out, Mexico had already seen enough of the "personal freedom" allowed by the liberal constitution of 1857, with its extravagant, utopian visions that could not be realized in workable social programs.

5.4.3.2   Shaky Empirical Support

It can also be objected that the *científicos*' agenda conflicted with two plausible empirical claims previously made by Mora. Since those claims were backed up with sufficient empirical support, it follows that the positivists' agenda was empirically wrongheaded. Mora's relevant claims were that (i) prosperity in Mexico required the creation of a substantial middle class in the country that could play a role akin to the role of the middle class of Britain or the United States, and (ii) the government itself should not be a source of individual wealth. The *científicos* acted in ways that show a commitment to rejecting both claims. To support this objection, let us briefly look at this period in Mexico's history, which represents the high noon of positivism in the country's modern politics. Whether from public office or the pages of their newspaper *La Libertad* (Freedom), the positivists were extolling the financial benefits of their positions in the government during the Porfiriato while disregarding any legislation that might help a middle class take root and flourish. Quite the contrary, they condoned labor practices that made large numbers of Mexicans poorer and more disenfranchised. For instance, while Minister of Finance under Díaz, positivist José Ives Limantour (1854–1935) condoned the *ejido*, an abusive system of exploitation of peasants in the *estancias* that resembled the *encomienda* system of servitude in colonial times. His policies brought wealth to Mexico, but this wealth benefited only the few.

Indeed, the positivists' agenda for Mexico's economy brought wealth mostly to themselves and to others of the ruling class – from government officials to local and foreign industrialists, landowners, financiers, and merchants. The autocratic rule of Porfirio Díaz served only the interests of Mexico's own small wealthy class and foreign investors. Meanwhile, the vast majority of Mexicans remained not only poor but absolutely powerless under a police state. The grand transformations of Mexican society that the *científicos* had envisioned never came to pass. It turned out to be just another impracticable utopian speculation – the very kind of thing positivists professed to despise. When at last the common people of Mexico rose up against Díaz's regime in the great revolution of 1911 led by Emiliano Zapata (1879–1919), Francisco Madero (1873–1913), and Pancho Villa (1877–1923), their rebellion was in a sense not only against the dictator but also against those who devised his regime's social, economic, and political agenda, the positivists. The revolution amounted to the last step of their experiment: their "scientific" plan had been tested and refuted. And they themselves entered history with the heavy moral burden of sharing responsibility for the evils of Porfirism.

5.5 The Upshot

Critics of nineteenth-century positivism in Latin America have tended to produce historical accounts that, whatever they may disagree on, at least agree on one thing: the movement primarily involved nation builders. On the topic of how to assess the movement, critics' focus has varied. Some emphasize the differences across countries, which might lead us to believe that we cannot really consider Latin American positivism as a single philosophical tradition (Ardao 1963; Subercaseaux 1980). Others focus on the movement's practical consequences, on occasion regarding these as so bad in countries such as Mexico as to suggest that perhaps we should give no credit at all to these positivists (Zea 1949; Levinson 2013). And although the positivists' take on the legacy of the conquest, which was by no means universal, is a topic that deserves more attention than it has received, some critics interpret Lastarria's view of that legacy as nothing more than a revival of the European Black Legend of the sixteenth century (Burke and Humphrey 2007). However, in light of the evidence reviewed in this chapter, these interpretations can be challenged. The first two seem only *in part* true, while the third claim is plainly false. Let us consider each in turn.

First, although it is true that in Latin America positivists' views developed in isolation and differed to some degree from country to country, we found some commonalities. To name a few, secularism, revisionism about the legacy of the conquest, philosophical eclecticism, and a pluralistic, consequentialist political theory in which order, prosperity, and freedom are the highest values. On these themes, any difference between, say, Lastarria in Chile and Justo Sierra in Mexico or Benjamin Constant in Brazil would be no greater than a difference between Lastarria and Bello in Chile.

Second, it is true that positivism had many adverse practical consequences in Mexico and elsewhere. But not all its consequences were negative. Zea may be right that positivists' agenda in his native country failed categorically, and was even unsuccessful in its efforts to persuade most people to abandon their reliance on supernatural explanations of natural phenomena. The positivists also failed in Brazil, where their movement had a strong anticlerical agenda. As Cruz Costa notes (1964: 92), the fact that Pereira Barreto defended the positivist theses is surprising since he "was well aware of the nature of the environment in which he lived and knew that they would not easily be accepted .... Contrary to what he believed, theology still had the strength to muster the same influence on which it had counted in the past."

But this is an area where positivism was not futile. After all, it succeeded in secularizing public education and introducing the study of the natural sciences and social sciences with empirical methods. At the academic level, as a result of the positivists' intervention, something of the magnitude of an actual 'paradigm shift' took place: namely, the fall of Thomism and its Scholastic method after more than three centuries of dominance in Latin American universities.[21]

---

[21] There is in fact consensus that this intellectual revolution was the positivists' greatest contribution to Latin American philosophy, probably only comparable to the introduction of Thomism during the conquest. For some related assessments, see e.g., Ardao (1963), Frondizi (1949), and Jaksić (1989).

Finally, let us consider what to make of some critical assessments of the legacy of the conquest by positivists such as Lastarria. Janet Burke and Ted Humphrey (2007: 52) interpret them as attempts at reviving the Black Legend. Strictly speaking, the 'Black Legend' refers to a set of fictitious accounts of the abuses of the conquest that circulated during the sixteenth century, especially promoted by the British with the purpose of damaging the image of their Spanish rivals. Since there is abundant evidence that grave moral evils did occur during the conquest, and no evidence at all that Lastarria's historical data amounted to a fiction, this is one of the issues where both the facts and morality seemed to have been on the side of the positivists. Another is the related issue of the Mexican positivists' critique of Iberian ultramontanism. I have argued above that they deserve some credit for that critique.

5.6   Suggested Readings

Amory, Frederic. 1999. "Euclides da Cunha and Brazilian Positivism," *Luso-Brazilian Review* 36(1): 87–94.

Good outline of the history of positivism in Brazil, covering (i) the introduction of Comtism by Benjamin Constant, political thinker, mathematician, and educator; (ii) the development of the Brazilian Positivist Church by the Comtean orthodox group of Miguel Lemos and Raimundo Teixeira Mendes; and (iii) Euclides da Cunha's replacement of Comtean theory with social Darwinism and Mill's utilitarianism in response to his country's social and political problems at the turn of the twentieth century.

Ardao, Arturo. 1963. "Assimilation and Transformation of Positivism in Latin America." *Journal of the History of Ideas* 2: 515–522. (Reprinted pp. 150–156 in Nuccetelli and Seay 2004.)

Excellent overview of Latin American positivism. Ardao suggests its grip on the intellectuals of Latin America between 1870 and 1911 was comparable only to that of Thomism until the 1870s. Its success in deposing Thomism was the result of a process that had been initiated by the Latin American political thinkers of two previous generations.

Regarding the distinct features of Latin America positivism, Ardao offers mostly a comparative analysis of its historical development, mentioning, among other differences, that while in Europe science triggered the development of positivism, in Latin America positivism triggered the development of science.

Bello, Andrés. 1997b/1844. "Commentary on 'Investigations on the Social Influence of the Spanish Conquest and Colonial Regime in Chile' by José Victorino Lastarria," pp. 154–168 in Bello 1997 (excerpts reprinted pp. 62–73 in Burke and Humphrey 2007 as "Response to Lastarria on the Influence of the Conquest and the Spanish Colonial System in Chile").

A classic source for the views of this author that are discussed in this chapter.

Burke, Janet and Ted Humphrey. 2007. *Nineteenth-Century Nation Building and the Latin American Tradition.* Indianapolis/Cambridge, MA: Hackett.

A reader featuring a broad selection of works by eighteen Latin American political thinkers, most of them written during the nineteenth century. It contains some of the primary sources examined in this chapter in either a complete or an excerpted form. The editors include their own translations preceded by a brief introduction to the volume. For their ascription of the Black Legend to Lastarria, which I discuss above, see footnote 7 on p. 81. For a full articulation of what they have in mind by 'Black Legend,' see their 2011 essay "The New Black Legend of Bartolomé de las Casas" (Burke and Humphrey 2011).

Candelaria, Michael. 2012. "Introduction," pp. 1–20 in *The Revolt of Unreason: Miguel de Unamuno and Antonio Caso on the Crisis of Modernity.* Amsterdam/New York: Rodopi.

Of some interest to those curious about what happened to Justo Sierra after the anti-positivist revolution in Mexican philosophy. Candelaria claims that Sierra later in life changed his mind about the plausibility of positivism, and especially about the value of a positivist education (pp. 5–9).

Cappelletti, Angel J. 1991. *Filosofía argentina del siglo XX.* Rosario, Argentina: Universidad Nacional de Rosario.

In spite of its title, this book offers a historical exploration of positivism in Latin America during the nineteenth century, with an emphasis on the cases of Mexico and Brazil. Cappelletti agrees with other historians about the existence of an autochthonous positivism in Latin America, which paved the way for a speedy reception of the European varieties in Latin America.

Clark, Meri L. 2009. "*The Emergence and Transformation of Positivism*," pp. 53–67 in Nuccetelli, Schutte, and Bueno 2009.

Historical account of the development of Latin American positivism from certain strains of nineteenth-century European positivism. Closely follows the development of the movement in Argentina, Mexico, Chile, and Colombia. Clark identifies a variety of Latin American positivism with roots in liberal idealism that later change into a kind of state authoritarianism. Although that variety is best illustrated of course by the positivism of the *científicos* in Mexico, it may also be exemplified by the positivism of Bello.

Clark, Meri L. 2013. "The Good and the Useful Together: Colombian Positivism in a Century of Conflict," pp. 27–48 in Gilson and Levinson 2013.

Examines some disagreements between Colombian positivists José María Samper Agudelo (1828–1888) and Mariano Ospina Rodríguez (1805–1885), arguing that like other Latin American positivists of the nineteenth century, they too were seeking solutions to social ills such as recurring civil wars, economic stagnation, and poverty. The existence of such ills acted as a motivation to undertake a critical exploration of Latin America's colonial past.

Gilson, Gregory D. and Irving W. Levinson, eds. 2013. *Latin American Positivism: Theory and Practice*. Lanham, MD: Lexington Books.

Up-to-date discussion of positivism in Latin America, especially in Mexico and Brazil. Offers nine essays that critically examine the theoretical and practical legacy of the movement. They are accordingly arranged in two parts, one with a focus on the positivists' core claims, the other on the practical consequences of positivist theories.

Jaksić, Iván. 2001. *Scholarship and Nation-Building in Nineteenth-Century Latin America*. Cambridge, UK: Cambridge University Press.

Insightful overview of liberalism and positivism in Latin America by a knowledgeable historian. Especially relevant to our discussion of the Bello/Lastarria controversy over what to make of the legacy of the Conquest. Even if broadly sympathetic to Bello's conservativism, it offers an objective presentation of Lastarria's comparative radicalism.

Jorrín, Miguel and John D. Martz. 1970. *Latin-American Political Thought and Ideology*. Chapel Hill, NC: University of North Carolina Press,

Excellent historical survey of positivism in Latin America. It shows that the movement had some distinct and some common features in the countries where it took hold, which were by no means all the countries of the region. Chapter 4 provides solid data about positivism in Mexico, Brazil, and Chile. There is also some reference to positivism in Argentina and Cuba.

Lastarria, José Victorino. 2007/1842. Investigaciones sobre la influencia social de la conquista i del sistema colonial de los españoles en Chile, *Memoria Chilena*, Biblioteca Nacional de Chile. www.memoriachilena.gob.cl/archi vos2/pdfs/MC0008961.pdf. (References to reprint in Burke and Humphrey 2007, pp. 81–91).

A classic source for the author's views as discussed in this chapter.

Miliani, Domingo. 1963. "Utopian Socialism, Transitional Thread from Romanticism to Positivism in Spanish America," *Journal of the History of Ideas* 24: 523–538.

Argues that Comte's early thought coexisted in Latin America with the ethical theory of European socialists as well as with the thought of Latin American Romantics. The latter were eager to accept any alternative to Scholasticism based on a more objective methodology of philosophical inquiry (see pp. 537–538). Comte's method for positivist sociology provided just that alternative. Argentina's friendly reception of Comte was facilitated by the utopian socialism of the Romantics. In later works, Sarmiento and Alberdi were full-blooded positivists.

Romero, José Luis. 1998. *El pensamiento político latinoamericano*. Buenos Aires: A-Z Editora.

Sets Latin American positivism in the broader context of the liberalism of the 1850s, with its characteristic quest for national identities. Good analysis of the historiography of the period. Provides textual evidence for the existence in post-independence Latin America of the conservative forces denounced by some positivists – as evident, for example, in Ecuador's first constitution, which required its people to be practicing Catholics in order to be able to vote or be eligible for citizenship. See especially pp. 242 ff.

Zea, Leopoldo. 1949. "Positivism and Porfirism in Latin America," in F. S. C. Northrop, ed., *Ideological Differences and World Order: Studies in the*

Philosophy and Science of the World's Cultures. New Haven, CT: Yale University Press. (Reprinted pp. 198–218 in Nuccetelli and Seay 2004.)

A much shorter version of Zea's 1974 account of the history of positivism in Mexico when it became intertwined with Porfirism. Zea contends that the positivists chiefly aimed at effecting a value change in the minds of ordinary Mexicans.

6 Martí's Liberal Anti-Positivism

By the end of the nineteenth century, a number of ways of thinking about Latin America stood in sharp contrast with positivism. José Martí (1853–1895), a Cuban thinker known mostly for his literary and journalistic work, developed one such alternative perspective. He did so in many writings, addressing, among other issues, the identity and sovereignty of the region, and the need to defend it, especially his beloved country, from both colonial and neocolonial powers. Shortly after joining a military invasion of Cuban exiles in the United States seeking the island's independence from Spain, Martí died in battle. But his indefatigable campaigns for the unity and freedom of the island and, by extension, of Latin America, resonated among many peoples of a wide range of political persuasions in the subcontinent. By the 1950s, his reputation had already acquired a mythical dimension that often obscured the more accurate understanding of his political thought. It was, I believe, decisively shaped by Krausism – and in this chapter I will put forth reasons to support this view.

6.1 Life and Work

Martí grew up in Cuba at a time when that country and Puerto Rico were the only remaining Spanish colonies in Latin America. He resented Cuba's lack of sovereignty as well as the social and economic injustices facing the Cuban people – and, in fact, most of the peoples in the former Spanish colonies. His anti-colonial attitude predates what later became a pervasive theme among both hard and soft socialists of subsequent generations in the region. But this attitude was not the product of any familiarity with Marx's theory, which Martí certainly

131

had at some point in his adult life.[1] Rather, it grew as a sentiment that appeared to have been formed while he was a student of Rafael María Mendive (1821–1886), an educator and reformer well known in his native Cuba for his opposition to the colonial regime. Perhaps because of his relationship with Mendive, Martí was viewed with suspicion by the local authorities. Arrested and condemned to hard labor in a dungeon at age sixteen, he soon fell ill. His mother pleaded with the authorities to release him and grant him deportation to Spain, which they did. But while in prison, he wrote letters that testify to his suffering there, as did those he sent later to family and friends from Spain, where he arrived in 1871. During this experience of forced exile, which would not be the only one for Martí, he pursued studies in philosophy and jurisprudence at the University of Zaragoza, where he earned a Bachelor of Arts degree in philosophy and literature and a degree in law in 1874. He also wrote poetry and published, among other essays, the famous pamphlet El presidio político de Cuba (Political Imprisonment in Cuba).

Martí had thus initiated the life of a Latino émigré. His new nomadic existence took him later to France, Mexico, and Guatemala before his return to Cuba in 1878. But troubles with the local authorities arose again, and the following year he left once more for Spain, traveling later to France, New York City, and eventually Venezuela, where he arrived in 1881. But there he again ran into trouble with local authorities when his presence came to the attention of the dictator Antonio Guzmán Blanco (1829–1899), for whom any free-thinker like Martí would have counted as a subversive. Shortly after Guzmán Blanco censored a cultural magazine,

---

[1] Martí's familiarity with Marx's theory is evident in, for instance, his "Memorial Meeting in Honor of Karl Marx" (1999/1883: 43–45). Since Fidel Castro's revolution of 1959, the socialist government of Cuba has regularly sought legitimacy by invoking a continuity with the nationalist revolution pursued by Martí. But there has been some controversy about whether Martí himself would have endorsed Castro's government. Among those who think he would have done is Juan Marinello (1975), an intellectual of the Cuban Communist Party (who before the advent of Castro's regime had argued against Martí). In the other camp are some critics who have denied a link between Martí's thought and Marxism such as Carlos Ripoll and Raymond Carr in their 1988 exchange "Marx & Martí."

the *Revista Venezolana,* that Martí edited, Martí returned to New York, a city where he would reside for fifteen years.

With only a few intervals of absence, he remained there until 1895, when he joined a group of Cuban patriots planning an invasion of Cuba to fight for its independence from Spain. He was killed in combat at Dos Ríos, in May 1895, about three years before Spain relinquished sovereignty over Cuba in December 1898. His popularity with Cuba's nationalists and revolutionaries earned him epithets such as 'Apostle,' 'Maestro' (teacher), and 'Cuban Patriot' (Mañach 1950; Gray 1962).

Yet Martí was not only a man of action. He was also a man of ideas. And these he expressed in powerful ways in more than 200 writings, many of which have been interpreted in conflicting ways by the political leaders of his native Cuba. As a result, there is now a need to set the record straight about exactly what Martí's political philosophy was.

6.2 Hispano-Krausism

As might be expected of a thinker of Martí's caliber, there is more to his philosophical side than first appears. A lesser-known aspect of Martí's work is his Krausism, a complex theory of political philosophy he shared with a number of Latin American and Spanish reformists of the time. Krausism was an ambitious philosophical system devised by Karl Christian Friedrich Krause (German, 1781–1832). In the first half of the nineteenth century, Krause developed a form of post-Kantian rationalism that came to be known as 'harmonic rationalism.' But the theory never gained wide acceptance among philosophers. Except for in Spain and Latin America, Krausism never had a significant following among philosophers during the rise of nineteenth-century idealism – not even in Germany. What, then, could account for its stunning success in the Spanish-speaking world? Before addressing this question, let us take a brief look at the theory.

A student of Friedrich Wilhelm Joseph von Schelling and Johann Gottlieb Fichte in Jena, Krause had to wait for a university post until literally the day of his death. As a result, his experience of the fellowship of the professoriate in philosophy was somewhat limited. Even so, he was able to support himself as a private tutor in philosophy and music. His overarching philosophy may be described as a neo-Kantian "theory of everything" in which all crucial areas of philosophy are related in some ways, from ethics, metaphysics, and epistemology, to philosophy of religion, political philosophy, and many more. In epistemology, Krausism seeks the "unity" or compromise between a priori or "conscience" knowledge of God and a posteriori or experiential knowledge of the world. In metaphysics and philosophy of religion, Krausism is heavily indebted to Spinoza, since Krause also vindicates a kind of panentheism,[2] construed as a combination of pantheism and theism. Krause, however, went a step further by explicitly arguing against monotheism, which he regarded as conducive to a theocracy.

According to the theory of panentheism, the whole universe is a divine organism or unity made up of smaller components, themselves unities of other components, with individuals at the bottom. Echoing Spinoza's conception of God as *deus sive natura*, Krause's God includes both nature and humanity – where Creation and Creator are one – and this is made up of individuals united in smaller and larger groups (racial groups, nations, etc.). Thus individuals and their ultimate collection, humankind, are part of a divine universe – something that has moral consequences for individuals and humankind. Relevant to Martí's political thought are Krausism's implications that (i) *capital punishment* is wrong, (ii) punishment is permissible only when conducive to improvements, and (iii) what we now call 'liberal democracy' is the only form of polity compatible with the ideal of justice. Furthermore, moral wrongdoing occurs exclusively when individuals disrupt the harmonious unity of the whole.

Note that such claims about morality seem neither Kantian nor positivist (think, for example, of classical utilitarianism) but are quite idiosyncratic to Krause. Equally idiosyncratic is Krause's nonprogressive conception of personal and collective evolution according to which the history of an individual and that of humanity each unfolds in three stages: two "ascending" and one "descending." In the case of an individual, their evolution after conception toward childhood and adulthood represents the two ascending stages while their decline toward death is the descending stage. Humanity likewise evolves toward a mature, ideal stage in

---

[2] According to Dierksmeier (personal communication), Krause himself coined the term 'panentheism,' which is also used to refer to Baruch Spinoza's view.

which all individuals would reach unity (Zweig 1967: 365). But owing to Krause's much-criticized tendency toward jargonizing and mysticism, it is far from easy to explain how all his claims make up a system. Charitably read, we may think of them as making up an early version of communitarianism, one that emphasizes the value of each individual and their contribution to the global community of humanity and nature.

At any rate, as we will see, this interpretation is consistent with many of Martí's statements about the value of individuals and groups (Cubans, Latin Americans, minorities in the United States, etc.). Plausibly, Martí had become familiar with Krausism during his studies in Spain, where the movement first flourished before spreading also into the former colonies as Krausist students, lecturers, and books crossed the Atlantic. Julián Sanz del Río (1814–1869) had introduced it to his native country upon return from a research scholarship in Heidelberg, Germany, where he went in 1844 to study political philosophy. During his residence abroad, he fell under the philosophical influence of some disciples of Krause in Germany and Belgium.[3] The success of Sanz del Río's dissemination of Krausism is puzzling in light of the deep obscurity of the European version of the doctrine. A key instrumental factor might have been the need in Spain to break the centuries-long stranglehold of Scholasticism and the Catholic Church. Since Krausism was hostile to both, defenders of the status quo disliked it. The Church in particular disliked Krause's panentheism, which appeared to them either pantheist or atheist. But when the Church decided to add to its index of forbidden books Krausistic writings, including some by his disciples, this made them essential reading for Spain's avant-garde intellectuals.[4] In addition, since Spain had turned its back on both rationalism and empiricism during the Enlightenment, allowing only developments within Scholasticism, by the second half of the nineteenth century Spanish philosophers felt a desperate need to catch up with the rest of Europe.[5] In

---

[3] According to Arnulf Zweig (1967), the disciples of Krause who influenced Sans del Río were Heinrich Ahrens in Brussels and Herman von Leonhardi in Heidelberg.

[4] Claus Dierksmeier (2009).

[5] Historians of the movement who often cite these factors include Abellán (1989), Dierksmeier (2009), and Jiménez García and Orringer (2009).

addition, Spanish thinkers who were craving a philosophical change at the time apparently contemplated only two options in philosophy: either harmonic rationalism or empiricist positivism. Since they disliked the commitment of positivists to scientism and their hostility toward religion, they opted for harmonic rationalism, a philosophical theory they regarded as offering a compromise between rationalism and the empiricist side of positivism, with neither the scientism nor the secularism of positivism. Very soon there was a new hybrid doctrine in Spain expressing this choice, now called 'Krausopositivism.'

But Sanz del Río tried to stay close to Krause's original works on harmonic rationalism which he translated and edited, and on which he provided commentary. From a theoretical perspective, given harmonic rationalism, there is a moral core to values of any kind (e.g., epistemic, prudential, and legal values) since their "full" realization requires a free moral examination of one's own conscience, not only at the personal but also at the societal level. All values concern both the individual and society. From a practical perspective, the doctrine prescribes the pursuit of laws and institutions that would promote individual and social values by means of education, respect for the environment, individual rights (including women's rights), and distributive justice based on impartiality and equality. Consistent with these values, the Spanish Krausists believed in the possibility of improvements at the individual and societal level through evolution by peaceful means, not through revolution. Such improvements require respect for individual and social rights as well as free institutions and a limitation on state power – all tenets that were sharply at odds with the fascist worldview that later gained the upper hand in Spain after the Spanish Civil War with the rise of Franco.[6]

In any event, the strand of Spanish Krausism that took steps toward the achievement of some such practical goals is known as 'Krauso-institutionism.' Its representatives, mostly interested in enacting legal and institutional reforms, were primarily active in education, jurisprudence, and public policy. Salient among them in Spain was Francisco Giner de los Ríos

[6] Needless to say, Krausism came under siege during Franco's dark chapter in Spanish history. But by then the movement had already left an indelible mark not only on Spain's thought and culture but also on its institutions. For more on this see Jiménez García and Orringer (2009).

(1839–1915), who is often credited with having created the first private institution in the country to offer an academic education free of control by Church and state: the highly successful Institución Libre de Enseñanza (ILE, Institute of Free Education). Nelson R. Orringer, in the section he wrote for Jiménez García and Orringer 2009, provides a detailed account of the reforms pursued by Giner de los Ríos and his colleagues. For Orringer, it was the Krauso-institutionists' innovations in pedagogical institutions that was responsible for the cultural boost in Spain known as the 'Silver Age.' The reforms in their agenda included achieving academic freedom, coeducation, and student-centered institutions that made extensive use of dialogical methods akin to Socratic-style conceptual analysis. As a result of these reforms, institutions like the ILE began offering an education that was secular, more tolerant of novel views, and less authoritarian. Measures to bring about these reforms included the elimination of both corporal punishment of students and the distinction between primary and secondary education (a division that the Krauso-institutionists opposed on the basis that an individual's education moves gradually through *unified* stages). Giner de los Ríos was a key figure in articulating a philosophy of education along these lines.

On the other hand, the term 'Krauso-positivism' has come to denote a strand of Krausism most interested in enacting a scientific update in Spain by introducing theories and entire disciplines ignored by Scholasticism, such as evolutionary biology and scientific psychology. The Krauso-positivists concocted a hybrid doctrine that attempted to make Krausist rationalism compatible with the empiricist epistemology of positivism, using the one to counterbalance the excesses of the other. For them, on the one hand, positivism provided a restraint on Krause's speculative view of nature; and on the other, Krausism had a rationalist metaphysics and epistemology that acted as a counterweight to the radical scientism of strict positivism. But the Krauso-positivists also held positivism valuable because of their opposition to the dogmatism of Scholasticism and to the extreme reliance on speculative methods characteristic of late modern philosophers. The resulting combination of doctrines is not incoherent, unless it can be shown that there is a contradiction between an anti-realist metaphysics and an empiricist epistemology. In fact, Bishop Berkeley in modern philosophy and the logical positivists of the twentieth century have upheld that conjunction, while surviving attempts at refutation on the grounds of contradiction (a complex question that falls beyond our interest here).

But according to some historians of the movement there appears to be a third strand of Spanish Krausism, which we might call 'Krauso-perspectivism.' It includes the fundamental doctrines of José Ortega y Gasset (Spanish, 1883–1955) and his followers both in Spain and Latin America. For Claus Dierksmeier (2009) and some others, Ortega's perspectivism is a form of relational metaphysics indirectly influenced by Krause. True, Ortega's references to Krause are scarce, but a number of his theses in metaphysics and political philosophy are consistent with Krause's philosophical system. Dierksmeier mentions these:

> (1) [Ortega's] socio-political postulates in search of a liberalism for all classes and beyond the fray of political parties ..., (2) his program of advancing political progress through improved education (see his "Pedagogía social como programa politico"), and (3) his overall anti-revolutionary "reformismo" based upon his "pragmatismo idealista." (Dierksmeier 2009: 119–120)

It should be added that Ortega's famous aphorism, "I am myself and my circumstance ..." can be read as capturing the Krausist claim of unity between the individual on the one hand, and humanity and nature on the other. Of course, Ortega had a great impact in Latin American philosophy. But the influence of Krausism in the region, which was very intense by the turn of the twentieth century (and if Dierksmeier is right, continued to be so well into that century[7]) predates Ortega. For it goes back to the Puerto

---

[7] The spread of Krausism in Latin America at the turn of the twentieth century has to do with its appeal to those who, unlike the socialists and anarchists of the time, wished to bring about social reform by peaceful means. Accordingly, Krausism was the philosophical framework of many politicians and lawyers. In the former group were two presidents who explicitly adopted that framework – one in Argentina (Hipólito Yrigoyen, 1852–1933), the other in Uruguay (José Batlle y Ordóñez, 1856–1929). Later waves of populism and dictatorships appeared to have wiped out Krausism from the region, especially during the 1960s and 1970s. But Dierksmeier (2009) provides evidence from the Unión Cívica Radical (UCR) of Argentina for the view that it might only have been dormant, since it continued to inspire politicians seeking a peaceful solution to the problems of the region. His evidence includes writings by Raúl Alfonsín (1927–2009) of the UCR, who was President of Argentina from 1983 to 1989.

Rican educator Eugenio María de Hostos (1839–1903), and Martí, to whom I now turn.

6.3   The Elements of Martí's Krausism

Although there is debate about how to classify Martí's philosophical framework, that it was indeed Krausist is supported by both historical and textual evidence. First, not only did he studied jurisprudence and philosophy in Spain at the peak of that country's interest in Krausism, he endorsed the philosophy of Krause explicitly in his writings. Some of Martí's notes from a course in the history of philosophy that he delivered at the University of Guatemala support precisely this conclusion. In one such note, the endorsement of Krause comes after Martí rules out the philosophy of Fichte and Schelling – Fichte's because it "studied man as a subject in itself and remained focused on that subject," Schelling's because it "regarded man as analogous to his environment and thus confused subject with object." Martí then writes that Krause, "the best," managed to relate subject and object: "I had such a great pleasure when I found in Krause a philosophical compromise or means between two extremes that I attempted to call it 'relational philosophy.'" In other writings Martí gives evidence of his knowledge of the Spanish Krausists, of whom he said that they "Krausify the study of law but are . . . true sons of grave mother science" (cited in Vales 1996).[8] Again, it would be unusual if someone like Martí, who was interested in law and education and has studied in Spain in the late nineteenth century, failed to praise the Krausists.

But, most important, in Martí's more than 200 writings (including journalistic articles, speeches, and other short pieces) there are numerous claims consistent with the ideals of the Krausists in Latin America. For example, one such ideal has it that individuals as well as the groups they make up have equal intrinsic moral worth. If so, then each has rights, individuals and groups, and any attempt to deprive them of their rights as in racism and other forms of discrimination is wrong. In addition, humanity as a whole and nature have moral worth too since they are essentially (in

[8] My translations of quotes in Vales (1996), cited from Martí's *Obras Completas*, Havana: Editorial de Ciencias Sociales, vol. 19, p. 367.

fact, divinely) related. In the case of individuals, Krausists upheld their rights to be free and unite with other individuals in groups (nations, ethnic and racial groups, and humanity as a whole). Martí accordingly often engaged in passionate vindications of values for Cuba and Latin America such as sovereignty, unity, and cultural uniqueness. On Latin American peoples, he thought that, like any member of the human family, they deserved an adequate education that could allow them to reach freedom and happiness. They also deserved equal rights – that is, human rights independently of their skin color or socioeconomic status. On his optimistic view, Latin American nations are not an exception to the Krausist belief in a universal harmony: they will change for the better, but by peaceful social reform rather than by revolution. Except of course in the case of Cuba, whose independence has proved impossible in light of Spain's indifference to reasoned argument of the sort Martí forcefully outlined in the "Manifesto de Montecristi," a speech cowritten with compatriot Máximo Gómez in the Dominican Republic just before they led the invasion to free Cuba in 1895. Let us now take a closer look at how Martí argued for those Krausist ideals.

6.3.1   Populist Nationalism and Latin Americanism

Krausists believed that a nation's unity and freedom are its chief social values. As we will see here, Martí gave a populist twist to such nationalism. That he was a populist nationalist is evident in his unflagging zeal for the cause of Cuban independence and his almost romantic faith in the common people's unity in pursuit of that independence. In Latin America, however, his populist nationalism was in conflict with the prevailing political philosophy of the positivists, for whom order and progress trumped other social values: on their view, Latin America was not ready for unity and independence from the neocolonial powers of the West. Martí of course warned Latin Americans against neocolonialism. Also unlike the positivists, Martí remained suspicious of any authoritarian style of government, and he took the absence of freedom to be antithetical to a harmonious society. In addition, he trusted that the people of Latin America would eventually enact the reforms needed in their nations by means of a democratic system of government. These reforms would inevitably occur – so the argument went – once Latin Americans came to realize their common talents and values, which they could do with the right kind of education. Again by contrast with the positivists, Martí trusted the instincts of the plain, unpretentious people of the land: the peasants and workers, and all who struggle to live a simple, yet happy, life.

But in expressing his passionate commitment to populist nationalism, at no point did Martí invoke either 'class struggle' or any other revolutionary concept familiar from the lexicon of nineteenth-century socialist and anarchist movements. Rather, like other Krausists of the time, he thought that change would result from promoting the right kind of education – which, as we will soon see, would have to consist not only in imparting practical knowledge but also in developing some moral virtues conducive to social cohesion.

Martí also campaigned for "Latin Americanism," promoting awareness of the value of Latin Americans' unique *mestizo* identity, and of their membership of and equal rights with other members of the human family. According to Latin Americanism, Latin Americans should neither try to emulate European and North American values and ways of life in detriment to their own, nor assume that the people of Madrid or Paris or New York are somehow superior. In "Mente Latina" (The Latino Mind), for example, after mentioning the comparative brilliance of Latino students in the United States, he contended that it is the lack of practical skills in the region's university curriculum that "kills South America." The situation would be different "[if] South Americans were educated, not for living in France, given that they are not French; or in the United States, which is the most productive bad fad, given that they are North Americans; or in colonial times ... But for living in South America ...."[9]

Furthermore, Martí directed many recommendations to fellow Latin Americans to promote their awareness of the interference of foreign powers in the region. He of course denounced Spain's lingering colonial rule over Cuba and Puerto Rico, but also warned Latin Americans about the growing power of the United States. They should be on guard given its ambitions in the region, which posed a serious threat because North

---

[9] Martí (1997–2015/1884b). Martí often argued that Latin Americans should both develop practical skills and avoid thinking of themselves as inferior to other people.

America, like Europe, could not possibly understand the nature of the Latin American people. On his view, "[n]either the European nor the Yankee could provide the key to the Spanish American riddle" (1999/1891b: 117).[10] But if the chief task facing Latin America is that of becoming truly independent – which means being free from *any* form of colonial rule, whether old or new – then education must figure prominently in any "to-do list" for the region.

6.3.2   Other Antidotes to Oppression

In his 1894 essay "The Truth about the United States" Martí (1894b) outlines such a "to-do list" along Krausist lines. First, he takes education and knowledge to be the best antidote to oppression due to either foreign domination or local authoritarianism. He construes education as a means for people to acquire not only the skills necessary for life but also some desirable traits of social character. There is no doubt that, just as in the case of the Latin American positivists, Martí championed education. But contrary to what Mañach (1950) contends, he was not fully on board with the positivists on education: he coincided with them on some points, but also had substantive differences. For one thing, unlike the positivists, Martí did not understand education as a tool for instilling habits in people that are conducive to the *progress* and *order* of their nation. And he did not think that *all* Hispano-American values were flawed or in need of replacement with the values of more developed nations. True, like the positivists of his time, Martí did favor the teaching of science and opposed any instruction in Catholicism – an opposition that was in accord with his own, Krausist, anticlericalist convictions. He wrote: "No one has the right to teach either the Catholic or *anti-Catholic religion in schools*; honor should be the greatest virtue in religion, and as long as the schools promote it they will be religious enough" (cited in Gray 1962: 53, my emphasis).

These remarks are consistent with Martí's Krausist view of the value of science and the general disvalue of organized religion. But the rejection of organized religion neither conflicts with the panentheism of his Krausist

---

[10] Additional evidence for this standard interpretation of Martí on Latin America and the United States can be found in his "Our America" (1999/1891b) and "Mother America" (1999/1889), among other essays.

philosophical framework nor commits him to the naturalist ontology of the positivists. In addition, his conception of the best education for the Latin American nations and rulers could not have been farther from the conception of the positivists, who conceived education as modeled on foreign systems (Sarmiento, for example, imported teachers from the United States to impart such systems in Argentina). Moreover, Martí explicitly distinguished education aimed at false erudition from education that aimed at developing practical skills, as well as understanding one's own cultural identity (Martí 1999/1891b: 113). He of course favored the latter type of education.

Accordingly, Martí also had some related views on what public officials should do about education. In setting up their systems, he believed, those who wish to guide the Latin American nations toward their unity and freedom should value ideas grounded on their own experiences within their own cultures (as opposed to imitating dubious Western values, such as progress and prosperity at all costs). They should be mindful that people must learn some of the practical skills needed to move forward in an increasingly competitive world.[11] To achieve this goal, he called degree programs in theology and any other subject unsuitable to this goal to be eliminated from the curriculum. They needed to be replaced with science and technology, whose teaching should be geared toward practical applications in nature, construed narrowly to mean the students' immediate environment. Thus, students from rural regions should learn agricultural skills, and city students should learn skills necessary for urban life, and not the other way around. In his essay "Maestros ambulantes" (Ambulatory Teachers, 1997–2015/1884a), he advocates sending schoolteachers to the countryside to instruct the farmers in practical matters concerning their work "with nature," as well as helping them develop the right traits of moral and social character. Education is required to be fully human – he argued – something that presupposes being free and having enough prosperity to be a good person. But the "only path to permanent and easy prosperity is that of knowledge, farming, and making use of . . . nature."[12]

---

[11] Accordingly, Martí writes: "Education must give the means of resolving the problems that life presents" (cited in Gray 1962: 53).

[12] As a good Krausist, Martí further declares: "Happiness exists on earth and we can conquer it with the prudent use of reason, knowledge of the harmony of the universe, and the regular practice of generosity" (1997–2015/1884a, my translation).

Here we have a mixed teleological argument in which knowledge is instrumental for prosperity, prosperity for being a good person, and being a good person for the ultimate goal of achieving human happiness. Only good people can be happy. Maybe a more consistent Krausist would instead take knowledge to be valuable in order for humans to have a harmonious relation with nature. In either case, though, knowledge is seen as instrumental or valuable for the sake of something else.

At the same time, since by the end of the nineteenth century emancipation from foreign powers was an unfinished business in Latin America, and the perils of US expansionism loomed large, Martí argued that educators should also be mindful of the need for Latin Americans to assert their own common identity as a people upon the world stage. So besides learning about the richness of their own culture, Latin Americans needed to learn that they all had a common identity, one determined by the region's history and its ethnic and racial diversity. Like Bolívar, Martí believed that a clear understanding of that identity was essential for anyone in a leadership position, whom he advised:

> Knowing is what counts. To know one's country and govern it with that knowledge is the only way to free it from tyranny ... The history of [Latin] America, from the Incas to the present, must be taught in clear detail and to the letter, even if the archons of Greece are overlooked. Our Greece must take priority over the Greece which is not ours. We need it more. Nationalist state men must replace state men ... (Martí 1999/1891b: 114)

6.3.3 The Rejection of Racism

Although Martí recognized that Latin Americans had a common identity, he did not fail to note their diversity in terms of race and socioeconomic status. Furthermore, he was aware of the region's long history of racial and ethnic prejudice. His Krausism committed him to rejecting that legacy while vindicating the intrinsic value of individual persons and groups.[13] Martí accordingly maintained that all groups of people deserve equal

---

[13] Krause's vindication of the dignity of individual persons and groups goes back to Kant's principle of Humanity-as-End-in-Itself, to which I return in Chapter 9 on liberation theology and philosophy.

rights, since there is in fact a single race: the human race. Given this view, any form of slavery or racism is morally wrong. He knew these two evils firsthand from his experiences: first, in Cuba where Spain had abolished slavery but tried to use racism as a tool to divide the revolutionaries, a stratagem that Martí denounced in his 1894 essay "El plato de lentejas" (A Lentil Plate). Yet his writings also show familiarity with the practice of racism in the United States. Particularly shocking for Martí, as denounced in "Indians in the United States," was US racism against the native people in that country; this was something he had not witnessed before, because the native inhabitants of Cuba had been wiped out during the early days of colonial rule.

The *locus classicus* for Martí's condemnation of racism is "My Race," whose major argument can be reconstructed in various ways. As a slippery-slope argument, it holds that, once the white racists proclaim their racial superiority over black people, then the white racists must accept that the black people too have the right to claim their racial superiority over others, including the white races – a conclusion that these should find unacceptable. Here is the argument in Martí's own words:

> What right do white racists, who believe their race is superior, who see something special in their own race, have to complain about black racists? What right do black racists, who see a special character in their race, have to complain about white racists? White men who think their race makes them superior to black men admit the concept of racial superiority, and thereby authorize and provoke black racists. (Martí 1999–/1893, my translation)

The argument as it stands appears weak, since racists of either group might reply (and have done so) by invoking empirical evidence in support of the alleged superiority of their race.[14] But Martí can meet this reply with the rejoinder that, so far, no evidence of that sort has proved compelling.

To add weight to his argument, Martí also invokes a Krausist conception of the moral importance of universal unity and harmony. Given that

---

[14] The lack of empirical evidence for racism is shown by extensive literature on the race and IQ debate. See for instance, Ned Block's "How Heritability Misleads about Race," *Cognition* 56(2) 1995: 99–128.

conception, another argument against racism gets off the ground, one that goes like this:

1. If people from an ethnic group [sic] proclaim the superiority of their group over another group, then that would incite the reaction of the other group and create discord.
2. Discord offends against universal unity and harmony.
3. Whatever offends against universal unity and harmony is wrong.
4. *Therefore*, it is wrong for people of an ethnic group to proclaim the group's superiority over another group.

Of course, this argument relies on the truth of premise (3), which encompasses Krausist doctrines many would reject (for example, Marxists and anarchists, with whom Martí is sometimes wrongly classified). A stronger argument against racism in "My Race" is one that need not rest on any Krausist assumptions, since it can be reconstructed as follows:

1. Peace demands of Nature the recognition of human rights.
2. People whose human rights are violated through discrimination will fight for them.
3. War is incompatible with peace.
4. Therefore, discrimination is contrary to Nature and the enemy of peace.

Here the Krausist assumptions are those invoking "Nature." But they can be easily ignored, thereby producing an argument that rests only on strong evidence from observation and common sense.

Once we take into account these small amendments, Martí has now offered us two strong arguments against racism: on the one hand, the racists have no reason or evidence for their claims of racial superiority; on the other, racism leads to war or other forms of social discord. These cause suffering, including pain and death, which are generally bad. Yet Martí optimistically believed that rational people will come to realize the inevitable conflict between racism and peace. This empirical claim, though it may be true in the long run, in the short run appears false. Many systems of government that have approved and even imposed racial or religious discrimination nonetheless have been able to survive in relative peace for a long time. Think for instance of the Spanish and Portuguese colonies in the Americas.

6.4 The Upshot

Martí's nationalism and Latin Americanism are evident in his passionate attempts to persuade, respectively, Cubans to fight for their nation's sovereignty and Latin Americans to become aware of the perils of US expansionism. I have argued that each of these doctrines has a Krausist philosophical foundation that prompted him to assign the highest value to freedom and unity (understood in terms of social harmony). Although not strictly a philosopher, as we have seen, Martí had some training in philosophy. But, more importantly, in countless writings he proved to be an original philosophical thinker, who not only took up the Latin Americanist tradition of Bolívar, but set it on a more progressive path. Central to his political philosophy was the conviction that an individual's happiness requires not only material well-being but also harmony with other individuals and nature. He was confident that with education of the right kind, Latin Americans would eventually appreciate the richness of their common culture, unite, and prosper within democratic nations. Like the peoples of other parts of the world, they should have leaders who understand their culture and are committed to the moral values that may allow them to flourish. The individualism he encountered during his North American exile appears to have reinforced his Krausist belief that unity and love are above material welfare.

True, on his view some level of material well-being is necessary if people are to be happy. As we saw, Martí thinks that happiness requires goodness, and goodness requires some level of material well-being. But material well-being is sufficient neither for goodness nor for happiness. Consider, for example, the case where people live in a society marked by economic inequality and racism. Whether or not that society had achieved material well-being like the United States, Martí would say that those peoples are bound to be at war with each other, or experience social discord of some other sort. In the absence of social harmony, those people cannot be happy.[15]

---

[15] Martí in fact had a mixed response to the United States, as evident in, among other essays, "The Truth about the United States" (1894) and "Letter to the New York Herald" (1999/1895a). On the one hand, he praised that nation's respect for individual freedom; on the other, he denounced its racism and expansionist foreign policy. He rightly perceived the latter as a threat to Latin America.

These claims amount to a kind of communitarianism opposite to both the individualism of ethical egoism and the class struggle championed in Marxism as a means of socioeconomic progress. If this interpretation of Martí's political thought is right, then, the common claim that the Latin American Marxists of the twentieth century are his ideological successors cannot be correct. There is abundant textual evidence from his writings to think that, faced with the increasingly acute social and moral problems of twentieth-century Latin America (racism, *machismo,* pervasive poverty, the destruction of the environment, foreign interference, etc.), Martí would have rejected a class-struggle strategy for resolving them.[16]

6.5 Suggested Readings

Dierksmeier, Claus. 2009. "Krausism," pp. 110–127 in Nuccetelli et al. 2009.

Outlines the chief theses of Karl Krause and their adaptation by his Spanish and Latin American followers at the turn of the twentieth century. Contends that some of those followers, especially in Uruguay and Argentina, were able to produce correct diagnoses and prognoses of sociopolitical problems in a number of areas, from women's liberation and animal rights to ecological sustainability and global governance. For a more recent work on the philosophy of Krause, see Dierksmeier (2019).

Fernández Retamar, Roberto. 1976. "La crítica de Martí," pp. 11–29 in *Para una teoría de la literatura hispanoamericana.* Mexico City: Editorial Nuestro Tiempo.

Written by a cultural figure and public official in Cuba's socialist revolution, this essay points to an evolution in the radicalization of Martí, especially noticeable in his writings on aesthetics. Fernández Retamar did not at first explicitly associate Martí's political thought with socialism. But later, in a prologue of a collection of essays about (Noble 2007), he counted Martí as a socialist.

---

[16] A famous poem by Martí, "Cultivo una rosa blanca" ("I have a white rose to tend"), captures this ideal of social harmony by means of the metaphor that he gives a white rose to either the true friend or the cruel enemy (verso XXXIX, *Simple Verses,* p. 306 in Martí 1999). The message thus conveyed is inconsistent with Marxism – and, depending on some assumptions, also with ethical egoism, a position about which I will have more to say in connection with my discussion of Arielism in the next chapter.

Fornet-Betancourt, Raúl. 1997–2015. "El pensamiento de José Martí. Estudio introductorio: Vida y líneas generales de su pensamiento," in José Luis Gómez-Martínez, ed., *Proyecto Ensayo Hispánico*. www.ensayistas.org/filosofos/cuba/marti/marti2.htm

Excellent outline of the evolution of Martí's thought since his first important publication from early in his life, *El Presidio Político en Cuba* of 1871. Argues that Martí was not a Marxist since he did not invoke class struggle for the solutions of the problems facing Cubans and all oppressed peoples; rather, he started out as a Romantic who relied instead on the power of love and continued to uphold that view later in life.

Horan, Elizabeth. 2010. "Whose José Martí?" *American Quarterly* 62(1): 181–189.

Focused on Martí's years in New York, where he produced numerous translations (from English into Spanish), manifestos, notebooks, poetry, newspaper articles, and cultural commentaries. Besides providing interesting biographical data, Horan argues that Martí's thought was not positivist but rather a mix of Cuban nationalism and the "transnational" approach of Latino *émigrés* in the United States. On this interpretation, Martí would be an antecedent of "border" writers such as Gloria Anzaldúa.

Jiménez García, Antonio and Nelson R. Orringer. 2009. "Del krausismo al krausopositivismo," pp. 67–78 in Garrido et al. 2009.

Well-informed survey of the reception of Krausism in Spain, from the introduction of the movement by Sanz del Río to the constitution of Spanish institutionist and positivist varieties of Krausism.

Krause, C. Chr. F. 1871. *Ideal de la Humanidad para la vida, con introducción y comentarios por Julián Sanz del Río*. Madrid: Imprenta de F. Martínez García, (2nd ed. available online at www.cervantesvirtual.com/obra/ideal-de-la-humanidad-para-la-vida–0/).

This mostly consists of Sanz del Río's translation of Krause's 1811 work *Urbild der Menschheit*, misleadingly introduced by Sanz del Río as if it had been written by him. But contains those of Krause's ideas that became the most popular among Spanish American Krausists.

López-Morillas, Juan. 1981. *The Krausist Movement and Ideological Change in Spain, 1854–1874*. Cambridge, UK: Cambridge University Press.

Argues that Krausism, in Spain first, and then in Latin America, played the role of ridding the culture of the conservative values of the Counter-Reformation, which had isolated the peoples of these regions from modern European thought. It considers Krausism to be a form of positivism similar in some respects to utopian socialism, but without the explicit atheistic agenda of socialism.

Mañach, Jorge. 1950. *Martí: Apostle of Freedom*. New York: Devin-Adair. www
    .latinamericanstudies.org/1895/manach.pdf

A mostly accurate outline of Martí's life and work. But its interpretation of his philosophy of education as an outgrowth of positivism is questionable based on the evidence provided in this chapter.

Martí, José. 1999/1889. "Mother America," *El Partido Liberal*, December 19, 1889,
    pp. 101–110 in Martí 1999.
    1999/1891b. "Our America," La Revista Illustrada, January 1, 1891, pp. 111–121
    in Martí 1999.
    1999/1893. "My Race," *Patria*, April 16, 1893, pp. 160–162 in Martí 1999
    (references to "Mi raza," in Gómez-Martínez 1997–2015).
    1997–2015/1894a. "El plato de lentejas," *Patria*, January 2, 1894a, in Gómez-
    Martínez 1997–2015, www.ensayistas.org/antologia/XIXA/marti/marti6
    .htm
    1999/1894b. "The Truth about the United States," *Patria*, March 23, 1894b, pp.
    172–176 in Martí 1999.

Short articles illustrating most of the elements of Martí's philosophy discussed here.

Ripoll, Carlos. 1984. *José Martí, the United States, and Marxist Interpretation of Cuban
    History*. New Brunswick, NJ and London: Transaction Publishers.

Argues that Martí's campaigns for the independence of Cuba and Puerto Rico were motivated by nationalism rather than socialism or communism. As evidence, Ripoll invokes writings from Martí's US period, where he expressed admiration for the protection of personal freedoms in the United States as well as concerns about that country's expansionist international agenda. Agrees with early intellectuals of Cuba's Communist Party, such as Juan Marinello, who before the advent of Castro's revolution had contended that Martí favored a pluralistic democracy over a dictatorship of the proletariat.

Roig, Arturo Andrés. 1998. "Etica y liberación: José Martí y el 'hombre natural,'" in *Etica del poder y moralidad de la protesta: La moral latinoamericana de la emergencia*. Mendoza, Argentina. (References to reprint in Gómez-Martínez 1997–2015, www.ensayistas.org/filosofos/argentina/roig/etica/etica18.htm)

An interpretation of Martí's political philosophy, especially as presented in the essay "Nuestra América," that is incompatible with the Krausist interpretation proposed in this chapter. According to this interpretation, Martí turns out to be a proto-liberation philosopher who in that essay is concerned with the history of the "struggle" for the liberation of the oppressed in Latin America. But see also Roig (1969).

Schutte, Ofelia. 2011b. "Undoing 'Race': Martí's Historical Perspective," pp. 99–123 in Gracia 2011.

Defends Martí's use of terms such as 'white' and 'black' from the charge that it connotes a white-supremacist view. Holds that in doing so, he was following a view that separates the corporeal or visible from the spiritual or invisible which had been commonly accepted since the Enlightenment. Vaguely characterizes Martí's philosophical framework as a "humanist idealist perspective" without identifying it with Krausism.

Vales, José Francisco. 1996. "La influencia de la cultura alemana en la formación del pensamiento de José Martí," *Iberoamericana* 20(1): 5–25.

Broad study of the influence of German literature and philosophy on Martí. Provides evidence of his interest in philosophy in general and in the philosophy of Krause in particular. Good secondary source for Martí's notes for his lectures in the history of philosophy.

7   Utopian Latin Americanism: Arielism and *Mestizofilia*

By the late nineteenth century, José Martí had sent a strong message to Latin Americans: the culture of the United States has many strengths that deserve praise, but it is not a culture that can produce a truly good and happy society. The thinkers considered in this chapter, José Enrique Rodó (Uruguayan, 1872–1917) and José Vasconcelos (Mexican, 1882–1959), go a step further in their rejection of US values and vindication of Latin America's cultural identity. Rodó in fact went so far as to declare US values not worth emulating. And Vasconcelos advanced a utopian vision of a Latin American race that would have superior values.

These thinkers belonged to two consecutive generations of Latin American intellectuals who were jaded with the ill-conceived social and political adventures of positivism. It seemed to many of them that the Comtean and Millian experiments had come crashing down in failure, and that it was time for Latin Americans to assert their own distinctive identity in a way that would make a secure place for them in the world. Their doctrines developed at times of international unrest and realignment of power among nations, which affected the subcontinent deeply. By the end of the nineteenth century, the European crisis that precipitated World War I was in the making. That war, together with the even more terrifying enormity of World War II, seemed to put to rest any remainder of the positivist-inspired optimism that had led some thinkers to dream of uninterrupted, universal progress and order. Already Spain had lost its last colonies in the Americas, and the United States was moving steadily toward becoming the new imperial threat to Latin America that Martí had predicted. Some such developments had a dramatic effect on the consecutive generations of Latin American intellectuals represented by Rodó and Vasconcelos. For better or worse, they carried out a reassessment of the role of the positivists in their native countries, as well as of the place of their young nations in the world. Yet at the end of the day, if I am right in the discussion that follows, none of these views on Latin American identity and values is compelling. But Rodó's views are far less defensible than Vasconcelos's.

7.1 Rodó's Elitist Anti-Positivism

By the turn of the twentieth century, some intellectuals in Latin America began to be dissatisfied with the cultural policies of local politicians, which were usually inspired by one or another positivist movement among several that had become fashionable in the region. In this context, it is hardly surprising that *Ariel*, a narrative essay targeting positivist values, was to assume in the early 1900s the status of an anti-positivist manifesto. Published in 1900, *Ariel* offers its critique of such values by focusing on what it sees as the weaknesses of North America's democracies and their underlying utilitarian outlook. At the same time, *Ariel* offers a passionate defense of what I take to be a Eurocentric model of Latin American identity. I will analyze these two aspects of *Ariel* after having a quick look at its author's life and work.

7.1.1 Life and Work

Born in Montevideo in 1872, Rodó belonged to the modernist generation of literary writers that came after Martí's. Although unlike Martí Rodó never obtained a university degree, by means of self-education he acquired extensive erudition, especially in literature – a subject he taught at Uruguay's National University in Montevideo. Through his own readings, he became familiar with the modernist aesthetic of his time as well as with positivist and anti-positivist European doctrines. By the time he published *Ariel*, he was already convinced that positivist moral and social philosophy was wrongheaded. Arguing for this negative thesis was his main goal in the book, which was by far Rodó's most important work. Among his other books with philosophical aspirations are *Motivos de Proteo* (*The Motives of Proteus*, 1909) and *El mirador de Próspero* (*The Gallery of Prospero*, 1913).

But it was not only philosophy that concerned Rodó, who held a number of key positions in Uruguay's institutions. He served twice in the Chamber of Deputies, and – owing to his considerable erudition, which ranged from literature to philosophy and the history of Western culture – the same year *Ariel* came out he was appointed director of the country's national library, a position of great distinction in Latin American countries. Rodó also played a crucial role in Uruguay's literary and cultural development in other ways. For example, he did so through his founding in 1895 of what was to become a highly regarded cultural magazine, *La revista nacional de literatura y ciencias sociales*. In 1916, just a year before his death in Italy, he accepted the position of foreign correspondent for a highly regarded news and culture magazine that was popular in Latin America, *Caras y caretas* (*Faces and Masks*).

The factors that prompted the development of Rodó's political thought are likely to include, first, some noticeable attempts by the United States to interfere with the economies and political institutions of Latin America. Second, the state of social unrest that began to affect nations of the region under the ostensible influence of positivist politics, especially in neighboring Brazil.[1] Third, the fact that in 1898 Spain lost its remaining colonies in Puerto Rico, Cuba, and the Philippines. Carlos Fuentes, a contemporary Mexican thinker and literary figure, has summarized some relevant historical events surrounding *Ariel*'s publication as follows:

> Spain, our old empire, was defeated and dismantled by the United States, our new empire, in 1898; the Philippines and Puerto Rico became North American colonies, Cuba a subject state. Our sympathies shifted to the defeated empire: the United States desatanized Spain while satanizing itself. Walker's takeover in Nicaragua, the mutilation of Colombia so that the Panama Canal could be held independently of Latin America, the intervention in Mexico in 1914 and again in 1917, Marines in Haiti, Honduras, Nicaragua, and the Dominican Republic. In the center of the period . . . Rodó's *Ariel* appears as the emotional and intellectual response of Latin American thought and Latin American spirituality to growing North American imperial arrogance, gunboat diplomacy, and big stick policies. (Fuentes 1988: 16)

[1] Among especially relevant factors is the 1896 unrest in Brazil that culminated in a peasant revolt against the liberal Republic in Canudos. Euclides da Cunha, who as we saw in Chapter 5 was initially a Comtean positivist, captured this event in his 1902 novel, *Rebellion in the Backlands*.

Fuentes plausibly contends that *Ariel* acted as a vindication of the values of Latin American culture in contrast with the values prevalent in US culture. So Rodó's views, like those of his positivist predecessors, were not merely theoretical but had some practical consequences. They caused, at least in part, some changes in the attitudes, policies, and institutions of Latin America.

Among such changes is, first, the formation in October of 1909 of a group of young intellectuals in Mexico City who were willing to voice their objections to positivism, the so-called Ateneo de la Juvendud (Athenaeum of Youth), which counted Vasconcelos among its participants and was soon to spread to other Latin American countries.[2] Furthermore, *Ariel* might have played a role in helping some positivists rethink the truth of their theories.[3] In addition, *Ariel* became popular within student movements of the 1910s throughout Latin America that were seeking a democratization of the universities. Of all these, the University Reform Movement in Argentina was the most inspirational because it obtained a clear victory in 1918, when President Yrigoyen of the Union Civica Radical party signed into law the autonomy of the National University in Buenos Aires.[4] But the puzzling issue for us here is what, exactly, was the message of *Ariel* that could have had an impact on such a diverse series of events?

7.1.2 Rodó's *Ariel*

In *Ariel*, although the narrative opens with a reference to Shakespeare's *Tempest*, Rodó is less indebted to that work than to Joseph-Ernest Renan's 1888 *Caliban*, a "philosophic drama" by a relatively obscure

---

[2] The *Ateneo*, an organization credited with having enacted an anti-positivist cultural revolution before the military revolution of 1910 (Vargas Lozano 2010), first operated under the name 'Sociedad de Conferencias' (Association of Conferences). Initially its members were figures such as Dominican Pedro Henríquez Ureña (1884–1946) and besides Vasconcelos, Mexicans Antonio Caso (1883–1946), Alfonso Reyes (1889–1959), and others. Their average age was twenty-five.

[3] For example, as the story goes, reading *Ariel* led Justo Sierra to have second thoughts about the objectivity of science.

[4] By 1921, the branches of the National University of Argentina in the provinces had also adopted the reform. They were to be run by students, administrators, and professors. But not for long. A military coup in 1930 overturned the democratic rule of law, preventing Yrigoyen from completing his second term in office.

French author, historian, and philosopher of religion (1823–1892).[5] After all, Rodó's characters in *Ariel* bear a resemblance to the evil character, Caliban, and good characters, Prospero and Ariel, as they appear in Renan's work. Caliban symbolizes democracy, which with some magical help from the positivists, ultimately defeats Prospero and Ariel, who symbolize the political will of the aristocracy favored by Renan. At the beginning of Rodó's narrative (1988/1900: 31), Próspero is sitting near a statue of Ariel, the character in Shakespeare's *Tempest*. He is ready to reveal to his audience of young students what it takes for a life to go well – which he does in a series of prescriptions about their education that take center stage from page 41 on. It is a farewell meeting, since he is retiring and seems to fear for the future of Latin American youth, to whom Rodó dedicates the book. In essence, Próspero's advice to his students seemingly consists in a series of prescriptions to the effect that they should: (a) embrace the moral and aesthetic virtues constitutive of their own Latin American culture; (b) avoid a dogmatic acceptance of cultural values from the North; and (c) practice being self-critical. Only when (a) through (c) are satisfied, can Latin American youth avoid falling into the trap of utility and practicality, the not-worth-pursuing "values" of an evil character, Calibán.

Of course, as in the case of Renan's symbolic characters, Rodó's characters too have a number of connotations in the book. Calibán connotes the unexamined life that can only lead to the acceptance of the cultural values of the United States. Although Rodó does not explicitly equate Calibán with the United States, he explicitly ascribes to that nation the utility and practicality of Calibán, which he deems bad traits of individuals and groups. At the same time, Próspero connotes the young nations of Latin America, which he claims share a unique, Mediterranean culture with roots in ancient Greece and Rome as well as Christianity. According to Rodó, from ancient Mediterranean culture, especially from Greek culture, Latin Americans inherited the ideal of beauty, which is a superior concept,

---

[5] Rodó offers many praises for Renan in *Ariel*. For example, on page 57 he is said to be "one of the most agreeable masters of the modern mind" and the reader is told that if they read him (something Rodó strongly recommends) "you will revere him as I do" (See also 1988/1900: 33, 36, 41, 51, 63–64, 65, and 88).

connected to reason; while from Christianity they inherited the ideal of charity.[6]

But how could the peoples of Latin America possibly have such roots? What about the Amerindians and the Afro-Latin Americans? Do they too have those cultural roots? Since Rodó does not say, we may plausibly assume that he is counting only the Spanish cultural heritage. Although this assumption in itself represents a departure from the aversion to Spanish values of the positivists, it also invalidates the assimilation of his Latin Americanism with the multiethnic, *mestizaje* model of Latin American identity of Bolívar and Martí.

Once these assumptions become explicit, it is clear that Rodó, like Sarmiento, believed that the Latin America of his time was facing a civilization-versus-barbarism dilemma. But unlike Sarmiento, he placed the United States on the barbarism side and the ancient Mediterranean empires of Greece and Rome on the civilization side. Understood as a conflict of cultures, on the civilization side of the dilemma are the higher cultural values of Próspero; on the barbarism side are the lower cultural values of Calibán. Understood as an inner conflict facing each individual, on the civilization side is the "spirit" or intellect of a person and on the barbarism side the "instinct." In addition, from a social perspective, Próspero represents the leadership of the intellectual elite, who know how to subordinate materials needs and instinct to higher, spiritual values – while Calibán represents, among other things, the "appetites" of the masses and a type of popular culture Latin Americans should reject.

7.1.3 The Critique of the United States

Rodó's *Ariel* is often interpreted as holding that, while the culture of the United States has many strengths that deserve praise, it is not to be emulated by Latin Americans, who have their own valuable culture (Symington 1988; Miller 1999). A *qualified critique* of the United States along these lines might truly apply to a thinker like Martí, who repeatedly expressed his admiration of some aspects of US culture (e.g., its freedoms) yet criticized

---

[6] Rodó's positive remarks about the aesthetic and moral values of ancient Greece are at their peak on pages 43–44 of *Ariel* (Rodó 1988/1900). But see also pages 35 and 52–53. His praise for the value of Christianity is most explicit on page 79.

that country's expansionism in matters cultural and economic. However, it is difficult to find textual evidence for a qualified critique of the United States in Rodó. In his *Ariel* we find instead generalizations, such as that North Americans regard the relentless striving for material gain as an end in itself. Because of this, the argument continues, there is a certain coarseness in North American culture that is absent in Latin American culture. American society is simply materialist at its core and so all its titanic strivings and technological achievements are made, in the end, for the sake of no ideal that can give a true purpose to human life.

This is all due to the influence of positivism, or as Rodó calls it, 'utilitarianism.' North Americans are consumed with the desire to advance their own immediate self-interests (at which they are spectacularly successful), but seem blind to the spiritual impoverishment this brings. Even worse is the North Americans' aesthetic sense, for the populist spirit that drives their democracy is a leveling impulse that enforces mediocrity in all things.[7] Somewhat speculatively, we may wonder what Rodó would say of the greatest patrons of the arts in the United States? What would he say of the financiers and captains of industry who have endowed the art museums and musical institutions, or the curators of those museums, or the art professors? Do they too have only a coarse and crude aesthetic sensibility? He seems committed to giving some counterintuitive responses here, such as that the true subtlety of great art eludes *all* North Americans but not Latin Americans. These North American plutocrats want art only to glorify themselves, not for its own intrinsic value.

In any case, according to Rodó, this sorry situation facing the United States might be remedied, if only the American school system could instill in the young a discriminating sense of high culture and good taste. Education should aim at developing a broad range of moral and aesthetic attitudes and sentiments, such as appreciation of real excellence in thought and in the arts. But this the United States refuses to do, since it is dedicated only to the cause of propagating mediocrity: it wants only to see the most widespread proliferation of basic literacy, but cares not at all about students' learning to recognize true quality, beauty, or wisdom. For Rodó

[7] See, for example, Rodó (1988/1900: 75–79, 83, 86, 88, and 90–92).

(1988/1900: 40–42; 82), specialization in education leads to a willful narrowness of the understanding.

North American conceptions of morality he sees as similarly shallow, since they are based, not on "selflessness" and the cultivation of the virtues, as Rodó believes they should be, but on a more prosaic notion of ordinary duties rooted in honesty and prudence in day-to-day dealings with others. He cites Benjamin Franklin's simple moral code as an example of this, implying that, while it can account for obligations, it allows for no moral categories going beyond that – and thus cannot account for the special regard in which we hold saintly or heroic actions (Rodó 1988/1900: 83–84).

On the issue of the prevailing moral outlook in North America, in *Ariel* Rodó takes it to be one doomed to a certain pedestrian incapacity for nobleness of character because it aims at mere concord among self-interested individuals and neglects "true principles of selflessness" (1988/ 1900: 83). Although he calls that outlook 'utilitarianism' (on p. 57 and elsewhere) and even mentions John Stuart Mill (p. 83), it is clear that he fails to understand the classical utilitarianism of Bentham and Mill, since for him the term 'utilitarianism' does not denote a normative ethical theory based on the principle of utility.[8] As you may recall from Chapter 5, according to that principle, roughly, an action is morally obligatory when among possible actions in the circumstances it is the one that maximizes the balance of happiness over pain for most individuals affected by it – otherwise, it is either morally neutral or forbidden. In *Ariel,* however, 'utilitarianism' and related terms are sometimes used in the vulgar sense of "acting for the sake of expedience rather than duty," and at other times refer in fact to ethical egoism, an opposing consequentialist theory that takes right action to be that which maximizes the agent's own interests. This confusion leads Rodó to level objections to "utilitarianism" that actually misfire. For example, he objects that utilitarianism "would never give rise to either sanctity or heroism" (Rodó 1988/1900: 83). Quite the opposite, as often pointed out. For, according to utilitarianism, an agent has the moral duty to always take the course of action that maximizes happiness over pain for the majority of those concerned. Sometimes that action would favor the interests of the agent, other times it would not. So, in

---

[8] See *Ariel* (Rodó 1988/1900) pages 57–59, 65–67, and 76–78 among others.

utilitarianism, neither ethical altruism nor ethical egoism is true. To illustrate, consider the common case of some agents who, after work, appear to have a choice between, say, taking it easy at home watching TV or volunteering at a homeless shelter. According to utilitarianism, they must do the latter since that would produce more overall happiness in the world. It follows that agents must always strive to act according to what is standardly considered to be beyond the call of duty. Contra Rodó, a familiar objection to utilitarianism along these lines charges that utilitarianism is too demanding since, according to this moral theory, the moral agent must be (and *can only* be) either a saint or a hero.

Finally, Rodó thinks democracy itself, in the North American model, must inevitably be corrupt, insofar as it invites a tyranny of the majority (as Tocqueville famously feared), and encourages demagoguery of the worst sort. Thus public life is coarsened as political policies are dumbed down to appeal to the semiliterate masses. In such an environment, he believes, civic valor and noble leadership are impossible. Rodó (1988/ 1900: 57) blames utilitarianism and science for the rise of democracy in the nineteenth century, and at the same time appeals to Renan's argument that democracy is bad because it has led "humankind toward a Sacred Empire of utilitarianism." So it appears that he holds a chicken-and-egg view of the relation between utilitarianism and democracy that cannot be taken seriously since, first, it rests on an exceedingly weak appeal to unqualified authority (Renan), and second, the form of polity that he thinks most conducive to "aestheticism and selflessness" is plain and simple elitism.

7.2 Vasconcelos's *Mestizofilia* Anti-Positivism

Like Rodó, Vasconcelos too was curious about the question of Latin American identity, which may be broadly construed as: 'Is there a common identity that links all Latin Americans (and perhaps the Iberians) as well as their descendants throughout the world?' And, like Rodó, he answered 'Yes' and set out to contrast that identity with the collective identity of North Americans. However, as we will see here, there are also some significant differences between these two thinkers on the question of what to make of these identities.

7.2.1 Life and Work

A key figure of the Arielist movement in Mexico City, José Vasconcelos was born in Oaxaca, central Mexico, in February 1882. For much of his life, however, he was also a part-time resident of the United States. While growing up, he crossed the border almost daily to attend school in Texas. Later in life, during periods of political turmoil in Mexico, he sought temporary exile (sometimes voluntarily, sometimes not) in various US cities – including Chicago, New York, Washington DC, and San Antonio.

In 1907 he finished law school in Mexico and soon abandoned his early positivism partly as a result of his conversion to Arielism, which took place in the Ateneo de la Juventud, a discussion group of prominent intellectuals and artists in Mexico City that was active between 1907 and 1913. During the Mexican Revolution against the dictator Porfirio Díaz, Vasconcelos gave his support to the Pancho Villa and Francisco Madero factions. Like some other leading figures of post-revolutionary Mexico, he was deeply concerned with the tasks ahead in the formation of the nation and became attracted to a strand of Latin Americanism he defended in his writings, most famously in *La raza cósmica* (*The Cosmic Race*), a 1925 monograph that will be our focus in the next section. For now, note that the relevant type of Latin Americanism here amounted to a *mestizaje* view of the collective identity of Latin America that was gaining popularity among Mexican intellectuals in the early part of the twentieth century.

Vasconcelos had a lot to do with that development. Toward that end, he was active on several fronts, becoming a prolific writer as well as an active politician and public figure. On the writing front, he produced numerous essays and books, sometimes insisting on the same theses within a year of publication (e.g., *La raza cósmica* of 1925 and *Indología* of 1926). In 1935, when he was still in his early fifties, he published the first installment of a five-volume autobiography, *Ulysses Criollo*, of which an abridged version appeared posthumously in 1962, *A Mexican Ulysses*. His philosophical books, in addition to the ones already mentioned, include *Tratado de metafísica* (*Metaphysical Treatise*) of 1929, *Ética* (*Ethics*) of 1931, and *Lógica orgánica* (*Organic Logic*) of 1945.

In his work for public service, he occupied key positions in education. He was named chancellor of Mexico's national university in 1920 (a predecessor of the Universidad Nacional Autónoma de México), secretary of education in 1921, and director of the national library in 1946. From the ministry of education, he was able to make a contribution toward education reform and the promotion of Mexican art, especially the muralists of the time. Students from Colombia, Peru, and Panama initiated the practice of honoring his contribution in this area by referring to him as 'Maestro de la Juventud' ('Teacher of the Youth').

Less successful was his career as a politician. In 1929 he was an unsuccessful candidate for president of Mexico, probably hampered by election fraud on the part of his rivals, and in 1940, during the early years of World War II, he publicly supported the Germans with his own articles in the pages of a pro-Nazi magazine, the *Revista Timón*, of which he served as editor-in-chief.[9] Once a staunch defender of the virtues of *mestizaje*, Vasconcelos had now turned to an ideology of the purity of race that he had previously tried to debunk. This dark chapter in Vasconcelos's life did not, however, preclude him from continued work on the topics of his interest, which he carried on with almost until his death in Mexico City in June 1959.

7.2.2   Vasconcelos's *Cosmic Race*

Among Vasconcelos's writings on the cultural identity of the Americas, the most widely read appeared in 1925 under the long title *La Raza Cósmica: Mission de la raza iberoamericana. Notas de viaje a la América del Sur* (The Cosmic Race: Mission of the Ibero-American Race. Notes from a Trip to South America). As its original title suggests, the book has two distinct parts, one devoted to Vasconcelos's take on the *mestizaje* model of Latin American identity, the other to his recollections of a recent diplomatic

---

[9] There is abundant evidence of the *Revista Timón*'s pro-Nazi tendencies. For instance, Paz Salinas (1997: 29) quotes a headline of May 25, 1940 that reads, "We foresee the victory of Great Germany, and we are making it known to our readers." The magazine regularly tried to get Mexico aligned with Germany, or at least to remain neutral. It also justified the Nazis' conquests, featured photos of Hitler and his high command, and criticized the United States, which it considered to be governed by "Jews and Masons."

trip to Brazil and Argentina. For us here, the first part "Mestizaje" – initially the book's preface but later included as chapter 1 – turns out to be most relevant.

Vasconcelos's view of the Americas has much in it that agrees with Rodó's – for both of them vindicate the Spanish and Christian origins of Latin America, neglect to take into account the moral wrongs committed by Iberians during the conquest, and make quite a fuss about the "perceived" evils of standard science and its positivist supporters. In particular, Vasconcelos sternly defends the civilizing role in Latin America of Christianity and the Spanish colonization, by contrast to the evolutionary theory and other positivist developments of the "Anglo-Saxons." He writes, for example,

> Christianity preached love as the basis of human relations, and we now begin to see that only love is capable of producing a superior Humanity. The policies of states and the science of the positivists, directly influenced by those policies, declared that it was not love that was the law, but antagonism, struggle, and the survival of the fittest, with no criterion for judging fitness other than the curious *petitio principii* contained in the thesis itself, since he who survives is fit, and only the fit survives.[10]

Like Rodó, Vasconcelos is confident that Latin Americans will develop a philosophy and science that is superior to positivist philosophy and Anglo-Saxon science. About the latter, he thinks that "[t]his science that came to invade us along with the products of conquering commerce can, however, be fought in the same way that every imperialism is fought, by opposing to it a superior science, a broader and more vigorous civilization" (ibid.: 81). That civilization is of course that of Latin Americans, whose superiority to the Anglo-Saxons is the point he attempts to substantiate in "Mestizaje."

Rodó would of course, so far, agree with Vasconcelos. But they part company on the issue of who in fact counts in this seemingly superior Latin American culture: where Rodó discounts the Amerindians and the

---

[10] Vasconcelos (2011/1925: 84). A few pages earlier, he laments that Latin Americans "have been educated under the humiliating influence of a philosophy devised by our enemies, sincerely perhaps, but with the aim of exalting their own purposes and crushing ours" (ibid.: 81–82).

Afro-Latin Americans completely, Vasconcelos is willing to take them into account. Somehow putting aside the contribution of many other groups of native peoples, he argues that due to the greatness of the Aztecs and Incas, and the (Catholic?) spirit of colonial Spain, all the races that met in the subcontinent began a valuable process of intermingling. Somehow also putting aside the Atlantic slave trade of colonial Spain, Vasconcelos contends that the mix of blood from peoples of African descent, Amerindians, and white Spaniards during the colonial period initiated a process of multiracialism that is of the first importance in biological terms for the future of human societies. For he sees a pattern of development through human history, with each race playing a distinctive role individually in a social evolution toward a final culmination of history in a "cosmic race" that will be a synthesis of all existing races.

In addition to this evolutionary speculation, "Mestizaje" presents a philosophy of history that is at the same time a controversial philosophy of race whose consequences continue to be at the center of debates (von Vaccano 2011, 2012; Hooker 2017a; Nuccetelli 2017). According to that philosophy, humanity is composed of four principal races, the African, the East Asian, the Amerindian, and the Indo-European (though there are of course distinctive national and ethnic subgroups within these general categories). The last of these to be dominant is the European, with the northern European group having been historically the most powerful of all. Yet this is simply the last hurrah of a decadent race doomed to fail. After all, the greatest representatives of that subgroup (the English-speaking North Americans and British, who have been so influential in the economic life of the world) are themselves, given this account, representatives of only a narrow and egoistic individualism, far inferior to the broadly cooperative and aesthetically sensitive culture that flourishes in the Spanish- and Portuguese-speaking Americas. Accordingly, Vasconcelos writes:

> We have, thus, on our continent all the elements for the new humanity,
> a law that will select the factors for the creation of the predominant types
> and that will not be guided by national criteria, as a single conquering race
> would have to be, but by criteria of universality and beauty, and we also have
> the space and the natural resources. No European people, no matter how
> well endowed, could replace the people of Ibero-America in this mission, for

each of those peoples has an already constituted culture and a tradition that is a hindrance in tasks of this kind. No conquering race could replace us, because it would necessarily impose its own characteristics, even if only out of the need to exercise violence to maintain its conquest.[11]

On this theory, Latin Americans cannot be replaced, simply because most of them are *mestizos* and more *mestizaje* is underway. As a result, they have the singular advantage of mixed blood: they are typically not of a single race but of two or more. And this cannot fail to animate and strengthen their bloodlines in a way that will in the end lead to the most significant turn in history: the final synthesis of all races in a genetically superior form of human being. This "cosmic race" will arise in a "Promised Land" comprising "Brazil, Colombia, Venezuela, Ecuador, part of Peru, part of Bolivia and the northern part of Argentina" (Vasconcelos 2011/1925: 69). In that region people of all ethnic groups, attracted by the tolerant, racial pluralism of Latin America, as well as the warm climate and abundant natural resources that give the region its boundless potential, will come together to make a new race.[12] This fusion of all the different races of the world, Vasconcelos insists, will incorporate the distinctive strengths that are characteristic of each race, thus overcoming the limitations of mono-racial identity that are the Achilles heel of even the currently triumphant Anglo-Saxons. He particularly argues against segregation of blacks in the United States (Vasconcelos 2011/1926: 100 and ff.).

Supplementing this philosophy of race is a conception of three periods in the historical development of human culture, in which different principles regulate the associations among people: the "material or military, the intellectual or political, and the spiritual or aesthetic" periods (Vasconcelos

---

[11] Vasconcelos (2011/1925: 87–88). The above-quoted paragraph ends on page 88 with the racist remark that "Neither can the peoples of Asia fulfill this universal mission; they are worn out, or at least lack the boldness for new undertakings."

[12] Vasconcelos believed the process of mixing necessary for the constitution of the cosmic race had already begun during the colonial period. He gives as examples the controversial "wedding" of Hernán Cortès and Malinche – a native woman of Mexico given as a present to Cortès – as well as Inca Garcilaso de la Vega of Peru, who had a Spanish father and an Inca mother (Vasconcelos 2011/1926: 96–97). But in his attempt to vindicate the Spanish Crown's open-mindedness about interracial marriages, he omits to mention that by the time of Inca Garcilaso, there were already laws against such marriages and his parents were forced to separate.

2011/1925: 73). In the first period, the principle is simple survival in response to power; in the second, it is reason; and in the third, free choice based on taste. Only when human associations transcend the second period (our present condition according to Vasconcelos) and move to the third can the final synthesis of races be accomplished.

7.3   The Upshot

As we have seen, Rodó's thought should be assessed in the context of the intellectual frame of mind of Latin America at the turn of the century, a point in time when the cultural and economic expansionism of the United States in the region denounced by Martí and other modernists was evident. Rodó reacted against a set of values he ascribed to this nation, including its standards in science and utilitarianism (the theory he wrongly identified as its prevailing moral theory). Yet, as often pointed out by anthropologists, judgments about a culture other than one's own may sometimes be distorted by ethnocentric bias. To meet this inevitable objection, Rodó should have brought to light more compelling grounds for his critique of US values. His chief argument for rejecting North American culture in *Ariel* founders on misinformation and a strawman fallacy. The latter fallacy arises because, first, it is doubtful that utilitarianism was at the time (or is now) the prevalent moral theory in North America. But, most important, utilitarianism simply is not committed to the principle of ethical egoism that Rodó ascribes to it. In fact, utilitarianism and ethical egoism stand in the relationship of contrariety: they could both be false, but if one is true, the other must be false.

Another central claim in *Ariel* that lacks support concerns the identification of Latin America with a nobler continental ideal whose roots are in Christianity and the great ancient civilizations of the Mediterranean. Rodó takes this for granted and repeatedly urges Latin Americans to retain their Mediterranean heritage and avoid wasting their lives in the ignoble pursuit of material well-being. Of course, in Rodó's time many in the United States might have considered the unflagging pursuit of material wealth praiseworthy, while many Latin Americans might have been more interested in religiosity, artistic enjoyment, erudition, or any other goal that Rodó regarded as more valuable. However, there is something dogmatic in vindicating certain goals for Latin Americans without offering good reasons for pursuing them. Contra Rodó, we should reply emphatically, first, that Latin Americans should not pursue certain cultural forms simply because they were the values of Christianity or colonial Spain, or ancient Greece and Rome. Second, by omission, Rodó's prescription for Latin American youth disvalues the culture of vast numbers of Amerindians and people of African descent. These peoples in some countries of the region made up the majority of the population. But in light of his pervasive social, political, and cultural elitism in *Ariel*, it is not surprising that he discounted their contributions.

However, on the issue of the tasks facing Latin American intellectuals, Rodó's claims might have some support when charitably construed. For who might object to the position that intellectuals should set a good example, both in the moral and the cultural sphere? Or produce guiding ideas that can help shape a better society? Or promote education? Yet, for the reasons just outlined, it would be wrong to think, as suggested in *Ariel*, that intellectuals have the duty to help preserve every element of the region's cultural past. After all, some elements of that cultural past are definitely not worth preserving: for example, dogmatic scholasticism in science and philosophy, racism, sexism, and religious and moral ultramontanism. In attempting to rid the region of some of these, there is no doubt that the positivists scored better than Rodó.

Let us now turn to Vasconcelos's celebration of the mixed racial and cultural identity of Latin Americans. On my view, it is a more progressive model not only compared with the Anglo/Eurocentric model of the positivists and Rodó, but also with the segregationist model prevalent in North America in the 1920s. Vasconcelos took issue with US segregationists in "The Race Problem in Latin America," a speech delivered at the University of Chicago in 1926. Surely, the objections facing his vision of a cosmic, Latin American race are many, ranging from its being grounded on pseudo-biology, armchair sociology, and distorted history (especially of the Spanish conquest and colonial rule) to its exhibiting a number of biases against ethnic groups that can be construed as nothing other than racism.[13]

---

[13] Following Peter Singer's definition of speciesism as the bias of thinking that species boundaries determine moral worth, I define racism as the bias of thinking that race determines moral worth. For evidence of racism in Vasconcelos's work – especially but

Yet, more recently some scholars have charged that any *mestizaje* model, Vasconcelos's included, faces a 'racial democracy' objection that runs this way:

1. According to the *mestizaje* model, there is racial democracy in Latin America.
2. Racial democracy is incompatible with racial discrimination.
3. There is racial discrimination in Latin America.
4. *Therefore,* the *mestizaje* view of Latin American identity is false.[14]

By 'racial democracy' proponents of this argument mean racial equality or justice. Although they are right that racial justice is incompatible with racial discrimination, of which there is much in Latin America, their argument rests on the weak premise 1. For the *mestizaje* view is compatible with there being racism in Latin America when understood as making a normative claim: the model does not merely describe what Latin American identity is, but prescribes what it should be. Once this is noticed, it becomes clear that it is preferable to its competitors of the time – such as the Alberdian transplantation model or the US segregationist model.[15]

Putting aside Vasconcelos's pseudoscientific racial commentaries – together with the exegetical issue of whether he in fact intended to provide a utopian vision of the future of Latin America (Zea 1993) or a biological theory – it seems that some version of his *mestizaje* model made a contribution to Latin American thought. At the very least, it provided a theoretical framework for raising the cultural and racial self-image of the region. I know of no such celebrations of mixed races and ethnicities coming from high-ranking public figures in the United States at the time of Vasconcelos or the predecessors of his model – among whom I place Las Casas, Bolívar, and Martí. In North

not limited to antisemitism and anti-Americanism – see his "Mestizaje," and also the data from the *Revista Timón* provided in Dana (2015).

[14] The 'racial democracy' objection to the *mestizaje* model might even claim that this model has been a tool for hiding the racist nature of Latin American society. Both versions have been advanced by scholars from Latin American studies (De la Fuente and Andrews 2018; Mitchell-Walthour 2018). For a different take on the *mestizaje* model, see Hooker (2017) and Nuccetelli (2017).

[15] See, for instance, Andrews (2004) and Vinson (2018).

America, there are no parallel figures in positions of power like these, who celebrated the cultural and racial contribution of Native Americans and blacks to the region's identity. Of course, I am aware that this very tentative hypothesis is in need of support by hard data from history and the social sciences.[16]

7.4 Suggested Readings

Bar-Lewaw, M. Itzhak, ed. 1971. *La revista "Timón" y José Vasconcelos*. Mexico: Casa Edimex.

Classic source providing textual evidence of Vasconcelos's support of National Socialism in the 1940s.

De Beer, Gabriella. 1966. *José Vasconcelos and His World*. New York: Las Americas.

One of the most comprehensive biographies of Vasconcelos. Good account of his growing up near the United States–Mexico border, his commute to Texas for schooling during this period, and the intermittent periods of residence in various parts of the world, including New York, Washington DC, Chicago, San Antonio, Texas, and California in the United States.

Devés Valdés, Eduardo. 2000. *Del Ariel de Rodó a la CEPAL (1900–1950)*. Buenos Aires: Editorial Biblos.

Chapter 1 offers the standard interpretation of Rodó's *Ariel* as an anti-imperialist manifesto. With no critical analysis of the limitations of this manifesto (e.g., its elitist and racist implications), the chapter focuses on drawing connections with predecessors and successors of Rodó in the task of warning Latin Americans against US cultural imperialism and praising the virtues of their culture. It also contains a chapter mostly devoted to historical analysis of the work of Vasconcelos.

Fuentes, Carlos. 1988. "Prologue" pp. 13–28 in Rodó (1988/1900).

Very charitable, though not always faithful, reading of *Ariel* by a prominent Mexican novelist and thinker. Argues that Rodó's idealization of Europe

---

[16] Elsewhere I have argued that the *mestizaje* model best accounts, at least in part, for African Americans' and Afro-Hispanics' contrasting attitudes in the face of controversies such as the one surrounding the film *Nina* in 2012. For more on this, see Nuccetelli (2017).

amounts to a utopia. Like Rodó, Fuentes conflates utilitarianism as a philosophical doctrine with the pursuit of one's "immediate self-interest."

Hooker, Juliet. 2017. *Theorizing Race in the Americas: Douglass, Sarmiento, Du Bois, and Vasconcelos*. New York: Oxford University Press.

A chapter on Vasconcelos takes issue with the claim that there is or has been racial democracy in the region. For Hooker, Vasconcelos – together with Brazilian Gilberto Freyre – championed that claim without providing sufficient evidence for it. He also assumed without hard evidence that the process of racial mixing had begun with the conquest. In spite of her criticism, she ultimately vindicates the role of Vasconcelos's model on the grounds of its departing from the model of white identity prevalent in Latin America at his time.

Jaksić, Iván. 1996. "The Machine and the Spirit: Anti-Technological Humanism in Twentieth-Century Latin America," *Revista de Estudios Hispánicos* 30: 179–201.

Historical analysis of the notion of progress in Rodó, which he understood in a generally non-positivist way as a tendency toward embracing high aesthetics and moral values. Looks into the humanism behind his critique of mainstream science (see *Ariel*, pp. 37 and ff.).

Mariátegui, José Carlos. 1922. "'Indología' por José Vasconcelos," *Variedades*, Lima, October 22.

Review of Vasconcelos's sequel to the *Cosmic Race*, *Indología (Indology)*, a 1926 monograph. Mariátegui has much praise for Vasconcelos's utopian idea of a cosmic race. In particular, he ascribes to Vasconcelos the claim that white racism is a product of "Anglo-Saxon" culture – or in his words, "an imperialistic prejudice of the Anglo-Saxons" (my translation). Neither Vasconcelos nor Mariátegui provide any evidence for this dubious claim.

Miller, Nicola. 1999. *In the Shadow of the State: Intellectuals and the Quest for National Identity in Twentieth-Century Spanish America*. London: Verso.

Chapter 5 of this well-informed book devotes considerable attention to different strands of anti-imperialism in Latin American political thinkers. It includes a section on "The *Arielist* Response to Imperialism" in which Rodó's Latin Americanism is contrasted with Martí's. Since Martí had rejected US cultural and economic expansionism, he could defend both Latin Americanism and nationalism. But since Rodó had only rejected US cultural expansionism, he could not consistently reject US economic interference in his country.

Paz Salinas, Maria Emilia. 1997. *Strategy, Security, and Spies: Mexico and the US as Allies in World War II*. University Park, PA: Penn State Press.

Historical study of Mexico–United States relations during World War II. Its chapter 2, "Mexico and the Axis Threat," describes the creation of the *Revista Timón* with Vasconcelos as its editor. Provides textual evidence that this magazine was an instrument of Nazi propaganda masquerading as a voice calling for "freedom of the press."

Rodó, José Enrique, *Ariel*. 1988/1900. Austin, TX: University of Texas Press.

Classic source for Rodó's conception of Latin American identity and his reaction against positivism.
Salles, Arleen. 2011. "Rodó, Race, and Morality," pp. 181–202 in Gracia (2011).

A comprehensive discussion of Rodó's views on Latin American identity throughout his works. Although Salles notes his racism by omission (p. 196), she seems to explain it away as part of an attempt to "elevate a region that had been historically relegated." As a result, she merely laments that Rodó "promoted a distorted view" of Latin American identity (p. 197).

Vasconcelos, José. 1997/1925. *The Cosmic Race: A Bilingual Edition*. Baltimore, MD: The Johns Hopkins University Press.
    2011/1925. "Mestizaje," pp. 45–90 in Stavans (2011) (references to reprint pp. 7–40 in Vasconcelos (1997/1925)).

Classic sources for Vasconcelos's anti-positivist, *mestizaje* model of Latin American identity as discussed in this chapter.

von Vacano, Diego A. 2011. "Zarathustra Criollo: Vasconcelos on Race," pp. 203–226 in Gracia (2011).

Account of Vasconcelos's political philosophy that is quite sympathetic to his *mestizaje* model of Latin American identity. But it claims without support that Vasconcelos placed equality as the central concept in his political philosophy (p. 225). In light of my discussion above, this seems highly unlikely, owing to his antisemitism and anti-Americanism.

    2012. *The Color of Citizenship: Race, Modernity and Latin American/Hispanic Political Thought*. Oxford: Oxford University Press.

Argues that Vasconcelos's "synthetic" paradigm of race, the most prominent among the *mestizaje* models in Latin America, competed with a "domination" and a "dualistic" paradigm of race in Europe and the United States, respectively. Attempts to trace the influence on Vasconcelos of the Nietzschean concepts of 'aesthetic' and 'synthesis.'

8   Soft and Hard Socialism

The waning of positivism in Latin America during the early twentieth century revived the debate about the racial and ethnic identity of the region. José Enrique Rodó and José Martí illustrate two different traditions within which those questions took on a new urgency, and they both developed their answers in part by contrasting the values predominant in Latin America with those of the United States. Yet of these two, only Martí clearly saw the problems facing the region: lack of social justice, economic underdevelopment, and the imperialist threat from industrial powers – above all, the United States. For this reason, the socialist political thinkers whose theories about how to solve these problems are the topic of this chapter often vindicate Martí, even when he embraced Krausism, a philosophical doctrine incompatible with the theoretical framework of these thinkers, Marxism.

I outline that framework in Section 8.1 below, which readers familiar with Marxism may skip to go directly to the sections on the hard socialism of José Carlos Mariátegui and Ernesto "Che" Guevara, and the soft socialism of Salvador Allende and Víctor Raúl Haya de la Torre. Mariátegui put that framework to work in accounting for the urgent problems of his native Peru, among which he singled out "the problem of the Indian" and "the problem of the land," both considered in Section 8.2. In the sections that follow I turn to views of another hard socialist, Guevara, and then two soft socialists, Allende and Haya de la Torre.

8.1 Marxism

Marxism is in fact a set of economic, social, and political doctrines related through family resemblances.[1] Although they share only a few features,

---

[1] Many contemporary political philosophers who have reflected on Marxism would agree with this point. See for example, Hindess (1995), Kymlicka (2002), and Stephen Lukes (1987).

they belong to the family because their central doctrines are relevantly related to the various doctrines offered by the nineteenth-century German philosophers Karl Marx (1818–1883) and Friedrich Engels (1820–1895). These doctrines appear in a number of works, of which the most notable include *The Communist Manifesto* (coauthored by Marx and Engels, 1968/ 1848), *Das Kapital* (Marx 1967/1867) and the "Theses on Feuerbach" (Marx 1968/1845). Here I will not attempt to summarize Marxism but rather paint with a broad brush the Marxist doctrines that might have fueled Mariátegui and Guevara's proposals.

In Chapter 5, I have listed Marxism as a kind of positivism, owing to the fact that it vindicates the characteristic theses of positivism, broadly construed: namely, naturalism, secularism, and empiricism. In addition, it also amounts to a physicalist or materialist type of naturalism, a scientist type of empiricism, and a revolutionary type of determinism. These connections with nineteenth-century positivism will become evident upon reflection on the Marxist doctrines outlined next.

8.1.1   Marxism and Positivism

Marxism radically rejects the social and political ideals of the Enlightenment, especially the theories of John Locke (British, 1632–1704) about the natural rights of individuals and the legitimacy of the state, as offered in his *Second Treatise of Civil Government* (1690). For example, Locke considered life, liberty, and property to be basic natural rights, to which all humans have an equal claim. Many other revolutionary thinkers from Britain, France, and America agreed without questioning the compatibility of those rights. But Marxists question their compatibility: on their view, the principles of individual liberty and private property of capitalist societies interfere with economic equality. In addition, they question the universal legitimacy of the capitalist state. Although Locke and Thomas Hobbes (British, 1588–1679) attempted to ground its legitimacy in a social contract, Marxists would reject such accounts as mere speculation with no basis in facts.

By challenging the liberal and libertarian Western traditions on the rights of individuals, Marx and Engels made a U-turn in political philosophy. They rejected the standard arguments European and American political thinkers had given for liberal democracy and capitalism after the three principal political revolutions in modern history. Consistent with their skepticism about the existence of human rights such as the Lockean natural right to property and liberty was Marx and Engels's critique of most doctrines that make up the political philosophy of the Enlightenment.

The Marxists' views on property and liberty rights may be either relativist or nihilist, depending on whether they are interpreted as holding that the justification of those rights may vary at different stages of a society (so that they can be justified in a capitalist society but not in a socialist one) or as holding that they are never justified. As for equality, Marxism is committed to saying that exploitation precludes the capitalist system from delivering *true* equality. Only communism, the stage that follows socialism, can do that. After all, there is no equality when the means of production are in the hands of a few and others need to sell their labor to survive. Marxism in fact predicts that when a society reaches its mature state, namely, communism, inequities will disappear. Any communist society will function without private property and thus, without economic classes, because the means of production will be owned by the society as a whole. Marx himself describes the nature of communism in *Critique of the Gotha Program*, where he contends that, owing to a communist society's elimination of class struggle and its abundant economic wealth, each person would contribute according to their ability and be compensated according to their needs.

With regard to how a society moves from capitalism to socialism, and after that to the final stage of communism, Marx predicted that a society would reach socialism by revolution and communism by peaceful transition. His account of these transformations is reminiscent of August Comte's law of three stages, which we discussed in Chapter 5, and has some elements of the philosophy of history of G. W. F. Hegel (German, 1770–1831). The positivist strand of Marxism is evident in its determinism about social change; while in Comte such determinism concerned the development of thought, in Marx it concerned the ownership of the means of production. For either of them, though, a society's transformation unfolds according to scientific laws and only in one direction, except for temporary setbacks.

The Hegelian element of Marx's progressivism resides in his thesis that, before reaching the communist stage of development, socioeconomic and political transformations occur invariably because of the contradictions inherent to each stage of a society – except for the last stage of communism, in which there are no such contradictions. The difference rests on the belief that prior to communism, there is class struggle between a certain dominant economic class and those in its grip. At some point the oppressed classes will stage a revolution and throw off their oppressors, thereby becoming the next dominant class, and so on. Thus each society in the stage prior to communism contains within itself the elements that will destroy it and thus move "the wheel of history" forward. During the era of medieval feudalism in Europe, for example, nobles and hereditary monarchs were the dominant class, and were later overthrown by the bourgeois class (the middle class) that had been growing in the cities. These were the capitalists, the investor class of entrepreneurs, who later made up the dominant class of Western democracies. In explaining why social progress should occur in this way, Marx adapted Hegel's philosophy of history, especially his doctrine that history unfolds in a thesis/antithesis/synthesis cycle. According to this adaptation, roughly, except for socialism and communism, any previous historical period (i.e., the thesis) contains the seeds of the next period (the antithesis), which will in turn produce a new society (the synthesis). The socialist revolution, the one that will inevitably occur in capitalist countries, Marx thought, will arise out of the internal contradictions of capitalism. For in it, the *proletariat* (i.e., all industrial workers and farm laborers who do not own the means of production) are engaged in a class struggle against the dominant economic powers (i.e., those who own the means of production).

Furthermore, although initially more productive than feudalism, capitalism is ultimately doomed. At some point it will become less productive than its socialist alternative.[2] But the change from one stage to another

---

[2] The problem for capitalism, as described by Marxists, is economic at its root: briefly, because gains and losses are cumulative in capitalism, the wealthy are in a better position to compete in the market. It also favors them in the surplus offered in the labor market, which causes low wages. In addition, the Industrial Revolution produced a considerably larger labor force than was needed. For an analysis of the Marxist critique

cannot be achieved through peaceful means: like other radical social changes of the past, it will involve violence because of the class struggle inherent in every capitalist society.

8.1.2   Marx on Philosophy, Morality, and Religion

Marx considered philosophy an applied activity aimed at promoting social change. In "Theses on Feuerbach" he famously wrote, "[t]he philosophers have only *interpreted* the world, in various ways; the point, however, is to change it" (1968/1845). Depending on what exactly Marx meant by "change" here, the quote appears an overstatement. After all, if not his predecessors, certainly quite a few of his contemporaries actively pursued social change in various ways. Among them, the utopian socialists, the classical utilitarians, and the Comtean positivists would agree with Marx's skepticism about morality and religion, even if they would not invoke Marx's further view that morality and religion belong to the ideological "superstructure" of any society that is characterized by class struggle. Since, Marx predicted, in communism socioeconomic classes will disappear, morality and religion will then be transcended. There will be no need for it since people will have no vices but only social virtues such as solidarity. The moral traits held as preeminent in capitalist societies such as liberty or justice will become obsolete, since, for example, in a communist society no problem of distributive justice could arise. Given this account, it is very puzzling that Marx himself refrained from explicitly referring to a communist society as one in which social injustices do not occur. In fact, in his writings he never associated communism with a just system or capitalism with an unjust system. This omission has puzzled some critics such as Stephen Lukes (1987), who accounts for it by claiming that, according to Marx, communism transcends justice.[3]

On religion, Marx offered a secularist account that places it in the ideological superstructure of any society still waiting for the socialist

---

of capitalism, see Nathanson (1998), especially Chapter 4, "Socialism and the Critique of Capitalism."

[3] Other hypotheses about the absence of justice talk in Marx can be found in Kymlicka (1990), Wolff (2017), and Wood (1981). For a detailed coverage of the evolution of Marx's moral theory, see Kain (2011).

revolution. Its role to play in any such society, as he metaphorically put it, was to be "the opiate of the people." That is, religion is a useful story to protect the status quo by lulling the oppressed into a kind of sedation that helps them cope with the two social ills he associated with class struggle, exploitation and alienation.

In a capitalist society, exploitation occurs when people are compensated less than the whole value of what they produce, and alienation is a kind of estrangement that workers suffer because they are separated from what they produce, have no ownership of the means of production, and accordingly become commodities whose labor is traded at the market value. Although Marx emphasized the evils of alienation only in his early works, the concept quickly caught on among Marxist thinkers. Both Mariátegui and Guevara, each in his own way, added the notion of *solitude* to explain the roots of alienation. For Mariátegui, it is the solitude of the Amerindians who have been estranged from their lands, states, cultures, and religions by the Spanish Conqueror; for Guevara, it is the solitude of the North American workers who are pitted against each other in a brutal competition for work and are left with no other reason for their labor than a material incentive. As we will see next, these paradigm Latin American Marxists also took to heart Marx's emphasis' on philosophy's power to transform the world.

8.2   José Carlos Mariátegui

8.2.1   Life and Work

José Carlos Mariátegui (Peruvian, 1895–1930), though not a philosopher by training, stands out as one of the most creative philosophical thinkers within the Marxist tradition of Latin America. Mostly self-educated, early in life Mariátegui engaged in political activism and demonstrated great talent in a number of the humanities, from literary criticism and poetry to sociology and political thought. In 1926 he founded *Amauta,* an art and culture journal that played a central role in spreading early twentieth-century avant-garde literature in Latin America. While editing this journal and taking an active role in the politics of Peru, Mariátegui wrote many speeches and articles devoted to the analysis of the major political issues of his day, including the plight of Amerindians and women, the struggle for socialism in Latin America, and even the existence of a characteristically Latin American school of thought. He died at the age of thirty-five, after years of ill health, disability, and political persecution. Early in life his work as a progressive journalist and support for a general strike by textile workers put him at odds with the Peruvian government, and he was sent into exile in Europe. From 1919 to 1923 he lived in Italy, France, and Germany, where he deepened his acquaintance with the ideas of Marxist and socialist theorists and literary figures. Crucial influences at this time came from Henri Barbusse, Antonio Gramsci, and Maxim Gorky among others. Upon his return to Peru, his radical convictions were firmer than ever: "I share the opinion of those who believe that humanity is living through a revolutionary period. And I am convinced of the imminent collapse of all social-democratic, reformist, evolutionist theses" (1996/1923: 7). To ignite such a revolution, he first joined a popular revolutionary front, the Alianza Popular Revolucionaria Americana (APRA), but in 1928 he went on to organize the more radical Communist Party, whose agenda was more in line with Mariátegui's own view that socialist revolution was the only option that could solve the central problems of Peru.

These, as we will soon see, he located in the oppression of the indigenous peoples and ultimately, in the *latifundio*, a semifeudal distribution of the land rooted in the Spanish colonial period. In many of his writings Mariátegui presents this conception of Peru's two central problems. But he was also an outspoken critic of the imperialist menace to Latin America coming from the United States, and of the capitalist, totalitarian doctrines advanced by Italian Fascists and German National Socialists, then increasingly popular in Europe. In 1925 we find him urging Latin American intellectuals to rally together against these forms of totalitarianism in his pioneering essay "La escena contemporánea" ("The Contemporary Scene").

8.2.2 An Eclectic, Humanist Marxism

Latin American theorists of Marxism and socialism during the early twentieth century are criticized often for their tendency to focus on general questions of theory while neglecting to analyze the socioeconomic problems at home. Mariátegui, however, would in no way be vulnerable to this charge, since although he did have an internationalist agenda and an interest in theory, he carefully adapted his theoretical framework to account for issues of social and economic justice in Peru.[4] But not only was Mariátegui closer to the utopian socialists than to Marx in this respect. On his view, considerations of justice have a significant role to play in the fight for a change from a capitalist and neocolonial society to a socialist society in which human values can flourish.[5] For this reason, Augusto Salazar Bondy, a sympathetic critic, argues that Mariátegui advocated a "moral" or "humanist" kind of socialism (1967: 320–322).

In addition to its humanism, his socialism was eclectic. It found inspiration not only in Marx's writings but also in other sources, both Peruvian and European which included the utopian socialists, novelist Henri Barbusse, and Georges Sorel, a theorist of syndicalism influenced by Bergson. Its Peruvian influences reduce to two radical thinkers: Manuel González Prada y Ulloa and Víctor Raúl Haya de la Torre. González Prada (Peruvian, 1848–1918) had an extreme Catholic education against which he reacted, first by endorsing British liberalism, and later, in writings such as *Páginas libres*, transitioning to an extreme secularist form of anarchism (Cappelletti 2017: 179–191). About Haya de la Torre, I will have more to say shortly. But for now, note that he was a social reformist who became leader of the Peruvian Student Federation at a time when university students throughout Latin America were staging protests in pursuit of educational reform.[6] He later founded the political party, APRA). After his return to Peru from a forced exile in Europe, Mariátegui began a collaboration with Haya de la Torre, mostly at a distance because Haya himself took exile

---

[4] The practical aspect of Mariátegui's political thought is evident in the essays edited in *Siete ensayos de interpretación de la realidad peruana* (Seven Essays Interpreting Peru's Reality) of 1928 (Mariátegui (1971/1928). See also the essays in Pearlman's *Meaning of Socialism* (Mariátegui 1996; ed. by Michael Pearlman).

[5] Recall that, motivated perhaps by the need to distinguish "scientific" from "utopian" socialism, Marx himself never actually invoked considerations of justice in his writings – not even to contrast capitalism and communism.

[6] In the late 1910s, university students staged numerous protests throughout Latin America with the goal of democratizing the still-authoritarian structure of universities. In Argentina, those strong protests brought about the Reforma Universitaria (University Reform), a law sanctioned in 1918 that gave students representation in the government of public universities, thereby democratizing them.

in Mexico in 1923, and stayed there until 1931. But finding the APRA insufficiently radical, in 1927 Mariátegui created Peru's Communist Party.

Mariátegui's writings comprise papers speeches, articles, and edited volumes. They mostly offer studies of the history and culture of Peru, and aim at producing what has been termed "a national regeneration through socialism" (Hale 1996). He thought that Latin America, especially the Andean region, had never undergone a full-fledged capitalist national process. In the early twentieth century, an incipient capitalism coexisted there with two kinds of colonialism: the remnants of old Spanish colonialism, which had crippled the development of full-fledged capitalism, and the neocolonialism that resulted from foreign interference, especially from the United States, a country that benefited from the prevalence of semi-feudal economic relations in the region. Thus, for him, the socialist struggle against capitalism in Peru was intertwined with a struggle against old and new colonialism.

Among the peculiar features of Mariátegui's recommendations for the success of a socialist program in Peru was that it should include an almost religious element in its practices. He thought that to rally the masses for the revolution, not only were arguments needed but also myths. Such useful fictions could carry a persuasive advantage because of their epistemological directness, which they shared with images and intuitions.[7]

The main protagonists of Peru's national regeneration through socialism, the masses that need to be persuaded to carry it out, were the Andean Indians. But of course their success would depend on the ability of leaders like Mariátegui to provide an adequate diagnosis of the problems to be resolved – which, one way or another, for Mariátegui were always related to what he interchangeably referred to as "the problem of the Indian" and "the indigenous question."

8.2.3   Andean Indians, Land, and Religion

Mariátegui also differed from other Marxists and socialists of his time in his diagnosis of the problems facing Peru and other Andean nations such as

---

[7] For a sympathetic analysis of Mariátegui's theory of myths, see Salazar Bondy (1967: 317–320).

Bolivia and Ecuador. When he set out to analyze the central problems of Peru, rather than invoking the general flaws of capitalism, he actually looked at the reality at home. And what he saw was the extreme destitution of the most neglected people, the Andean Indians. So he determined that this problem was the central one, and needed to be solved by the Andean Indians themselves. But a durable solution could come only through an understanding of the socioeconomic reality that had caused the problem in the first place. On Mariátegui's diagnosis, the Indian problem is the direct effect of "the problem of the land," though it relates derivatively to racism and religion, which are factors Marxists locate in the ideological "super-structure" of a society. The problem of the land has its roots in the Spanish colonial system and its feudal distribution of the land stolen from the Amerindians. The *latifundio*, the economic system of land distribution insti-tuted in Peru during Spain's colonial administration, carried deep disadvan-tages for the native peoples. In Mariátegui's time, he contended, a remnant of colonialism still trapped those peoples: *gamonalism,* an arrangement whereby the local landowners or chieftains took economic advantage of, and made political decisions for, the Andean Indians working for them.

According to Mariátegui's analysis, then, (i) the Indian problem, the most urgent for Peru, was the causal effect of the land problem; and (ii) a socialist revolution was the only possible solution to both problems. In one of his articles devoted to defending thesis (i), "The Problem of the Indian," Mariátegui, after offering a sympathetic analysis of the extreme poverty and unjust treatment of the indigenous peoples, argued by induc-tive elimination for thesis (ii). The factors he ruled out as possible causes of the Indian problem included morality, religion, legislation, education, and race. He wrote:

> Any treatment of the problem of the Indian – written or verbal – that fails or
> refuses to recognize it as a socioeconomic problem is but a sterile,
> theoretical exercise destined to be completely discredited. Good faith is no
> justification. Almost all such treatments have served merely to mask or
> distort the reality of the problem. The socialist critic exposes and defines the
> problem because he looks for its causes in the country's economy and not in
> its administrative, legal, or ecclesiastic machinery, its racial dualism or
> pluralism, or its cultural or moral conditions. The problem of the Indian is
> rooted in the land tenure system of our economy. Any attempt to solve it

with administrative or police measures, through education or by a road building program, is superficial and secondary as long as the feudalism of the *gamonales* continues to exist. (Mariátegui 1971/1928: 239)

Let us consider in turn several of the factors that Mariátegui rules out as solutions to the Indian problem in this passage, beginning with morality. Just as Marx rejected "human rights" talk, Mariátegui finds the conventional liberal arguments on behalf of the Andean Indians' rights equally specious because of their uselessness in achieving socioeconomic change. As for religion, he thinks it is more part of the problem than of its solution: religion is as futile as morality, for even when in the hands of someone well intended such as Bartolomé de las Casas, religious intervention in Peru had resulted in nothing more than a few benevolent laws that were never enforced. On education and culture, the means for social reform preferred by positivists, Mariátegui thought that they would not solve the Indian problem so long as the society that did the educating and enculturating remained fundamentally unchanged. Mariátegui argued that the content of public education offered in Peru in his time was contaminated with the same bourgeois values that had kept the Andean Indians in thrall. Note that this argument rests on the Marxist assumption that the prevailing values of a society are always those of its dominant economic class, and that it is these values that will inevitably be inculcated by the school system.

8.2.4   Racism

Mariátegui added to the standard Marxist account of racism a link between this social evil and the Indian problem. He believed racism in Peru began in colonial times, introduced by the Spaniards to serve the purpose of igniting competition among various groups of marginalized peoples (especially, the Amerindians, blacks, *cholos*, mulattos, and *zambos* of the region) in order to keep them under conditions of extreme exploitation. After all, he reasons, tensions among the workers could only benefit the ruling classes. Thus Mariátegui's account of racism in Peru is consistent with the Marxist account that explains racism in terms of its function within societies characterized by class struggle. Accordingly, for Mariátegui the racism of twentieth-century Peru was a specific form of discrimination rooted in a class struggle traceable to the Spanish Conquest. It was causally related to the colonial socioeconomic system, and thus, to the problems of the Indian and the land. He believed that the racism instituted in colonial times, rather than disappearing with the defeat of the Spaniards in the early nineteenth century, shifted and came to favor the *criollos*, who did nothing to eliminate it. On his view, the Peruvian *criollos* and even the so-called *cholos* (mestizo people of Indian and Spanish ancestry) were in the end no less to blame than the Spaniards for having inflicted on the indigenous peoples a "debasing oppression" grounded partly in racial prejudice.

Of course, racism can be construed in various ways. Mariátegui takes it to be the belief that certain races have some inferior physical or psychological traits – a belief that he finds easily refutable by counterexample since, contrary to what some social Darwinists of his time were claiming, no such trait can be proved essential or inherent to a race. "If such were the case," he argues, "[then the allegedly inferior trait] would have expressed itself in the same way in all the periods of history." But it did not, therefore "[t]he obvious inference is that the 'nature' of races is constantly changing with the conditions of their existence. But these conditions are determined by nothing more nor less than the relation between society and nature, i.e., the condition of the productive forces" (1996/1929: 98–99).

We may illustrate this antiracist argument by selecting at random a trait of character a racist might adduce as indicative of the racial inferiority of the Andean Indians – say, that they cannot govern themselves, as supporters of the Spanish Conquest often alleged. Any such claim would stand refuted by the evidence, for example, from the great Inca Empire. And since other refutations along similar lines could be run any time the racist ascribes an inferior trait of character to a group of people, Mariátegui is entitled to conclude that racism stands refuted by comparative analyses of historical data. Let us also note that Mariátegui also rejected primitivism, a sentimental attempt to romanticize the indigenous peoples by considering them racially or culturally superior. The right attitude toward these people, he thought, was instead that of assisting their economic progress by overturning the feudal Peruvian system of land distribution. For "whether the Indians will raise themselves materially and intellectually depends on a change in their socioeconomic conditions" (1996/1929: 99)

At the same time, on Mariátegui's view there is historical data suggesting not only that the Andean Indians are in no way inferior to *criollos* and *cholos*: they are also prime candidates for a socialist uprising that will lead to the national regeneration of Peru. He holds this view based on evidence about their communal ownership of the land in pre-Columbian times and their unified conception of state and religion.[8] That pre-Conquest religious conception, Mariátegui believes, predisposes them to arise in a socialist revolution once they understand what is at stake in it. Although that conception has by now been either transformed or rejected in the minds of the Andean Indians to fit Catholicism, Mariátegui hopes it can be recovered. He claims that Inca religion was both temporal and materialist rather than atemporal and spiritual like Catholicism. For the Inca people, religion and state were in fact one. Their ceremonies and symbols, the priests and officials, were tangible tokens of a divinity that was not transcendent but immanent in them. From these premises, Mariátegui concludes that the Andean Indians would likely accept "historical materialism" (i.e., Marxism) once it was explained to them. At that point, they would support a political revolution to overthrow the country's political system and its semifeudal economic order.

The argument appears to be that the Inca people were traditionally accustomed to live in a society in which religious and political leaders were the same. From this empirical premise he concludes these people would be on board for a socialist system featuring no religious authorities external to the political authorities. But this argument does nothing to support its conclusion. After all, socialism comes with enforced secularism and the Incas were no secularists. Unsurprisingly, other Marxists omitted reference to this argument of Mariátegui's in a prediction to the effect that socialism would be rapidly endorsed by Andean Indians.

---

[8] In his essay, "The Religious Factor" (2004b/1928), Mariátegui also engages in some reflection about Christian religions since their introduction to the Americas. He speculates that, in North America, Protestants were more interested in their own personal salvation than in converting the natives, so the native peoples were simply driven off the land by force – and, where needed, massacred – rather than converted. But in Spanish and Portuguese America the Conquest was in part also a mission of converting the native peoples to Catholicism.

But they repeated Mariátegui's other argument to the same conclusion: namely, that in pre-Columbian times, the Andean Indians had a communal economic structure, remnants of which still existed in their traditional societies. Therefore, they could not fail to be moved by the call for a socialist revolution once they understand this system. But then Mariátegui appears to fall into a contradiction, because it is not logically possible that while education is useless to solve the problem of the Indian, socialist education is nevertheless useful. After all, socialist education is a kind of education. Of course, he would reject this charge by drawing a line between capitalist education and socialist education.

Of course, as a Marxist secularist interested in understanding the reality of his country in order to change it, Mariátegui also thought about the history of the relations between Church and state in Peru. On his view, Catholicism has already reached the peak of its power as a part of the bourgeois liberal ideology that is fundamental in a society dominated by privately owned means of production.[9] In the end, Mariátegui's speculations about the impact of mainstream Catholicism and underground Inca religions in Latin America seems to have had many receptive readers in thinkers of the Latin American left such as Ernesto Guevara, a known admirer of the Peruvian Marxist.

8.3 Ernesto "Che" Guevara

8.3.1 Life and Work

Ernesto "Che" Guevara (Argentine, 1928–1967) was a medical doctor who came to be known first for his participation in the revolutionary Cuban movement, led by Fidel Castro, that fought against dictator Fulgencio Batista and eventually deposed him in January 1959. Their new revolutionary government in Cuba turned socialist in the early 1960s. According to scholars of this movement (Llorente 2018: 6), it was not until April 16, 1961

---

[9] Mariátegui predicted that with the rise of Peru's native peoples and workers, the power of the Church and the prestige of Catholicism in Latin American nations will accordingly wither. He would surely be surprised to learn that none of this has come to pass, and that by the later part of twentieth century there had emerged a movement within the Church, liberation theology, whose political and social views were close to his. I discuss this doctrine in Chapter 9.

that Castro announced publicly for the first time that a socialist revolution was taking place in Cuba. Before that date, although neither he nor Guevara described the revolution in those terms, they most likely knew in advance where the revolution was going. After his death in Bolivia in tragic circumstances, Guevara became a symbol of liberation for both socialists and nonsocialist progressives alike around the world.[10] Contributing to Guevara's fame (or notoriety, depending on who you read) was his international visibility in connection with anti-imperialist movements, not only in Cuba, but also in Africa and South America. Eventually, he left his position in Castro's government to command a guerrilla group in Bolivia, where special Bolivian Army soldiers, acting jointly with CIA operatives in the country, apprehended him in 1967 and had him shot.

While in Cuba, besides his active role in the guerrilla movement that led to the socialist revolution, Guevara served in several high-ranking positions in the new government, serving as president of the National Bank, Minister of Industries, and preeminent envoy abroad. In addition, over the period 1959–1967, he did a great deal of writing in the form of speeches, reports, notes, letters, and essays of various kinds. In some of these works there appears a normative moral theory that gives an interesting twist to Marx's succinct remarks on morality discussed above. It is a theory of what Guevara called "the new man" referring in fact to "the new human being" (as others call it today), who is a socialist being.[11] This theory is the focus of the sections on these thinkers that follow.

[10] The mythical status the figure of Guevara acquired after his death is something often noted by biographers and critics. See for instance Anderson (1997), Castañeda (1997), Llorente (2018), and Löwy (2007).

[11] See for instance Llorente (2018), a work that also contains details about TNHB. In examining this theory, we should bear in mind that Guevara was not a philosopher. Furthermore, he wrote about his struggles with philosophy while waiting in Africa to travel incognito to Bolivia. Guevara read some standard sources in the history of Western philosophy, but apparently was not prepared for their level of difficulty. This prompted his confession to a friend: "During this long vacation I buried my nose in philosophy books, which is something I'd been meaning to do for a long time. And I came across the first difficulty: there is nothing published on the subject in Cuba, if we exclude those long, dull Soviet tracts that have the drawback of not letting you think, as the party already did the thinking for you, and all you must do is digest it . . . " (cited from Vincent's 2012 online review of Guevara's *Apuntes filosóficos*).

8.3.2   The Theory of the New Human Being (TNHB)

Although Guevara consistently held this theory and frequently invoked it either directly or indirectly throughout the 1960s, he best articulates it in "Socialism and Man in Cuba," an essay that first appeared in the Uruguayan magazine *Marcha* (March) in 1965 with the title "From Algiers, for March. The Cuban Revolution Today." Guevara takes this theory to be a "refutation" of the following claim of the enemies of socialism:

The Anti-Socialism Claim – "Socialism abolishes the individual for the sake of the state."

Guevara offered no direction about how to interpret this objection to socialism. As I read it, it is analogous to a Rawlsian objection against classical utilitarianism: namely, that this moral theory cannot accommodate the separateness of persons. In spite of Marx's rejection of classical utilitarianism, the moral theory that Marxists seem to hold for a society that has reach a socialist stage of development also appears to face the problem the objector has in mind simply because classical utilitarianism and Marxism share the following three theses:

Impartialism – Every person counts as morally the same, neither more nor less than anyone else.

Perfectionism – There is at least one human excellence that must be promoted whenever possible.

Maximizing consequentialism – Whatever that excellence is, in a situation in which a person must decide what to do morally, the right action is the one that produces the greatest balance of that excellence for all concerned.

While for the classical utilitarians the human excellence that matters is happiness, for the Marxists other excellences matter, as we will see in Guevara's response to the anti-socialist claim, which is the theory of the new human being (hereafter, TNHB).

As a response to the anti-socialist claim, the TNHB does not count as a rejection of that claim but rather as a counterclaim holding that there is nothing wrong in refusing to respect the separateness of persons – since the principle underwriting that objection amounts to a capitalist myth created to protect what in fact are exploitative economic relations. Such relations might affect the workers of developed capitalist countries, or an entire nation of the underdeveloped world when it is under the grip of an imperialist capitalist nation. For Guevara a prime example of an imperialist nation is the United States, which amounts to a paradigm of the ills of capitalism.[12]

The primary moral values of the new human beings, by which Guevara means the socially minded individuals who are going to make the transition from socialism to communism in Cuba (or elsewhere) possible, are *social* values such as solidarity and abnegation for the sake of the revolution. To support his socialist moral theory, Guevara describes the behavior of two groups of people, the leaders and their base, during the long fight for the revolution in Cuba, where the guerrilla war lasted roughly from July 1953 to January 1959 when Castro and his forces declared victory against the dictator Batista. During that war, Guevara contends, moral character did not reveal itself in all members of the Cuban oppressed class, but rather in the fighters themselves, who then influenced the "still sleeping mass." These groups were the two fundamental characters of the revolution. Although at first the fighters engaged in actions individualistically, as they fought to achieve common goals, and received their ranks according to merit, their actions generated "revolutionary consciousness and militant enthusiasm." Guevara seems to think that during this "first heroic stage," combatants learned to do their work, fighting for the revolution, *for the good of the revolution*, independent of any personal benefit to be obtained. That selfless attitude, Guevara thinks, is the hallmark of "the man and woman of the future." On this account, then, the virtuous moral character consists of certain social traits that develop first in the leaders and include complex attitudes and sentiments such solidarity, self-abnegation, sacrifice, and courage.[13] The masses respond with trust to

---

[12] Guevara endorses Lenin's theory that imperialism is the last stage of capitalism. According to this, in the imperialist capitalists' countries the exploitation of developing countries favors the workers themselves, who then become free riders in reaping the benefit from that imperialistic exploitation and lose their "spirit of working-class internationalism." See Guevara (1987/1965 and 1967).

[13] Guevara also claims that "the new human being is guided by feelings of love," and a duty of "proletarian internationalism" (1987/1965).

these virtues of their leaders, Guevara thinks, but never follow them like a flock of sheep.

It is by means of education and "moral" incentives that members of the masses will eventually also acquire the right moral character. These two types of stimulus aim at developing the tendency to sacrifice oneself for the benefit of society as a whole, as illustrated for example by the willingness to engage in voluntary, unremunerated work. On this Marxist ethic, morality is a social matter that is mostly transferred in a top-down fashion: the masses learn by emulating their leaders and also by means of education and voluntary work.[14] But it also includes a bottom-up element, since when the leaders make mistakes "one notes a decline in collective enthusiasm due to the effect of a quantitative diminution in each of the elements that make up the mass." This interaction between leaders and masses will eventually result in everybody having the moral character of the new human being.[15]

By contrast, individuals in a capitalist society must elbow their lonely way forward in a "contest among wolves," while the new human beings of socialist nations "no longer travel completely alone over lost roads toward distant aspirations. They follow their vanguard, consisting of the party, the advanced workers, the advanced individuals who walk in unity with the masses and in close communion with them" (1987/1965). They are part of a society in which everyone acts toward the same goal. Becoming a new human being is a process in which direct and indirect education matters, together with the person's conscious willingness to undergo self-education. It is not an easy process, since "[t]he new society in formation has to

---

[14] Another Marxist political philosopher who assigned a primary developmental role to *work* was Engels (1996/1879), though for Engels this consisted in producing the evolution from ape to human.

[15] According to the TNHB, capitalist societies engender alienated human beings because "the laws of capitalism, which are blind and are invisible to ordinary people, act upon the individual without his or her being aware of it. One sees only the vastness of a seemingly infinite horizon ahead. That is how it is painted by capitalist propagandists who purport to draw a lesson from the example of Rockefeller – whether or not it is true – about the possibilities of individual success. The amount of poverty and suffering required for a Rockefeller to emerge, and the amount of depravity entailed in the accumulation of a fortune of such magnitude, are left out of the picture, and it is not always possible for the popular forces to expose this clearly" (Guevara 1987/1965).

compete fiercely with the past." The key to explain these contrasting scenarios is the difference between the capitalist and socialist economic systems. In Cuba, for example, the development of a new human being was, on his view, contingent upon the economic changes that were taking place: " we can see the new man and woman being born … the process goes forward hand in hand with the development of new economic forms."

In sum, like other Marxists, Guevara regards economic class relations as defining every stage of human society except for communism as determinants and as the ultimate explanation of radical moral differences across societies. This is a general, ethical relativist principle that Marxism seem to share. But Guevara gives his own twist to it by adding an account of the socialist virtues, and the role in developing these virtues of both education and voluntary work. On that account, what makes the higher moral conscience of the socialist human beings possible is that they do not need to sell their labor force in the market, but rather work for the benefit of all, which is their social duty. But Guevara acknowledges that although individuals in a socialist society no longer need to sell themselves as "commodities," some "coercive" aspects still exist even when work is voluntary. So he in fact offers a relativistic response to the claim that socialism does not respect the needs of individuals: in a socialist society, respecting those needs has no moral force.

8.3.3 Some Reactions to the TNHB

Although some critics are quite sympathetic to Guevara's theory of the new human being (Martinez-Saenz 2004; Löwy 2007; Llorente 2018), there seem to be some obvious objections facing his TNHB. For one thing, it fails to accommodate a number of related, commonly accepted intuitions about morality – as illustrated by Guevara's own commitment to becoming a new human being. After all, he went to fight the revolution in two continents leaving behind not only parents and friends, but even a spouse and children, and the latter were soon to become fatherless. From a moral point of view, his situation makes us think of painter Paul Gauguin, whose family was left destitute in France while he was producing great art in French Polynesia. A non-negligible intuition here is that this is not the kind of person that we should strive to emulate. Of course, Guevara could reply that, without Gauguin's experience in French Polynesia, we would all now be much the poorer for the lack of his marvelous works. But this reply is insufficient because it seems counterintuitive that Guevara could have had stronger duties to help Cuban society than to help any of the individual people who were nearest and dearest to him. Suppose I am a Cuban worker who is expected to do voluntary work at the factory that makes shoes for children who need them. If I decide instead to stay home to make shoes for my own children who also need them, according to the TNHB, my decision is morally impermissible. That seems the wrong verdict. Or suppose I have been assigned voluntary work cutting sugarcane in Cuba but decide instead to take it easy and go to the beach. If the social duties of the new human being trump all other considerations, my decision would again be morally impermissible according to the TNHB. This suggests that under the TNHB, morality becomes unbearably demanding, something only for saints and heroes, not for ordinary humans.[16]

I am aware that Guevara would have had a rejoinder to each of these objections, one that explains away what in fact are common moral intuitions about cases of this sort. He would have pointed to their reliance on a capitalist conception of moral character. But this rejoinder looks quite dogmatic.

8.4   Soft Socialism: Haya de la Torre and Allende

As with the political thought of Guevara or Mariátegui, that of the Latin American left during the twentieth century favored radical social changes for the region on grounds of social justice, national development, and independence from imperialist powers. But not all thinkers who accepted these premises shared Guevara's or Mariátegui's position on the necessity of armed struggle to produce the necessary changes. Some were "soft" socialists confident that genuine progress could occur within the system of liberal democracy. To this category belong the two political thinkers and activists considered here: the Chilean socialist Salvador Allende (1908–1973), and the Peruvian social reformist Haya de la Torre, whom

[16] Of course, this line of objection is commonly offered against classical utilitarianism. Yet given the similarities between utilitarianism and Guevara's moral theory that I have pointed out above, they equally apply to the TNHB.

I introduced above in connection with the APRA, a political party he created in 1924 that was initially supported by Mariátegui. Allende put into practice some of the views about social change earlier proposed by Haya. For on his view, at least in some Latin American countries, the ballot box was the best political strategy for remedying the widespread poverty and social injustice affecting their people (especially, the industrial workers and farm laborers). With Haya and Mariátegui, Allende shared the view that in Latin America the imperialism of the twentieth century had undermined national development, and exacerbated the land problem in the countryside. But he did not put a comparable emphasis on the plight of the Amerindians, who in the case of his native Chile were mostly the Mapuche.

Nevertheless he agreed with Haya that electoral success required building a political front that united all the classes and groups that stood to benefit from those reforms, which constituted the majority of Chileans. Among the likely supporters of such a front would be workers, peasants, middle class, and an incipient bourgeoisie whose development had been hindered by rural and city oligarchs and imperialist powers, especially the United States. "Our aim is socialism," declared Allende to a reporter, "but the changes will be made within the democracy of the *bourgeoisie*."[17]

Allende's coalition backing this program, the Unidad Popular (Popular Unity), won Chile's general elections in 1970 and he assumed the presidency on October 24. Soon afterwards, he began warning about the obstacles facing the front's program for a peaceful transition to socialism. Allende linked them to the interests of those who stood to lose most from the changes contemplated in his program: the owners of vast parts of Chile's countryside, some industrial and commercial monopolies, and foreign imperialist powers, especially the United States. In a 1972 speech to the General Assembly of the United Nations, he declared: "Our problem is neither an isolated nor a unique problem. It is the local manifestation of a reality that's overwhelming and encompasses the Latin American continent as well as all the Third World."[18] About a year later, forces under the command of General Augusto Pinochet staged a bloody *coup d'état* that terminated Chile's democracy and prompted Allende to take his own life

---

[17] Interview with the French magazine *L'Express* in April 1971, cited p. 82 in Etcheverri (2007), my translation.

[18] Speech delivered on December 23, 1972, pp. 82–83 in Etcheverri (2007).

when the air force began to bomb the presidential palace, La Moneda, where he was resisting with some loyalists. Before killing himself, he delivered a radio message to the Chilean people in which he seemed confident that socialism through democracy would be viable at some future time: one day it will be possible "for the free individual to build a better society" in Chile.[19]

Haya de la Torre would have agreed, since similar convictions fueled his reformist program for Peru. He began his activism as a student leader and later ran for the Peruvian presidency a number of times without success. His program for social reform included measures to alleviate the exploitation of the native peoples of his country by means of an agrarian reform, restrictions to foreign interference in local politics and the economy, and the promotion of a national regeneration program aimed at reducing poverty. He intended the APRA to be a front uniting a variety of progressive social classes and ethnic groups behind political candidates committed to implementing such reforms.

But those supporting the program had to face the fact that, for most of the twentieth century, democracy in Peru and other Latin American countries was a fragile idea. Haya's own attempts to win the presidency in democratic elections landed him in serious trouble with the opposition, including defeats by electoral fraud and persecution that forced him to go into exile. Nonetheless, Haya remained a campaigner for social change by democratic means throughout his life. Accordingly, he argued forcefully against a longstanding charge that Latin America was not ready for democracy – as you may recall, a claim also made by some leaders of the wars of independence, such as Bolívar. In a 1943 article devoted entirely to countering that claim, he argues that it presupposes that Latin American nations are too culturally backward to be capable of democracy. That is, it presupposes that those nations are impoverished not only in the literal sense, but also in their political traditions because of a fundamental cultural inferiority, and so are not fit for the rule of law.

On Haya's chief argument, such presuppositions are not only offensive but simply false. To debunk them, he invokes reasons perfectly consistent

[19] Farewell radio speech to Chileans, delivered on September 11, 1973 a few minutes before the air force started bombing La Moneda, pp. 88–89 in Etcheverri (2007), my translation.

with a Marxist account of why dictatorship repeatedly crops up in Latin America. Given that argument, if one examines the history of the relationship between Latin America and the wealthy democracies of the northern hemisphere, one finds that there is in fact an economic explanation for the prevalence of dictatorship and oligarchy in Latin America. The explanation finds the cause of this phenomenon in the interference of powerful financiers and industrialists in the United States, for whom the protection of their considerable investments demands social stability in the countries of Latin America. And these forces assume that in this part of the world it can be achieved only through autocratic military rule. It is not in the interest of US corporations and banks to tolerate experiments with democracy "in their backyard," and the political openness this brings, since it could potentially lead to social unrest and popular uprisings against the propertied classes and US interests. Since those classes, after all, depend upon the investors in the northern hemisphere, they serve them in return by maintaining political stability in their countries by any means (though the levels of poverty and exploitation sometimes render that stability very fragile). In this explanation, it is ultimately the power of wealth in the imperialist center, and the extent to which that wealth is derived from investments in Latin America, that ultimately keeps Latin American dictators in office.

Yet since Haya was a social reformist but not a Marxist, he was quick to offer a carrot to those powerful forces, which on his own account are responsible for the lack of democracy in Latin America. He departed from the Marxist narrative by warning the local ruling classes and imperialist powers that the relationship between North and South, as described above, "ends in being a bad deal" for them too in Latin America, where the propertied classes are a tiny minority nearly everywhere, and the vast majority of the population is poor. After all, although the masses have at present no voice to resist the unjust relations with oligarchs and generals, they *will* have it in time – and when this happens, the ensuing unrest will be bad for all concerned, including US interests. To win their support for liberal democracy in Latin America, Haya further compares the military regimes of Latin America with the Nazis and Fascists of Europe. Since the United States and its allies have opposed those European regimes so energetically, consistency requires that they similarly oppose their Latin American counterparts – or so Haya, the optimist reformist, suggests. Of course, hard socialists, like Guevara or Mariátegui, would point to the end of the Allende administration in Chile to reply that democracy has not yet proved itself to be the road to socialism in Latin America.

8.5   The Upshot

The first thing to notice about the soft and hard socialists considered in this chapter is that their attitude toward philosophical thought was in line with Marx's prescription that philosophy should be at the service of changing the world rather than merely contemplating it. But while Marx's "scientific socialism" was supposed to have no link to justice or any other moral value, our thinkers are heavily invested in talk of moral values, especially justice. Nevertheless, the political theories of hard socialists reviewed here, those of Mariátegui and Guevara, who identified themselves as Marxists, seem to rely heavily on comparative assessments of justice. This is evident in Mariátegui's account of the Indian problem, even when he explicitly denies that morality (together with religion and education) plays any part in its solution. Given his account, those who stood to suffer most injustice in early twentieth century Peru were chiefly the Andean Indians, who made up four fifths of the country's population according to his own estimate, which apparently was not too far off the truth (Miller 1999). On the other hand, Guevara's TNHB is a normative moral theory that relies explicitly on a comparative assessment of the unjust versus the just labor relations of workers in capitalist and socialist societies, respectively. Even soft socialists such as Allende and Haya de la Torre relied on considerations of justice, and therefore on moral considerations, to argue for the socioeconomic reforms they had in mind for their nations. But since Haya in particular was no Marxist, there need not be any inconsistency in his political framework: his proposed social reforms can ultimately rest on moral grounds. On my view, the Latin American hard socialists overlooked some theoretical problems with Marxist theory to which they were committed. For example, Marxism judges that socialism is *better than* capitalism while confining morality to an ideological superstructure, thereby implying that nothing is intrinsically morally better (or worse) than anything else.[20] The point is that if a socialist

[20]   That is, there seems to be an implicit moral element in the Marxist claim that socialism is better than capitalism – just as there is in the Spencerian evolutionist argument that, since creatures A are more evolved than creatures B, therefore creatures A are better

system is better than a capitalist one, this must be because a socialist system promotes some natural property that grounds a certain moral value, whether that property be aggregate happiness, economic abundance, or something else. But then there is some objective moral value worth pursuing for its own sake, and not merely as part of an instrumental, ideological superstructure. On the other hand, since soft socialists such as Allende and Haya de la Torre are not committed to all doctrines of Marxism, they need not face theoretical objections of this sort.

Finally, as I noted elsewhere (Nuccetelli 2002), the theories of both Guevara and Mariátegui make predictions that rest on romantic assumptions about human psychology. Consider Mariátegui's account of the problem of the Indian, which influenced Guevara's thought and action. Historical data shows that the Andean Indians have reacted to almost a century of attempts at socialist revolutions in the region in unsympathetic ways that defy Mariátegui's predictions. Quite likely, I submit, the problems facing these peoples are more complex than Mariátegui and Guevara thought. And of course, figuring out what they are has to involve the social sciences, not just armchair thinking based on Marxist premises that require empirical support.

8.6   Suggested Readings

Allen, Nicolas. 2018. "Mariátegui's Heroic Socialism: An Interview with Michael Löwy,"*Jacobin*, December 15. www.jacobinmag.com/2018/12/jose-carlos-mariategui-seven-interpretive-essays-peru-marxism-revolutionary-myth

Prompted by questions from the interviewer, Michael Löwy, a historian of the Marxist tradition in Latin America, gives his interpretation of Mariátegui's views and their significance within that tradition. For Löwy, Mariátegui's take on myth and Inca religion suggests the independence of his views from Marxist orthodoxy. Offers a glimpse of the Marxism of both Löwy and Mariátegui.

Anderson, Jon Lee. 1997. *Che Guevara: A Revolutionary Life*. New York: Grove Press.

---

than B. G. E. Moore (1993/1903) rightly objects that, had the environmental conditions been different, creatures B might have been more evolved.

Detailed biography of Guevara. Anderson's research famously led to the discovery that Guevara's body had not been cremated but buried in a mass grave. More journalistic than Castañeda's biography.

Becker, Marc.2006. "Mariátegui, the Comintern, and the Indigenous Question in Latin America," *Science & Society* 70(4): 450–479.

Gives evidence of Mariátegui's reluctance to uncritically obey directives from the pro-Soviet communist parties of Latin America. Becker points out the mix of orthodox and unorthodox views that Mariátegui held. On the one hand, he refused the directives of some regional comrades of the Comintern who wanted him to draw up a plan for building a separate indigenous republic of the South American Andes. And on the other, he offered an account of the oppression of the Indians along strict Marxist lines, in which factors such as race, ethnicity, and nationality play no relevant role.

Castañeda, Jorge G. 1997. *Compañero: The Life and Death of Che Guevara*. New York: Alfred A. Knopf.

Biographical account, provides more interpretation and textual evidence than Anderson's biography.

Chavarría, Jesús. 1979. *José Carlos Mariátegui and the Rise of Modern Peru, 1890–1930*, Albuquerque: University of New Mexico Press.

Offers a detailed account of the context in which Mariátegui developed his views. Its Part I looks closely at the intellectual context represented by, among others, figures such as social thinker Manuel González Prada and women writers Clorinda Matto de Turner and Mercedes Cabello Carbonera. Part II is completely devoted to historico-biographical facts concerning Mariátegui. It also contains discussion of his take on Marxism, indigenism, and critical position on Soviet orthodoxy. But caution is required before accepting unsubstantiated claims about his relation with Haya de la Torre and some other left-wing intellectuals of the time, for they appear designed to exalt Mariátegui's legacy.

Guevara, Ernesto. 1967. "Message to the Tricontinental." April 16. (References to reprint in the *Che Guevara Internet Archive*, www.marxists.org/archive/guevara/works.htm).

   1987/1965. "Socialism and Man in Cuba," pp. 197–214 in Deutschmann (1987). (References to reprint in the *Che Guevara Internet Archive*, www.marxists.org/archive/guevara/works.htm).

Classic sources for Guevara's views as discussed in this chapter.

Hale, Charles A. 1996. "Political Ideas and Ideologies in Latin America, 1870–1930," pp. 133–206 in Bethell (1996).

Contains a brief but well-informed section on Peruvian radical thought of the early twentieth century. Very helpful for locating it within the context of Latin American thought at the time.

Hanneken, Jaime. 2012. "José Carlos Mariátegui and the Time of Myth." *Cultural Critique* 81, 1–30.

Attempt at making sense of Mariátegui's attitude toward myths and Andean religion from the perspective of postcolonial studies. For writers in this tradition, his Marxism and anti-imperialism are attractive while his vindication of spirituality and myth are a puzzle. There is a positive proposal in this work, but its difficulties are those inherent to the postcolonialist tradition endorsed by the author. For another interpretation of Mariátegui within that tradition, see the first two chapters in Schutte (1993).

Haya de la Torre, Víctor Raúl. 1973/1943. *Aprismo: The Ideas and Doctrines of Víctor Raúl Haya de la Torre*, ed. Robert J. Alexander. Kent, OH: Kent State University Press.

Best source in English for Haya de la Torre's doctrines of political philosophy as discussed in this chapter.

James, Daniel. 2001. *Ché Guevara: A Biography*. New York: Rowman & Littlefield.

A biography of Guevara with some account of historical facts concerning his radicalization and later failed campaigns to bring the socialist revolution to Africa and South America. Also offers some facts mixed with speculations about whether Fidel Castro betrayed Guevara in Bolivia and what to make of the myth of Guevara.

Liss, Sheldon B. 1984. *Marxist Thought in Latin America*. Berkeley, CA: University of California Press.

One of the few anthologies offering readers the chance to access nonstandard primary sources of Latin American Marxism, though some its fifty-five entries are not representative of their authors' mature thought (e.g., the Argentine socialist Juan B. Justo). Contains a selection of primary sources from ten South American countries (minus Ecuador and Paraguay) and Cuba. Liss's introduction outlines some of the general doctrines of Marx, Engels,

Lenin, Trotsky, Mao Zedong, and Gramsci. His conclusion makes no attempt to (i) evaluate the primary sources featured in this anthology; (ii) indicate what made, say, Mariátegui's thought more philosophically interesting than the thought of Latin American Marxists who had an exclusively political agenda; or (iii) suggest what might be distinctively "Latin American" about the included primary sources. A missed opportunity to engage in reasoned argument with those sources.

Llorente, Renzo. 2011. "The Amauta's Ambivalence: Mariátegui on Race," pp. 228–248 in Gracia (2011).

Close analysis of Mariátegui on the so-called indigenous question and its relation to the question of race. Llorente argues that Mariátegui's approach to the problem of the Indian, an "economic model" consistent with Marxist theory, is unable to deliver an adequate account of that relation.

Llorente, Renzo.2009. "Marxism," pp. 170–184 in Nuccetelli et al. (2009).

Maintains that "the union of theory and practice" is more typically realized by Latin American Marxist philosophers than by their peers in Europe or North America. Llorente focuses on the themes of Marxist thought that have attracted most attention (the problem of the Indian, liberation, alienation, humanism, etc.) and on a number of Marxist thinkers. Among them, he takes Mariátegui to have offered one of the most distinctive versions of Marxism, which combines orthodoxy with ideas from Henri Bergson, Friedrich Nietzsche, and Georges Sorel, and applies these to Peru's social problems.

Llorente, Renzo. 2018. *The Political Theory of Che Guevara*. London: Rowman & Littlefield International.

Guevara's contribution to radical social theory has not been sufficiently evaluated. Llorente looks at textual evidence from a vast number of Guevara's writings and critics, making a comparative assessment of his views and those of classic Marxist sources (Marx, Engels, Lenin, etc.) But he makes no attempt to assess how Guevara's educational policies affected Cubans, something perfectly testable today, more than fifty years after Guevara's death. Are modern Cubans the new people those policies were geared to produce?

Löwy, Michael 1992. *Marxism in Latin America from 1909 to the Present: An Anthology, Atlantic Highlands*. NJ: Humanities Press.

Though somewhat outdated, this is still a collection of writings by Marxist political thinkers of Latin America that is serviceable to general readers and instructors looking for readers in this area. Generally focused on anti-imperialism and class struggle. Some writings address the question for Marxists of whether the economic system of the region is capitalist or feudal, generally siding with the former view. Löwy classifies Latin American Marxists in three periods, each characterized by questions about either (i) socialism and anti-imperialism in the region, roughly from 1920 to 1935; (ii) what to do during the national-democratic phase that, according to the Soviets during Stalin's regime, was the one America was undergoing (1935–1960); or (iii) how to produce socialist revolutions in the region, especially after the experiences of Fidel Castro in Cuba and Salvador Allende in Chile (from the 1960s onward).

2007. *The Marxism of Che Guevara, Philosophy, Economics, Revolutionary Warfare,* 2nd ed. Lanham, MD: Rowman & Littlefield.

Covers a wide range of topics related to Guevara's policies and thought, from his take on Marxism, commitment to guerrilla warfare and conception of the new person, to the material-versus-moral incentives and voluntary-labor questions crucial to his ethics for socialism. Mostly exegetical but provides data for those interested in a more nuanced reflection of Guevara's thought.

Marchesi, Aldo, 2018. "The Subjective Bonds of Revolutionary Solidarity: From Havana to Ñancahuazú (Bolivia) 1967," in *Latin America's Left: Rebellion and Cold War in Global 1960s.* Cambridge, UK: Cambridge University Press, pp. 69–100.

Good historical account of Guevara's attempt at expanding the Cuban revolution to other Latin American countries. It also provides an analysis of the impact of his anti-imperialist manifesto of 1967, published in the *Tricontinental* magazine.

Mariátegui, José Carlos. 1971/1928. *Seven Interpretive Essays on Peruvian Reality.* Austin, TX: University of Texas Press. (Also available at the *Marxists Internet Archive,* www.marxists.org/archive/mariateg/works/7-interpretive-essays /index.htm)

Contains most of Mariátegui's essays that are discussed in this chapter.

The Marxists Internet Archive. n.d. "Marxism and Anti-Imperialism in Latin America." *The Marxists Internet Archive.* www.marxists.org/subject/latinamer ica/index.htm

Selection of primary sources by Latin American Marxists in either the original Spanish/Portuguese texts, or their English translations. Includes writings by

Salvador Allende, Fidel Castro, Frantz Fanon, Ernesto "Che" Guevara, and many other socialist thinkers.

Márquez, Iván. 2008. *Contemporary Latin American Social and Political Thought*. Lanham, MD: Rowman & Littlefield.

Chapter 10 of this anthology offers selections from the writings of thinkers representative of the 'Latin American left' – a label commonly used to refer to views that have a Marxist component, from liberationism and dependency theory to hard socialism and the Zapatista movement.

Martinez-Saenz, Miguel. 2004. "Che Guevara's New Man: Embodying a Communitarian Attitude," *Latin American Perspectives* 31(6): 15–30.

Contends that Guevara's actions to promote revolution outside Cuba, especially in other Latin American countries, defined his own individual identity, one that was at the same time a social identity. His actions did more to show that identity than his writings. His conception of the new person reveals a conflict in liberalism between the individual and society.

McLaren, Peter. 2000. *Che Guevara, Paulo Freire, and the Pedagogy of Revolution*. Lanham, MD: Rowman & Littlefield.

Contains some chapters of interest for the study of Guevara's views and legacy. One concerns his death and the birth of the Guevara myth. McLaren suggests some lesson for Marxists to draw from the response to those events in the West. He also contrasts Guevara's socialist, and therefore, state-interventionist economic policies with the views of liberals and neoliberals. The other chapter concerns the legacy of Guevara and Paulo Freire for educators. Here some textual evidence for the author's claims seems necessary.

Miller, Nicola. 1999. *In the Shadow of the State: Intellectuals and the Quest for National Identity in Twentieth-Century Spanish America*. London: Verso.

Good source for the historical context of the so-called Peruvian radicals of the early twentieth century. Contains valuable information, especially about the views of Haya de la Torre and Mariátegui's controversies with contemporaries over the Indian problem.

Salazar Bondy, Augusto. 1967. "El pensamiento de Mariátegui y la filosofía marxista," pp. 311–342 in *Historia de las ideas en el Perú contemporáneo: El proceso del pensamiento filosófico*, vol. 2. Lima: Francisco Moncloa Editores.

Presents a very sympathetic reading of Mariátegui's Marxism, explaining with great clarity its commonalities and differences with standard Marxist theory.

Schutte, Ofelia. 1993. *Cultural Identity and Social Liberation in Latin American Thought*. Albany, NY: State University of New York Press.

Contains two chapters devoted to Mariátegui's Marxism, written from the sympathetic perspective of postcolonial theory. The author has done a close reading of Mariátegui's writings and points directly to what is most relevant in them.

9   Liberation Theology
        and Philosophy

From the early twentieth century, hard as well as soft socialists in Latin America made many attempts at explaining the deep socioeconomic problems facing the region, which ranged from economic stagnation and widespread poverty to political instability and endemic corruption and violence. These left-leaning accounts tended to run mostly in Marxist terms, invoking class struggle to explain the sharp contrast between the lavish living conditions and great political power of ruling elites on the one hand, and on the other, the extreme poverty and disempowerment of the majority of Latin Americans.

But in the 1930s and 1940s, Latin America experienced its first modern wave of populism, most dramatically illustrated by the rise to power of Getúlio Vargas in Brazil in 1930, Juan Perón in Argentina in 1945, and Lázaro Cárdenas in Mexico in 1934. At least partially under the spell of populism, some theologians and lay intellectuals of the region who were sensitive to the problems of concern to the political left attempted to account for social and economic disparities in ways that went beyond simply describing a struggle between proletariat and bourgeoisie. Their search for an account that better captured the conditions of oppression affecting the region led to the movements of liberation theology and liberation philosophy, which in fact have overlapping foundations. Because of their doctrinal commonalities, and the fact that liberation theology had a slightly earlier chronological development, my attention in this chapter will focus on that movement first. But I have also something to say about liberation philosophy.

9.1 Liberation Theology

9.1.1 Ethical Theory

Liberation theology, at least initially, emerged as a radical movement within the Catholic Church that challenged this transnational organization's centralized structure. Although some liberation theologians trace their movement to the sixteenth century, the combination of doctrines that characterizes it suggests instead that we are dealing with a twentieth-century intellectual development. Or so it would appear, since it is obvious that none of the three pillars of liberation theology is a product of the sixteenth century. On the one hand, the teachings of Christ, one of its pillars, long preceded that era. And on the other hand, Marxism and dependency theory, its two other pillars, appeared long after it.

Liberation theology, strictly speaking, first appeared in the 1960s when a group of Christian theologians (mostly Catholic priests) reacted to the social injustices facing the majority of people of Latin America by invoking an apparently inconsistent set of doctrines: the teachings of Christ, Marxism, and dependency theory. Their approach spread rapidly to the North and across the Atlantic, gaining in the process some support both inside and outside the Catholic Church.[1] Peruvian priest Gustavo Gutiérrez (b. 1928) labeled the movement 'liberation theology' in *A Theology of Liberation* (1973/1971).[2] In a later book (1993), Gutiérrez offered an account of the history of the movement that traces its roots to the work of some Spanish Dominican priests who in the 1550s questioned the morality of the Iberian conquest.[3] Prominent among them were Bartolomé de las Casas and Antonio de Montesinos, both outspoken opponents of the systems of slave labor that Spain and Portugal were enforcing in their American colonies.[4]

---

[1] Accordingly, the current webpage of the movement bears the title "Liberation Theologies." See https://liberationtheology.org/.

[2] Gustavo Gutiérrez's book first appeared in Spanish with the title *Teología de la liberación: Perspectivas* (Lima: CEP, 1971).

[3] For accounts of the history of liberation theology consistent with Gutiérrez (1993), see Boff and Boff (2000/1987), Dussel (1995), Petrella (2016), Hennelly (1990), and Vásquez and Peterson (2016).

[4] Liberation theologians regularly associate their own doctrines with those of the Dominican friars Las Casas and Montesinos, who, as you may recall from the discussion

Of course ascribing Marxism or contemporary dependency theory to either Las Casas or Montesinos would be an anachronism. But although these priests were not exactly a source of liberation theology, we can properly take note of some continuities in the underlying *motivation* and *moral theory* of, say, Las Casas (1992a/1537; 1992b/1542) and Gutiérrez (1993, 1999). For each of these thinkers rejected the indifference, and sometimes complicity, of higher officials in the Catholic Church toward the conditions of exploitation, poverty, and violence faced by most Latin Americans at the time. Moreover, in reacting to the reality of those conditions they both relied on an ethical framework consistent with Thomas Aquinas' natural law theory. Given this value-based moral theory, some ways of life amount to excellences that should be promoted because they lead to human flourishing, while other ways of life involve vices that undermine or hinder human flourishing and should therefore be avoided on moral grounds. In Gutiérrez's words (1990), some ways of life make people *more human*, while others make them *less human*: oppression makes people less human, as does poverty and violence. The sense of 'human' at work here is the same one invoked by Las Casas when he proclaimed the *humanity* of Amerindians – something that we would put today in terms of their having the moral standing of persons.

Liberation theologians also share with their Dominican philosophical forebears an interpretation of the mission of the Church according to which the institution should commit itself to helping resolve the problems of the neediest. But of course, unlike Gutiérrez, Las Casas could not have been sensitive to the familiar Marxist criticisms of organized Western religion as being focused solely on the afterlife. Gutiérrez and other liberation theologians embrace that criticism, holding that the Church as a transnational institution with a centralized rule from the Vatican should focus on global poverty, recognize it as a social sin, and try to elicit a response from those who truly hold Christian values (Boff and Boff 2000/1987, Gutiérrez 1973/1971). The Church, if it wishes to be consistent with its foundational doctrine, needs to grow more sympathetic to the needs of the poor. In Latin America, that entails getting involved in

of Lascasianism in Chapter 1, used a Thomistic natural law theory as their ethical framework for defending the human rights of Amerindians.

a struggle for the actual liberation of the people from oppression. That is, it entails becoming involved in politics, something contrary to the apolitical stance traditionally favored within the Church. Gutiérrez distinguishes two normative senses of 'politics': one that moves the layperson to join a political party, and another that moves the ordained and other clerics to engage in political participation without joining a political party. However, clerics should either favor some leftist option or at least withhold support from parties whose policies promote a less human-centered approach.[5]

To sum up, given the value-theory of liberation theology, a Christian ethic is bound to be a *this-world* ethic and to reject political oppression and poverty because these are conditions of life that dehumanize those who suffer them. An actual *this-world* liberation presents itself as an imperative for Christians: they must devote themselves to the elimination of social injustice and poverty in *this* world. This task first requires a correct account of the causes of injustice and poverty, which may involve the tools of the social sciences, including Marxism and dependency theory. But before examining how liberation theology makes use of these tools, let us briefly consider the historical conditions that made this unorthodox take on Christian theology possible.

9.1.2   Some Facts About the Development of Liberation Theology

Two types of historical development within the Catholic Church made the situation ripe in the 1960s for the development of liberation theology. The first type of development came about as a result of the Church's structure as a transnational institution with centralized rule by the Vatican. In the mid-twentieth century, a series of developments at the

---

[5] The fact is that liberation theologians do actively participate in the politics of their countries. To name but a few, Fernando Lugo, a bishop in Paraguay, ran for president in 2008, against the recommendations of the Vatican, and for senator in 2013. He was elected in both cases. Father Ernesto Cardenal, a member of Nicaragua's Sandinista party, was a Minister of Culture from 1979 to 1987. And Father Francisco Olveira of Argentina, a member of the Curas por la Opción por los Pobres with known sympathies with a left-leaning branch of Peronism, declared during a recent interview: "We Christians cannot vote for him [Macri, the incumbent candidate], because sin is not only individual: it is also social" ("Padre Francisco Olveira: 'Votar a Macri ser un pecado,'" *La Nación,* June 7, 2019).

highest level in the Church proclaimed certain ethical imperatives for Catholics that were to be central to liberation philosophy. Prominent among them was Pius XII's decision during his papacy (1939–1958) to re-evangelize Latin America, perhaps inspired by the fact that large numbers of Catholics already lived in the region.[6] To implement this decision, priests from North America and Europe were sent to Latin America and, as they became acquainted with their new environment, were struck by its widespread social injustices.

At the same time, local priests pursuing higher positions within the organization were encouraged to study in Europe, chiefly at the Catholic University of Louvain in Belgium. As a result, they were exposed, not only to some social and political theories standardly censored in Latin America, such as Marxism and socialism, but also to debates about religion between Catholics and intellectuals from other persuasions, including atheists and agnostics. Furthermore, in 1959 Pope John XXIII convened the Second Vatican Council, a high conclave on Catholic doctrine, in session between 1962 and 1965, and initiated a process of liberalization within the Church that had a great impact among Latin American theologians. Expressions such as 'the Church of the poor' and 'the preferential option for the poor' which became familiar after Vatican II, in fact captured the liberation theologians' view that Christians have a fundamental commitment to promoting social justice and assisting the poor. For the Church, that means that it is part of its mission to care about the needs of marginalized people and help eliminate social injustices. During the papacy of Paul VI (1963–1978), the process of liberal reform initiated during Vatican II continued, as is evident in some encyclicals emphasizing the Church's commitment to social justice for the poor.

---

[6] By the 1950s, Latin American Catholics accounted for 35 percent of all Catholics world-wide (Dussel 1996). According to a study by the Pew Research Center, in 2010, Catholics in Latin America accounted for 39 percent, and Brazil, with its 65 percent Catholic population, was the country with the largest number of Catholics worldwide (11.7 per-cent of the world Catholic population). Data cited in Ross Toro, "The World's Catholic Population (Infographic)," *LiveScience*, February 19, 2013, www.livescience.com/27244-the-world-s-catholic-population-infographic.html .

At the same time, some grassroots movements within the Church of Latin America were enacting changes related to those liberal reforms, notable among which were

- The emergence of informal "ecclesial" communities, usually made up of middle-class youth, which obtained some authority from the Church to engage in progressive social activism within their community;
- The empowerment of laypersons to take action under the umbrella of the Church's Catholic Action;
- The formation of Catholic trade unions; and
- The constitution of Christian Democrat parties which, pitched as alternatives to the extreme right and left, won presidential elections in Chile and Venezuela.

All these factors prepared the way for the growth of liberation theology following the declaration of the second General Conference of Latin American Bishops gathered in Medellin, Colombia, in 1968. The views underwriting that declaration were in sharp contrast with the traditional thinking of the Catholic Church in Latin America. Since the early 1800s and for more than a century, the Latin American church had been gradually becoming more conservative, perhaps in reaction to the regular challenges made by those secularist political thinkers who have questioned its power, beginning with the romantic socialists and liberals of the period of national reorganization, and later the positivists, the socialists, the anarchists, Marxists, and some others.[7] Be that as it may, by the early twentieth century the Latin American church, solidly aligned with the ruling elites, had established deep alliances with the region's major right-wing movements and dictators while at the same time claiming to remain "apolitical."

9.1.3   The Appeal to Marxism and Dependency Theory

Surely a reasonable requirement for any religious believers, including Christians, is that their attitudes and actions be consistent with their deeply held religious beliefs. Given that requirement, then, it seems we

---

[7] Among those who would explain the conservatism of the Catholic Church this way are Dussel (1996), Haight (1998), and Petrella (2016).

must accept the argument of liberation theologians that a Christian has a moral duty to care for the poorest and most vulnerable peoples in this world. But even non-Christians would face the same imperative if, for example, they accepted the premise that the evil of widespread poverty outweighs considerations such as the right to private property, inheritance, and the like. This point will become relevant to our assessment of liberation theology later. For now, however, note that liberation theology is not only concerned with the ethical problem posed for Christians by the conditions of the poor in Latin America. Commonly, liberation theology also attempts to explain its causes and develop solutions grounded on the "social sciences," by which it chiefly means Marxism and dependency theory.

In their view of Marxism, liberation theologians generally accept at least its critique of capitalism as an economic system bound to produce an unequal distribution of benefits and burdens in society. As is well known, Marx theorized that under capitalism the vast majority of people must earn a living by selling their labor, in the course of which they face burdens like poverty that do not affect the minority who own the means of production.[8] But liberation theologians generally stop short of endorsing Marx's conception of class struggle and revolution as the wheels of history. They think, instead, that Latin America is among the exceptions to that conception, as a result of certain historical factors such as colonialism and dependence that have determined that the chief struggle in the region is not between classes, but between those who benefit from the existing unfair distribution of wealth and those who do not. A group's precise role in this struggle is, according to liberation theologians, something to be determined by a left-leaning interpretation of dependency theory, first developed by Raúl Prebisch (Argentinean, 1901–1986).

In Prebisch's version of the theory, the dependence of Latin America on industrialized countries during the past century amounts to both a hypothesis that can be used for achieving a better understanding of the

---

[8] One might agree with the socialist view that capitalism fails to distribute wealth fairly, without fully subscribing to remedies such as the elimination of private property and the replacement of the liberal state with a state-controlled system that distributes goods according to need. Liberation theologians who align themselves with populist movements need not subscribe to full-fledged socialism, though many have done so – for example, Ernesto Cardenal of Nicaragua and Camilo Torres of Colombia.

widespread stagnation and poverty of the region and the development of successful strategies to mitigate economic underdevelopment. This early version of dependency theory attracted the attention of economists interested in the region during the second half of the twentieth century. The theory's wide reception was due in part to Prebisch's leadership of the Economic Commission for Latin America and the Caribbean at the United Nations from 1950 to 1963. In this original form, the theory is a kind of developmentalism that accounts for the underdevelopment of Latin America in terms of an international division of labor worked out during the twentieth century, whereby the countries of the world belong to either a "center" or a "periphery," contingent upon whether they are producers or consumers of industrial goods (Prebisch 1971). On the one hand, the industrialized countries of the center have a monopoly on manufactured products, which enter the international market at whatever price the center determines. And on the other, the underdeveloped countries of the periphery are the producers of raw materials, which also enter the international market at whatever price the center determines. That is, because of the periphery's need for manufactured products, it must accept the price fixed by the center for both industrialized goods and raw materials.

A left-leaning interpretation of the theory adds the claim that development and underdevelopment are two sides of the same coin: the countries at the center gained their place there at the expense of the countries on the periphery. By contrast with the developmentalist and Marxist understandings of Latin America's underdevelopment in terms of precapitalist structures, this version of dependency theory understands it as a consequence of an ultra-development of capitalism in the center that condemns some countries to remain forever on the periphery. Underdeveloped countries are thus doomed to remain in that condition *unless* they can get out of being chiefly producers of raw materials. On the issue of how to break out of that hopeless circle, the opinions of economists drawn to the theory have varied. While Prebisch suggested in the 1950s and 1960s that Latin America should adopt protectionist economies, some of his left-leaning successors in the 1970s and 1980s argued for the adoption of socialist economies.[9]

---

[9] A number of writers within the framework of dependency theory have addressed the issue of extreme poverty and super-exploitation of laborers in Latin America. They include Cardoso and Faletto (1969), Marini (1977), and Sunkel and Paz (1975).

The early liberation theologians tended to be sympathetic to this socialist version of dependency theory, for they viewed the economic inequalities of Latin America as the result of the growth of free-market capitalism in the countries of the center. Among those countries, the United States stood out as an imperialist force that benefited unfairly from trade in this part of the periphery. But liberation theologians today might include in their indictment other countries of the northern hemisphere too, similarly contending that these nation's economic growth and prosperity were obtained by means of exploitative global practices elsewhere. They are also responsible for widening poverty and displacement in poorer nations to the south. In Latin America, the mostly Amerindian rural population was first driven off their land during the Iberian conquest and later forced to work for the *latifundistas* under conditions of exploitation akin to slavery or servitude. The mechanization of agriculture in turn forced them to move to urban areas, where they have increasingly found themselves on the fringes of society. The plight of these poorest of the poor, the denizens of miserable shantytowns throughout Latin America, has been made worse, many liberation theologians now believe, by the effects of globalization. These people were the least prepared to participate productively in the capitalist economies that began taking root in their countries during the twentieth century. For many Latin Americans of the working and the middle classes, the transition to capitalism has not been easy, but, for the most marginalized and the poorest, the fruits of capitalism have been a bitter harvest of increasing deprivation.

Other key factors in explaining the causes of poverty in Latin American countries are to be found in (i) the alliance between ruling elites with the United States and other countries of the center; and (ii) the complicity of the Catholic Church with the unfair political systems resulting from that alliance. As mentioned above, challenged by the secularism of the nineteenth century, in the twentieth century the Latin American church became extremely conservative in both political and religious matters, often supporting authoritarian leaders from the right.

However, in the view of liberation theologians, the Church must go back to follow the path of Las Casas, Montesinos, and of the many other past figures who understood the conditions of the Latin American poor and took steps to remedy them. Once these conditions and the teachings of Christ are properly understood, so the argument goes, consistency demands that not only the Church but all Christians take up the mission of becoming advocates for the poorest and most vulnerable people. Although this mission may even require engagement in the political struggle on behalf of the poor, liberation theologians have generally avoided engagement in armed struggle. One of the exceptions was Camilo Torres (Colombian, 1929–1966), an early liberation theologian and professor whose frustration with the ability of institutions in his country, including the Church, to improve the situation of the poor eventually led him to join the guerrilla movement, the National Liberation Army (ELN). After receiving training, Torres was killed during his first engagement in armed combat.[10]

9.1.4 Some Problems Facing Liberation Theology

From its very beginnings, liberation theology had an explicit commitment to the position that Catholic clerics in Latin America have a moral duty to contribute to the liberation of the poor and oppressed. This message follows from liberation theology's interpretation of the teachings of Christ, which is a development that parallels, in certain ways, the "new theology" movement in mainline liberal Protestantism in the 1960s in the United States. Liberation theology conveys that message by means of a metaphor according to which it is precisely in the encounter with the sufferings of the poor in society that the individual comes face to face with the living embodiment of Christ in the modern world. The oppressed peoples of Brazilian *favelas* and other squalid slums throughout Latin America are the manifestation of Christ – before whom Latin American Christians are compelled to reevaluate their own priorities and acknowledge their moral

---

[10] Camilo Torres was among those liberation theologians who in the 1960s and 1970s favored arm struggle as a way to improve the conditions of the Latin American poor. A prolific writer, some of his phrases became slogans for guerrilla groups. For example, "The duty of every Christian is to be a revolutionary"; "Marxists fight for a new society, and we the Christians should be fighting with them"; and "Let's not discuss whether the soul is mortal or immortal, let's think instead that hunger is mortal and defeat hunger so that we can later discuss whether the soul is mortal or immortal." My translation, from "El Basilisco, revista de materialism filosófico," www.filosofia.org /ave/001/a230.htm. See also Torres (2016).

shortcomings. The degree of justice in Latin American societies is directly proportional to how they treat the poor and the oppressed among them.

But although liberation theologians cast these messages, at least in part, as concerning social justice, their ethical framework is not consistent with that casting. For like some of their sixteenth-century ancestors mentioned above, they subscribe to natural law theory and according to this theory, there are four fundamental moral values: life, reproduction, sociability, and knowledge. Justice is at best derivative of one or more of these. As a result, given natural law theory, any act or omission that promotes poverty would be wrong *if and only if* poverty is a condition that undermines or hinders one or more of the four basic values.

Now consider some scenarios whereby a course of action that can alleviate poverty or oppression may do so only by means of committing some injustice. Think, for example, of a scenario featuring an authoritarian government that helps the poor while also engaging in the illegal persecution of its political enemies. In that scenario, liberation theologians are committed to supporting the authoritarian government, a conclusion that is not surprising in light of the actual support liberation theologians provided to the left-leaning parties that came to power in Latin America with the return of democracy after the 1980s. Some of these governed in ways that made them vulnerable to charges of either authoritarianism, corruption, or both.

This suggests that the liberation theologians' ethical framework cannot accommodate an idea that has had a distinguished history in Western ethics and political philosophy: the primacy of justice, which means that justice must be regarded as the weightiest of all moral demands. According to the principle of the primacy of justice, this virtue trumps all other moral values. "If the happiness of the world could be advanced by unjust means alone," writes a contemporary advocate of the primacy of justice, "not happiness but justice would properly prevail. And when justice issues in certain individual rights, even the general welfare cannot override them" (Sandel 1982: 2).[11] The actual "praxis" of some liberation theologians has

---

[11] Western philosophers have cast the primacy of justice in different ways. For Aristotle, it is the highest social virtue; for deontologists, it is the grounds for the moral law itself (which is about what is right, independent of whether it promotes some good or end); and for classical utilitarians, it contributes to the maximization of social utility.

shown that they lack the philosophical resources to defend the primacy of justice.

9.2 Liberation Philosophy

9.2.1 Origins and Goals

Liberation philosophy (hereafter, 'liberationism') is a family of doctrines closely related to liberation theology in both historical roots and their interest in the socioeconomic problems facing Latin America. They were first developed in Argentina in the early 1970s, when a group of philosophers declared that, properly understood, philosophy in Latin America must not concern itself with the traditional problems of philosophy about what there is, whether we can have knowledge, and how to determine the moral thing to do in a situation. Rather, Latin American philosophy should concern itself with liberation from ideological domination and thus contribute to the liberation of the oppressed. Works by liberationists appeared as early as 1971. Some link the emergence of the movement to the changing political situation in Argentina at the time because the country was about to enjoy a short-lived democracy (1973–1976) after a military government (1966–1973). Democracy brought a revival of Peronism, the ideology of the country's major nationalist, populist political party whose left-leaning wing counted on the sympathy of liberationists. In 1976, another military *coup d'état* deposed the right-leaning Peronist government of Isabel Perón. Liberationists then reaffirmed their belief that philosophy should engage with "praxis" and be geared toward the economic, social, and ideological liberation of the oppressed.

   In this belief, liberationists were only echoing Marx's prescription in his "Theses on Feuerbach" according to which philosophers should redirect their focus: instead of attempting to understand the world, they should aim at changing it. Yet the liberationists did not construe the category of 'the oppressed' in exclusively Marxist terms (i.e., as referring exclusively to the proletariat). Rather, they equated the oppressed with the poor, including the Amerindians, and sought to contribute to their liberation by embracing a left-leaning version of the theory discussed above, *dependency theory*. On their view, Latin America was not a good model of capitalist class struggle because the relevant struggle was of the type commonly found in *dependent capitalism*. After the 1976 *coup d'ètat* in Argentina, many liberationists left for other Latin American countries and spread their doctrines elsewhere, especially in Mexico, where some of the movements' leaders sought academic posts. It now has followers in Europe and the United States, especially among Latino philosophers.[12]

Liberationists make up a group with a variety of philosophical interests and methods. Although they all profess to have an interest in Latin American philosophy, Arturo Roig and Leopoldo Zea are among the few who have actually done consistent work on this area of philosophy. Furthermore, although they all share an interest in German philosophy, their interests are diverse, ranging from neo-Hegelian idealism and Heideggerian phenomenology to Marxism and the discursive ethics of the Frankfurt school. And although the liberationists invariably take their interests in continental philosophy to be essentially critical, they also borrow a great deal from the theories they set out to criticize. As a result, it is appropriate to think of liberationism as one of the several offshoots of continental philosophy in Latin America. Classifying liberationism as a type of continental philosophy accounts in part for its hostility toward analytic philosophy, which is quite evident in the version of liberationism proposed by one of its founders, Enrique Dussel (Argentine, b. 1934), to be considered later.

In addition to the core doctrines mentioned above, dependency theory and Marxism, which liberationists in philosophy share with liberationists in theology, a core goal of their liberationism consists in some negative theses about the value of all traditions of Western philosophy. As far as I understand them, their objections to Western philosophy, which target its contents as well as its methods, consist in claims liberationists made in publications of the early 1970s, especially in a collective volume by Ardiles et al. that played a foundational role and may be considered a manifesto of the group.[13] It included a significant preface in which the editors identified all the contributors as young Latin American philosophers who were

---

[12] For a brief history of liberationism, see Scannone (2009).

[13] Ardiles et al. (1973). The volume included essays by thirteen representatives of liberationism and appeared in a series "Enfoques latinoamericanos" (Latin American approaches) that aimed to assert and define the domain of Latin American philosophy.

determined to end the *enjenación académica* (academic alienation) of philosophers from the region. Dussel and the other leaders of the movement were thus undertaking the task of undermining a tendency in Latin American philosophy to be imitative of European and North American traditions – a claim to be revisited in Chapter 10.

In any case, there appears to be more to the notion of academic alienation than its association with the lack of originality in Latin American philosophy. The manifesto's contributors also state that the alienation of mainstream philosophers in Latin America is noticeable in their attempts to capture "objective totalities," which thereby render their philosophies an instrument of oppression or domination. By contrast, the contributors' own liberationist philosophy attempts to capture the distinctiveness of the Other, who is "a concrete man in his inalienable differentiation" (Ardiles et al. 1973: 5). But it is difficult to discern what this dichotomy of objective totalities versus the distinctiveness of the Other might mean – a defect that, as we will see, also undermines the understanding of other liberationist claims.

Provisionally putting these negative claims aside, the liberationist manifesto also makes the positive claim that liberationism intends to develop an original Latin American philosophy which is also a 'concrete' or 'situated' yet 'absolute' philosophy of the praxis of liberation.[14] Some liberationists now assert that they have developed such a philosophy (Dussel 1980/1973; Scannone 2009). But it is unclear how liberation philosophy can be "concrete" and "absolute." The liberationists use the word 'absolute' as a modifier of the word 'truth' when they say that liberationism is "absolutely true" without being "universally true."[15] Dussel, for example, associates 'universal' with 'totality,' which in his jargon in turn equates with 'domination.' Surely, given relativism about truth, no claim can be

---

[14] I will leave for Chapter 10 a consideration of liberationist attempts to develop an original Latin American philosophy, such as that of Leopoldo Zea, who in the 1960s engaged in a controversy with another precursor of liberationism, Augusto Salazar Bondy. Unlike Zea, though, Salazar Bondy was led to a skeptical conclusion: Latin America, because of its economic and cultural dependence on Europe or the United States, could have an original philosophy only if it were to become independent of each of them.

[15] Vicente Medina pointed out to me that the term 'absolutely' makes no sense as a qualifier of 'truth,' since truth does not come in degrees.

universally true. Yet if relativism is correct, no claim can be absolutely true either, because that amounts to an objectivist claim incompatible with relativism. And if what the liberationists are saying is "no truths are universal, but my own theory is absolutely true," that of course would be self-defeating. As a result, either way the liberationist manifesto runs head-on into a contradiction.

9.2.2   Dussel's Liberationism and Its Problems

Dussel's liberationism adds to the above claims a lengthy critique of Western philosophy and philosophers, which includes critiques of analytic philosophers such as Karl Popper and Ludwig Wittgenstein, as well as entire branches of philosophy such as logic, philosophy of science, and philosophy of language (1980/1973: 152 ff.). He essentially charges that their conceptions of truth, knowledge, or value commit them to a "philosophy of domination," because it is a philosophy contaminated by ideology. To avoid this charge, Western philosophers must support liberationism for reasons considered in due course.

9.2.2.1   *Dussel's Master Argument Against Western Philosophy*

On Dussel's view, the chief error of Western philosophy is its universalism – that is, its objectivism about truth, knowledge, and value. Against such an objectivism, he offers some arguments that can be reconstructed as follows:

1. So far, theories of Western philosophy have provided only objectivist conceptions of truth, knowledge, or value.
2. Any objectivist conception of truth, knowledge, or value amounts to a philosophy of domination.
3. *Therefore,* so far Western philosophy has been a philosophy of domination.

Although this argument is valid, it has easily refutable premises and is therefore unsound. Counterexamples to premise (1) come from any Western philosophical theory that rejects objectivism, of which there are many – from the ontological relativism of Willard Van Orman Quine to the transcendental idealism of Immanuel Kant and many more. Premise (2) requires it to be demonstrated that *any* objectivist philosophical theory is committed to justifying or tolerating domination, understood as the oppression of some humans by other humans. But oppression need not be justified by any of the chief normative theories of Western philosophy. Consider for example Kantianism and its 'categorical imperative,' an inviolable moral rule that prescribes: "Act so that you use humanity, in your own person as well as in that of another, always also as an end and never only as a means" (Kant 1948/1785: 429). Since any oppressor would fail to honor this categorical imperative by using other humans as mere means, it follows that oppression is morally wrong. Other chief theories would yield similar results, therefore disproving premise (2) of my reconstruction of Dussel's arguments.

9.2.2.2   The 'Ideological-Contamination' Problem for Western Philosophy

As we have seen, according to liberationism, philosophy should aim at being mostly about praxis: a tool for liberation. On the liberationists' view, all branches of philosophy should be put at the service of seeking not merely the socioeconomic liberation of the poor but principally, the "integral liberation of humans." This would include philosophical liberation from domination of women by men, children by adults, dependent periphery nations by imperialistic nations from the center, and so on. But above all, for Dussel (1980/1973: 149–153), philosophical liberation requires liberating people from *ideological domination*, which in turn involves unmasking the widespread *ideological contamination* of Western philosophy.[16] As far as I can tell, a philosophical theory suffers contamination of this sort just in case (i) it explicitly or implicitly favors some form of oppression (of male over female, rich over poor, adult over child, imperialist country over periphery country, etc.); or (ii) it vindicates the existence of universal, objective truths.

Dussel undertakes the task of showing how Western philosophers have made themselves vulnerable to this ideological-contamination problem. On his view, those vulnerable to it also include Marx and other early socialists and Marxists whose ideas Dussel accepts. Of course, his list of

---

[16] Other liberationists agree. See, for example, Scannone (2009).

ideologically contaminated philosophy includes the works of Aristotle, John Locke, Thomas Aquinas, Immanuel Kant, Karl Popper, Ludwig Wittgenstein, the logical positivists, and all branches of philosophy that have flourished mostly under the effort of analytic philosophers – from logic and philosophy of language, to philosophy of mind and science.

Let us take a closer look at Dussel's attempt to substantiate his ideological-contamination charge against these major figures in the history of Western philosophy. In the case of Aristotle, for example, it is his theory of natural slaves that Dussel invokes as a reason for holding him vulnerable to the ideological-contamination charge. But this theory by no means amounts to one of Aristotle's major works in philosophy. As a result, the charge rests on an ungrounded assumption: namely, that Aristotle's major contribution to philosophy was the theory of natural slaves. This charge in fact rests on a combination of certain so-called informal fallacies. For the reasons outlined so far, it is certainly a straw man. In addition, it appears to be a case of 'beside the point,' since Aristotle's theory of natural slaves supports a criticism, but not the one offered by Dussel. Either way, Dussel's objection cannot be taken seriously.

But what about Dussel's case for the ideological contamination of Aquinas? This objection invokes a theological account attributed to Aquinas according to which the original sin of Adam and Eve is transmitted to offspring by the father, not the mother – a view that Dussel interprets as a sign of *machismo*, which you may recall is the equivalent of male chauvinism in Latin America. Yet once again, Dussel's objection is a straw man, since such a theological explanation can hardly count as Aquinas' major contribution to philosophy. In fact, on the points selected by Dussel, neither Aristotle nor Aquinas were doing *philosophy*. Rather, they were engaged in speculations on issues better left to the social sciences and theology.

And as directed against analytic philosophers, the ideological-contamination charge fairs no better. For the claim that the work of, say, Karl Popper suffers from the alleged problem rests on neither an argument nor any textual evidence from his work. Dussel simply declares that Popper's falsificationism is so contaminated – as he does in the cases of the alleged ideological contamination of logical positivists, Wittgenstein, Kant, and many others.

9.2.3 Other Objections to Liberation Philosophy

9.2.3.1 *Do Western Philosophers Have a Moral Obligation to Support Liberationism?*

Another criticism of Western philosophy that liberationists need to rethink involves Dussel's claim that philosophers from Western Europe and North America also have a liberation duty: namely, to have an attitude of solidarity with liberation philosophy. After all, Dussel holds, these philosophers are morally responsible for the imperialistic policies of their countries toward Latin America: "the philosophers of poor countries," writes Dussel, "will need the solidarity of the philosophers of wealthy countries, who are responsible for what their transnational corporations, their political leaders, and their armies cause outside their country's boundaries" (Dussel 1980/1973: 155). But once again the liberationist claim turns out to be exceedingly weak. For on the one hand, at least since Kant's moral theory, the dictum that 'Ought implies can' has been widely accepted in Western philosophy. If true, it means that any moral agent has a duty to do or believe something only if they can do it or believe it. That is, for an agent to have a duty to do x or believe x, so doing or believing it must be under their voluntary control. Thus a doctor or a firefighter has a duty to save a life only if that life can be saved. No one has a duty to do or believe what is beyond one's voluntary control.

Given that dictum, only those US philosophers who support or have supported imperialistic governments may in some sense be responsible for the actions of those governments. Since Dussel has provided no compelling argument against that dictum, his claim that all US philosophers are responsible for their country's imperialistic policies begs the question against Western normative theory.

9.2.3.2 *Who Are the Oppressed and Can Armchair Thinking Help Liberate Them?*

There is consensus among liberationists that philosophy must stand for the liberation of the Other. Falling within this category, which Dussel also refers to as 'alterity' and 'exteriority,' is anyone or anything that is oppressed, whether an individual or a group, an entire nation, or a continent. Thus among the oppressed are not only the poor, but also women, children, Amerindians, Afro-Latin Americans, African Americans in the United States, the region of Latin America itself, and many more. Here is how Dussel fleshes out this category and assigns the liberation role to all branches of philosophy:

> The oppressed are the poor in political terms (person, class, nation), the woman in the macho sexual system, the child, the youth, the people in the pedagogy of cultural domination. All the problems and topics of logic, philosophy of language, anthropology, and metaphysics acquire new light and new meaning when viewed from the absolute and nevertheless concrete (the opposite of universal) criterion that philosophy is the weapon of the liberation of the oppressed. (Dussel 1980/1973: 154)

Like other liberationists, Dussel too assigns to Latin American philosophers the duty to be the voice of the oppressed. How to discharge this duty is, however, anyone's guess. As far as I can see, a first step in the practice of a philosophy of liberation of the oppressed consists in ridding its philosophizing of two mistakes on the part of Western philosophy: namely, philosophizing from the first-person perspective, and establishing a dichotomy between the subject and the object of philosophizing. A major paradigm of such mistakes is René Descartes' response to skepticism about the external world, in which the famous dictum *cogito ergo sum* (I think, therefore I am) places the 'I' as the subject of thinking, which is its object. By contrast, liberationists wish to make 'the Other' the subject and object of philosophizing, so that the philosopher somehow does the thinking for the oppressed. If so, then the philosophers (i.e., the liberationists themselves) would speak for either the poor, the woman, the child, or the Latin American, as the case might be. Not only does philosophy thus become the thought of alterity but "the concrete other" renders it both situated and absolute at the same time (Dussel 1980/1973).

By contrast, as I interpret Dussel's use of the terms 'universality' and 'totality,' he believes that the thinking of Western philosophy consists of universal generalizations. On his view, philosophers proceeding with this kind of thinking are committed to egocentrism because they are unable to listen to the voice of the Other. Moreover, the egocentric Western thinkers are unable to recognize the Other as *distinct* yet sufficiently *analogous* to themselves. Such distinctiveness and analogy are conditions for being able to empathize with the Other and become its voice, which is the goal of liberationists. On the other hand, Dussel's *método analéctico* (anadialectical or analectical method) avoids egocentrism by using a method that combines analogical and dialectical reasoning.[17] The first type of reasoning allows liberationists to capture their similarity with the Other; the second, their differences. Dussel's followers regard this method as especially fruitful in ethics, where supposedly it "overcomes the thinking of totality that includes the critics of dialectics to become the philosophy of the poor, the philosophy of human liberation ... " (Rueda de Aranguren 2018). However, beyond obscure remarks of this sort, not much is known about how the anadialectical method is supposed to work. Liberationists need to state their positive doctrines clearly in order to show that they are in fact an improvement over those of their Western rivals. How might liberationists contribute to liberation from oppression? After all, make no mistake: liberationists are not experimental philosophers set to collecting empirical data from the oppressed in order to decide what needs to be done. Their aim is becoming the voice of the oppressed just by reasoning alone, and searching for the causes of oppression in Latin America with the "mediation" of theories such as Marxism, dependency theory, and Freudian psychoanalysis. This the liberationists can do from their armchairs, just by thinking. In addition, there is a paternalist attitude behind Dussel's idea that philosophy's role is to become the voice of the Other. This problem has been noted even by liberationists, such as Ofelia Schutte (1993).

9.3 The Upshot

Liberation philosophy grew in close connection with liberation theology, and the two have much in common. Since I have already drawn some conclusions about liberation theology's problem in terms of accommodating the primacy of justice, I need not rehearse here the similar problem that

---

[17] Although this expression literally translates as 'analetical method,' it appears as 'anadialectical method' in standard translations of Dussel, which I follow here.

liberationists in philosophy face. Of course, that objection falls short of amounting to a knockdown argument against liberationism of either kind. But it adds up to a series of problems that render liberationism quite weak. Prominent among them is the implausibility of dependency theory, a pillar of both liberation philosophy and liberation theology. In the Marxist version preferred by liberationists, this theory claims that Latin America's economic system is that of a *dependent capitalism*. As a result, the oppressed peoples of the region are made up not only of the proletariat but of many other groups. Latin America itself is the oppressed when compared with Europe and the United States, according to this theory's explanation of development in terms of the center/periphery dichotomy outlined above.

But there are strong reasons to think that is at least implausible and probably false. As noted by Michael Novak (1984), dependency theory's reliance on the equations 'center = producer of industrialized goods' and 'periphery = producer of food and raw materials' face counterexamples from industrial countries such as the United States and Canada, whose economies greatly rely on exporting food and raw materials, and developed economies such as Japan and Taiwan that were underdeveloped in the 1950s.[18] Although the soundness of these counterexamples is of course a matter for the experts to decide, at the very least they indicate the controversial character of dependency theory. Furthermore, the theory places all the responsibility for the underdevelopment of Latin America elsewhere, in the United States and Europe. If taken seriously, this claim entails that Latin Americans need not engage in a self-critical reflection on the causes of widespread poverty and stagnation in their naturally rich countries. Most crucially, by now the proponents of dependency theory can test its central hypotheses by examining the economic results of more than sixty years of socialist government in Cuba – as well as the several years of "anti-dependency" administrations in Argentina, Bolivia, Brazil, Ecuador,

---

[18] In his 1984 article, Novak offers counterexamples of two kinds against dependency theory. First, today "countries such as Canada and the United States have become far larger exporters of raw materials – grain, lumber, coal – than all of Latin America put together." Second, "such countries as Taiwan, Japan and South Korea of the East Asia rim, are far poorer in natural resources than Latin America, yet have in recent years been far more successful in building highly intelligent and dynamic free economies, overcoming poverty worse in 1945 than that of Latin America."

and Venezuela by the turn of the twenty-first century. An interesting case in point is the administration of Daniel Ortega in Nicaragua, to whom Dussel (1980/1973: 156) accords the status of paradigm leader of liberation. Ortega's return to power in 2006 was marked by unrest, brutal repression of the Nicaraguan people, and extremely conservative positions on matters of practical ethics and legislation such as abortion. Dependency theorists and their liberationist supporters need also account for the recurrent allegations of corruption and authoritarianism facing other left-leaning Latin American administrations.

In addition to these problems inherited from their appeal to dependency theory, liberation philosophers face a host of problems of their own. For one thing, they systematically offer misleading and often false reconstructions of theories and events. I have pointed out several strawman arguments that Dussel offered against major figures of Western philosophy. But even the liberationists' narratives about facts concerning the emergence of their own doctrines are affected by the problem of relying on an inflated historical account of the origins of liberation philosophy. Ofelia Schutte (1993: 176), for example, wrote that liberationism was "induced by the 'heterogeneous' political forces of Peronism" in Argentina, leaving us completely in the dark about what 'induced' is supposed to mean here. Her dates also do not add up, for she contends that the Argentine right-wing forces immediately saw the philosophy of liberation movement as a threat and mobilized paramilitary groups with the blessing of Isabel Perón to try to eradicate them. The repression against liberationists continued with the military *coup d'état* of 1976. However, as she recognizes, liberationism originated in an earlier historical context, with the appearance of articles in *Stromata*, a Jesuit journal published in 1970 and 1972, and in *Nuevo mundo*, a Franciscan journal, published in 1973. The third administration of Juan Domingo Perón started that year.[19]

---

[19] Schutte (1993: 176) also makes the puzzling suggestion that, in part due to the political pressures of the dictatorship period, after 1983 with the return to democracy in Argentina philosophy of liberation splintered into factions, one under the lead of Dussel and Ardiles (both identified as more hardline and ideological), another under the lead of Roig and Cerutti Guldberg (both identified as offering "a critical perspective on liberation").

Moreover, there is often the problem of figuring out what exactly the liberationists are saying, since their writings use so much Marxist, neo-Hegelian, Heideggerian, and postmodern jargonizing that it is literally impossible to know what their claims actually mean. Among the original liberationists, Dussel stands out as a prime offender on this score.[20] Even Schutte, a Dussel disciple whose prose is almost equally mind-numbing when she waxes philosophical, notices this problem in Dussel. At the end of the day, once the readers have made their way through the text, Dussel's writings have little to offer except for Marxist-sounding talk of oppression, ideological contamination, and Latin American Christian skepticism about the value of science and 'modernity' – all phenomena he associates with US and European cultural and economic hegemony. Finally, here is a strong ad hominem argument facing Dussel: in his most important work from the early period, *Para una ética de la liberación latinoamericana* (Towards an Ethic of Latin American Liberation), after criticizing *machismo*, Dussel at the same time underlines the traditional duty of Catholic nuns to remain celibate, to assert the independence of their own sexually from men's sexuality, and therefore be better positioned to reject *machismo* and devote themselves to the liberation of the oppressed. In so saying, he thus in fact sides with the Vatican on the controversy over the celibacy of nuns. Who, precisely, is being liberated here?

9.4   Suggested Readings

Arroyo Luna, Alejandro F. and Orlando Lima Rocha. 2013. *Filosofía en América Latina* (website). August 12. http://filosamericalatina.blogspot.com/

An online compilation of links to primary sources by liberationists and others. Features classic texts by a wide range of thinkers, from Alberdi, Frondizi, and Zea to Dussel, Scannone, Kusch, and many others. The unifying topic is whether there is an original Latin American philosophy.

---

[20] In Dussel's work, obscure and unsubstantial passages are not difficult to find. For instance, in explaining how the so-called anadialectical method is supposed to work, Dussel cryptically writes: "In the final analysis, it can be affirmed that the analectic moment of dialectics is founded on the absolute anteriority of exteriority over totality, even to affirming the priority of the Absolute Other as creative origin over creation as a work, as a finite and therefore perfectible totality" (1980/1973: 156).

Boff, Leonardo. 1995."Science, Technology, Power, and Liberation Theology," pp. 123–130 in *Ecology and Liberation: A New Paradigm*. Maryknoll, NY: Orbis.

A liberationist critique of technology consistent with Rodó's rejection of some characteristic North American values and of the vindication of the power of science that is often associated with those values. It shows skepticism about the uses to which science is put by the industrialized nations of the northern hemisphere. It laments that, where once science was practiced by individual scientists, working in their own laboratories, it has now become too complex and expensive to be pursued outside developed countries; and the uses to which it is put then reflect those countries' values.

Cerutti Guldberg, Horacio.1998. "Liberation Philosophy," in E. Craig, ed., *Routledge Encyclopedia of Philosophy*. London: Routledge. www.rep.routledge.com/article/ ZA011.

Outline of liberation philosophy, focused on its history since its first appearance in Argentina in the early 1970s. Breaks down the chief factors that brought it to the fore, including liberationists' concerns about the socioeconomic problems facing Latin America at that time, as well as examining the development of a liberation theology, and the development of a Marxist as well as a dependency-theory diagnosis and prognosis for the region.

Cerutti Guldberg, Horacio. 1983. *Filosofía de la liberación latinoamericana*. Mexico City: Fondo de Cultura Económica, available online at https://enriquedussel.com/ txt/Textos_200_Obras/Filosofos_Mexico/Filosofia_liberacion-Horacio_Cerutti .PDF

A longer outline of liberation philosophy. Includes chapters on each of the factors that propelled it, together with analyses of the different tendencies within the movement and what they had to say about the quality of Latin American philosophy. In addition, it features a foundational text, the "Salta Manifesto" of 1974.

Devés Valdés, Eduardo. 2000. "Antecedentes del proyecto modernizador cepalino," in *Del Ariel de Rodó a la CEPAL (1900–1950)*. Buenos Aires: Biblos, pp. 287–304.

Informative account of the history of the Comisión Económica para América Latina (CEPAL), which was created by the United Nations in 1947. Devés Valdés looks closely at the developmentalism of Prebisch and others, which he takes to have two pillars, one vindicating the importance of industrialization, the other encouraging states to take measures conducive to the development of the region. He argues that these claims had antecedents in the political thought of the early twentieth century.

Dussel, Enrique. 1978. *Ethics and the Theology of Liberation.* Maryknoll, NY: Orbis.

A paradigm of Dussel's version of liberation theology. Amounts to a good example of his critique of Western philosophy, including the charge that the latter suffers from ideological contamination, as well as his so-called anadialectical method and obscure style of writing philosophy.

Dussel, Enrique. 1996. "Note on Liberation Theology," pp. 275–286 in Bethell (1996).

Account of the history of liberation theology which also looks at the context within the Catholic Church of Latin America that made the movement possible.

Garrard-Burnett, Virginia, Paul Freston, and Stephen C. Dove, eds. 2016. *The Cambridge History of Religions in Latin America.* New York: Cambridge University Press.

A comprehensive collection of forty-nine essays on the different religions and religious practices of Latin America, from the pre-Columbian period to the present. Of particular interest for liberation theology are the essays on the history of Catholicism in the region.

Gutiérrez, Gustavo. 1973/1971. *A Theology of Liberation.* Maryknoll, NY: Orbis (references to excerpts pp. 93–106 in Márquez 2008).

A classic of liberation theology that is discussed in this chapter.

Haight, Roger. 1998. "Liberation Theology," in E. Craig, ed., *Routledge Encyclopedia of Philosophy.* London: Routledge. www.rep.routledge.com/articles/thematic/liberation-theology/v-1 A standard, sympathetic account of the emergence of liberation theology as a conjunction of phenomena in the early 1960s. Among these were: (i) the poverty and violence afflicting many people in Latin America, and (ii) the interpretation of Christian theology by priests who were sympathetic to those affected by such conditions. Absent in this outline is any criticism of liberation theology.

Love, Joseph L. 1996. "Economic Ideas and Ideologies in Latin America since 1930," pp. 207–274 in Bethell (1996).

Outlines dependency theory – especially as it was formulated early on by Raúl Prebisch – which turns out to be a developmentalist approach to the global economic disparity between countries at the center and those at the periphery. Besides explaining such disparities by invoking an international division of labor that is favorable only to the countries of the center, it advocates economic protectionism without committing itself to a socialist economic system.

Novak, Michael. 1984. "The Case Against Liberation Theology," *The New York Times Magazine*, October 21. www.nytimes.com/1984/10/21/magazine/the-case-against-liberation-theology.html

Criticizes liberation theology's reliance on Marxism and dependency theory, arguing that the incorporation of Marxism into Catholicism would legitimize Marxism. The author fears the political consequences of an alliance between Marxism and Catholicism, "two powerful symbolic forces," especially because of the large number of Catholics in the world. A more extensive critique of liberation theology from the perspective of mainstream Catholics can be found in Novak (1986).

Schutte, Ofelia. 1993. *Cultural Identity and Social Liberation in Latin American Thought*. Albany, NY: State University of New York Press.

Though of uneven quality, this work offers an outline of liberation philosophy from someone within the movement. Schutte traces it to its Argentinian origins in the 1970s, highlights the philosophical differences among its major proponents, and makes an effort to produce a critical introduction to it. She classifies the movement's internal divisions according to different parameters, including whether a proponent's general philosophical framework is Heideggerian (Dussel, Ardiles) or Hegelian (Roig, Cerutti Guldberg). If Schutte is right, her classification contradicts the liberationists' claim to a radical departure from Western philosophy.

Torres, Camilo. 2016. *Camilo Torres Restrepo, profeta de la liberación: antología (teológica) política*, eds. Lorena López Guzmán and Nicolás Armando Herrera Farfán. Buenos Aires: Editorial El Colectivo.

Offers a representative selection of writings by one of the founders of liberation theology, a Colombian Catholic priest and professor who eventually joined the guerrilla movement known as the National Liberation Army and was killed in his first engagement under fire on the battlefield.

Topics range from education, feminism, and religion in Colombia to democracy and social justice in Latin America. The editors' substantial introductions provide significant information about Torres's attempt to combine Marxism and Catholicism as well as his association with early liberation theology.

10 Skepticism and Anti-Skepticism About Latin American Philosophy

This chapter presents a meta-philosophical debate about the nature and quality of Latin American philosophy. The debate has today almost the same urgency it had when it first arose in the 1950s. It has drawn, and continues to draw to it, philosophers of many different theoretical persuasions who argue for a skeptical or an anti-skeptical position.[1] The chief arguments on offer on both sides of this debate are the focus in what follows. But first, I have something to say about a related meta-philosophical question: What is Latin American philosophy?

10.1 Latin American Philosophy, Latino Philosophy, and Hispanic Philosophy

The American Philosophical Association (APA) offers an annual essay competition in *Latin American* philosophy but publishes a newsletter on *Hispanic/Latino* issues in philosophy and has a regular Committee on *Hispanics*. This professional organization appears to use the ethnic-group terms 'Latin American,' 'Latino,' and 'Hispanic' as if they had roughly the same meaning and denotation. In doing so, the APA is following common practice in the popular and academic discourse of many Americans. But, as we will see, what exactly these terms mean and denote when applied to philosophical inquiry has often been unclear.

Let us first consider 'Hispanic philosophy,' once characterized by Jorge Gracia in terms of "the philosophy developed in the Iberian peninsula, the Iberian colonies in the New World, and the countries that those colonies

---

[1] See for instance Cruz Revueltas (2003); Hurtado (2006, 2007, 2010); Pereda (2006); Nuccetelli (2017/2013, 2017); Rabossi (2003, 2008); and the 2014 special issue of the *Inter-American Journal of Philosophy* edited by Andrea J. Pitts and Adriana Novoa.

eventually came to form" (1993: 475). Gracia was not alone in his proposal since some others too have identified Hispanic philosophy by appeal to a hybrid historical-cum-geopolitical criterion. For example, Jaime Nubiola (1998: 32) takes Hispanic philosophy to comprise "all the philosophical thinking that has been developed over the last few hundred years in Spain and Portugal, the Spanish colonies of the New World, and the countries which grew from them." Since Nubiola includes Portugal in the list, he needs to add at least its major colony in America, Brazil. Thus amended, his conception of Hispanic philosophy is extensionally equivalent to Gracia's. But without a further linguistic component to exclude from the category of Hispanic philosophy any philosophical inquiry from Texas or California (states that occupy lands that once belonged to Spain) the resulting characterization is inaccurate. Some accuracy can be gained by the following Gracia/Nubiola-improved characterizations:

Hispanic philosophy = The philosophy developed in Spain, Portugal, and what today are the officially Spanish- and Portuguese-speaking nations of the Americas, from the time they were under Iberian rule to the present.

Spanish American philosophy = The philosophy produced in either Spain or in the regions of America today occupied by nations whose official language is Spanish.

Latin American philosophy = The philosophy produced in the regions of America today occupied by nations whose official language is Spanish.[2]

These categories are consistent with the existence of related disciplines with a narrower scope such as Spanish philosophy, Brazilian philosophy, Puerto Rican philosophy, and so on. Initially, the classification works nicely: Chilean philosophy comes out as a subfield of Spanish philosophy, which in turn is a subfield of Hispanic philosophy and so on. But a problem soon appears, since it yields that Brazilian philosophy is a type of Hispanic philosophy, something which is doubtful.

   Yet since all definitions are likely to face counterexamples, we can retain the above criteria and add to them a criterion for:

---

[2] Corresponding to these definitions respectively are the Spanish labels used – for instance, Garrido et al. (2009) and Gómez-Martínez (1997–2015): *filosofía hispana* or *hispánica*, *filosofía hispanoamericana*, and *filosofía latinoamericana* or *iberoamericana*.

Latino philosophy – The philosophy produced by either people from the Iberian Peninsula and Latin America in the United States, or their descendants in the United States.

However, there are problems facing this definition. First, it is controversial that *US residents* from Spain, Portugal, or Brazil who engage in philosophical reflection are thereby engaging in Latino philosophy. Second, it is doubtful that such residents in the United States generally identify themselves as Latinos. Third, a resident of the United States who has Iberian or Latin American ancestry and engages in Latino philosophy might move to, say, the UK. Do we want to say that this person ceases to do Latino philosophy just because of the relocation? To avoid such counterexamples, let us redefine this kind of philosophy as follows:

Latino philosophy = The philosophy produced by anyone to whom the term 'Latino' definitely applies.

Note that 'Latino' is an ethnic-group term that definitely applies to people who reside in the United States and are from the mainly Spanish-speaking nations of Latin America by birth or ancestry.[3] With this construal of 'Latino' in mind, it becomes clear that our new definition of Latino philosophy also fails for at least two reasons. First, some Latinos practice mainstream continental or analytic philosophy on general issues that have little or nothing to do with their ethnic identity. Second, some practitioners of Latino philosophy might not be Latinos by ethnicity. Similar problems can arise for the attempt to define 'Latin American philosophy' and 'Hispanic philosophy' along Gracia/Nubiola-inspired criteria, which take into account a combination of factors such as language, geopolitics, and ethnicity. What are we to do?

[3] But the exact reference of 'Latino' is still under negotiation. While there is agreement that people who live in the United States and are from the mostly Spanish-speaking nations of Latin America definitely count as Latinos, not all count people from Brazil. Among those who do count them are Corlett (2007), Tammelleo (2011), and Alcoff (2005) – but Alcoff also includes under the denotation of the term all the non-US residents of Latin America. On the other hand, Gracia (2008) is unclear about whether Latinos on his view include US residents who are from Portugal and Spain (by birth or ancestry. Stavans (2000) includes only US residents who are from the Spanish-speaking world; yet this means that he classifies within the group people who are Spanish-born and who live in the United States – something that Corlett rejects on justice grounds because that would make people who are Spanish-born eligible for affirmative action.

We need a better conception of this family of philosophical inquiries, one that avoids both including works ordinarily excluded from them and excluding works ordinarily included. That is, we need a conception that neither excludes the work of philosophers who have no Iberian or Latin American ancestry but work in Latin American philosophy;[4] nor includes works by Latinos which fall exclusively within the scope of some general areas of philosophy such as metaphysics or philosophy of science (e.g., the works of David Sosa and Ulises Moulines). In addition, we should avoid a conception that is too broad in that it counts as Latin American philosophy the works of philosophers in Latin America that fall exclusively within general areas of philosophy.

The latter restriction suggests that there must be a content- or method-related element in any adequate conception of what Latin American and Latino philosophy are – something along the lines of this principle:

> To qualify as Latin American philosophy, a philosophical theory, argument, or problem must bear some relation in content or method to Latin America.

This principle seems to be supported by analogy since, for example, to qualify as a theory of practical ethics, a philosophical theory must have something to do with moral conduct, value, or virtue. Any theory relevant to *none* of these notions would simply fail to qualify. If this is right, then some works by philosophers of Latin American descent may not qualify as Latin American philosophy in any interesting sense, while some works by philosophers of no such descent may qualify.

10.2   Skepticism About Latin American Philosophy

10.2.1   The Origin of Academic Philosophy in Latin America

Philosophy of course exists in Latin America and meets current Western standards such as having a proper representation in educational systems, learned societies, associations, journals, presses, and so on. But when did it begin? If one condition for qualifying as philosophy is that it meets those

---

[4] For instance, Lawrence Blum's (2009) analysis of some philosophical theories on Latino racial and ethnic identity, James Sterba's (1996) moral reflection on Amerindians and the Spanish Conquest, and William Talbot's (2005) discussion of the moral evolution of Bartolomé de las Casas.

current Western standards, then it began in the early twentieth century. After all, there is consensus that it was not until then that philosophy in Latin America became an academic discipline, independent of the sciences and theology (Romero 1943, 1944; Frondizi 1949; Miró Quesada 1974, 1976; Rabossi 2008). Before that, Latin American philosophy depended on other disciplines, most commonly, theology, literature, politics, science, and education.

But if we do not require the meeting of current Western standards in order for it to qualify as philosophy, then Latin American philosophy began in the sixteenth century with the introduction of Scholasticism by Iberian educators and theologians.[5] Yet since we can set even broader or narrower conditions for demarcating our area, it is plausible to say that under some such conditions, Latin American philosophy has colonial or even pre-Colombian origins, while under other conditions it has contemporary origins.

However, there is no question that between the 1910s and the 1940s, a generation of philosophers known as the *fundadores* or *forjadores* (founders) devoted themselves to the practice of philosophy for its own sake and successfully turned it into an autonomous field of inquiry. Philosophy in Latin America then gained academic recognition and began to meet what today are current standards for academic disciplines. As a result, by the 1930s and 1940s it had reached what long-time resident of Argentina, philosopher Francisco Romero (Spanish-born, 1891–1962) called *normalidad* ('normalcy' or 'maturity').[6] By the 1950s, it was no longer an open question whether there was philosophy *in* Latin America. But was it any good? That is the question that led many to skepticism about Latin American philosophy.

10.2.2   Early Skeptical Challenges: Cannabrava and Frondizi

For the skeptics of concern here, the problem facing Latin American philosophy concerns its quality.[7] Since its early formulations in the mid-

---

[5] Works that claim a sixteenth-century origin for Latin American philosophy include Beuchot (1996), Hurtado (2007), and Nuccetelli (2002); while defending its pre-Columbian origins are León-Portilla (1963) and Maffie (2009, 2013), among other works.

[6] See Romero (1943 and 1944).

[7] Other skeptics are universalists who question the very idea of a *Latin American* epistemology or a *Peruvian* metaphysics, because these categories make no sense for these

twentieth century, the problem has been that for the most part, philosophy as practiced in Latin America has appeared to be of low quality. Among the first to formulate this challenge were Euryalo Cannabrava (Brazilian, 1906–1979) and Risieri Frondizi (Argentine, 1910–1985). Cannabrava (1949) charged that Brazilian and by extension Latin American philosophy rest on sophistry and a kind of literary method of reasoning. If this is so, it is completely unlike North American philosophy.[8] Consistent with this assessment is Cannabrava's explanation of the attractiveness of continental philosophy to Latin American philosophers, which at the time meant mostly contemporary offshoots of German idealism, including phenomenology and existentialism. He believed that Latin American philosophers were attracted to these philosophical traditions precisely because of their "lack of intelligibility," and their "metaphysical abuses and frequent violation of the rules of correct thinking." Latin American philosophy was at its worst when addressing issues in philosophy of science in the writings of, for example, Mexican anti-positivist Antonio Caso (1883–1946), who lacked any "real acquaintance with ... [science's] development or technique" (Cannabrava 1949: 114–117).

Evidently, Cannabrava intends to do more than merely describe some deficiencies of Latin American philosophy. He claims that it is of low quality and attempts to explain why by offering a genealogical account based on factors concerning the discipline's origins and evolution. On this account, our discipline developed in connection with other disciplines that do not pursue rigorous reasoning and linguistic clarity, such as literature and politics. He contrasts this history with the history of analytic philosophy in the English-speaking world, a style of philosophy that developed in close relation to the formal and empirical sciences.

In 1949, Frondizi also argued that there was reason to doubt the quality of philosophy in Latin America. On his view, only 10 percent of philosophy in Latin America was at the time original. Being familiar with philosophical

---

skeptics unless they are understood as epistemology *in* Latin America or a metaphysics *in* Peru. I am not concerned with skepticism of their kind here.

[8] The deficiencies that Cannabrava claimed for Latin American philosophy led him to conclude that "[i]n Latin America we do not have philosophers like Morris Cohen, Victor Lenze, Ernest Nagel, and F. S. C. Northrop, who have studied the sources of science and followed closely its development ..." (1949: 117).

publications in the region, he had factual evidence for his skeptical claim, which may be called 'originalism,' since it sets as a necessary condition for Latin American philosophy to have an acceptable quality that it have some novel elements. Unlike Cannabrava's genealogical account, Frondizi's originalism does not attempt to explain the deficiency he has found in Latin American philosophy. But Frondizi is not alone in drawing skeptical conclusions from evidence pointing to the lack of originality in the academic philosophy of Latin America: as we will see next, originalism has drawn some Marxists toward skeptical conclusions too.

10.2.3   The Marxist Challenge: Mariátegui, Coutinho, and Salazar Bondy

In 1925, the Peruvian thinker José Carlos Mariátegui expressed a similarly bleak view concerning the lack of originality in Latin American thought. He wrote:

> All the thinkers of our America have been educated in European schools. The spirit of the race is not felt in their work. The continent's intellectual production lacks its distinguishing traits. It does not have an original profile. Hispanic-American thought is generally only a rhapsody composed from the motifs and elements of European thought. To prove this, one need only review the work of the highest representatives of the Indo-Iberian intellect. (Mariátegui 1925: 113, my translation)

Adding to some Marxist assumptions his own belief about the cultural and economic dependence of Latin America, Mariátegui argued that for the region to develop any original philosophical thought it must first gain full independence. Other Marxist philosophers echoed Mariátegui's argument. For example, Afranio Coutinho (Brazilian, 1911–2000) observed that in the case of his native country Brazil and, by extension Latin America, there is a "colonial mentality" that precludes the development of original philosophical thought. This unfortunate situation, he predicted, would persist until Latin America had won "complete independence – economic, and cultural – from the imperialistic powers" (Coutinho 1943: 187–188). Salazar Bondy gave similar arguments in his debate with Leopoldo Zea about the nature and quality of philosophy in Latin America (more on this later). He held that as a result of pervasive colonialism, philosophy in this region has amounted to "a thought of the upper class or of a refined oligarchical elite, when it has not corresponded openly to waves of foreign economic and political influence. In all these cases underdevelopment and domination are influential" (1968: 241).[9]

But the Marxists need to prove that dependence of the kinds they have in mind precludes the development of original philosophy. For it seems false that political, cultural, and economic dependence always determine the absence of originality in philosophy. A prime counterexample comes from the philosophical doctrines concerning Latin America that were offered by Las Casas and Vitoria (discussed in Chapter 1), which were developed under conditions of extreme colonial dependence yet had the properties of originality, authenticity, and peculiarity – all of which are defined in the next section.[10]

10.2.4   Some Present-Day Analytic Challenges: Pereda, Ezcurdia, Hurtado, and Rabossi

Skeptics about Latin American philosophy often explain the absence of certain virtues in the discipline by invoking its practitioners' vices. One of the most elaborate versions of this charge is made by present-day Mexican philosopher Carlos Pereda (Uruguayan-born, 1944–) who points to several vices of these philosophers, all of which contribute to their general vice of "arrogant reasoning." Given Pereda's 2006 account, they have these vices whether their conception of philosophy is what I call 'distinctivist' or 'universalist' – where:

---

[9] Both camps in that debate had later followers among the liberationists. For example, Salazar Bondy's position had a follower in Arturo Roig (1981), who declared the work of founder Alejandro Deustua (Peruvian, 1849–1945) a prime example of the imitative attitude denounced by Salazar. And Zea's position has a follower in Ofelia Schutte who, as we saw in Chapter 2, claimed that Latin America's feminism would automatically exhibit a Latin American perspective.

[10] I have argued elsewhere that it is the so-called philosophical *pensadores* (thinkers) who have made the most original contributions in the history of Latin American philosophy. I will have more to say about this in my concluding remarks, but see also Nuccetelli (2018).

Distinctivism is the doctrine that philosophy can be peculiar to regions, persons, groups, or cultures.

Universalism denies distinctivism, holding that all philosophy is universal.

On Pereda's account, universalists are guilty of arrogant reasoning because of their "subaltern fervor" and "craving for novelty," and distinctivists because of their "nationalist enthusiasm." Either way, arrogant reason causes the "invisibility" (i.e., insularity) of Latin American philosophy, a dual problem that can be defined in this way:

External invisibility: Philosophers outside Latin America generally ignore the work of philosophers of this region.

Internal invisibility: Philosophers inside Latin America generally ignore each other's work.

On this account, philosophers in Latin America have a snobbish attitude toward each other. They are mostly devoted to importing philosophical theories from major centers of Western philosophy and following the latest philosophical fad, so that they have neither interest in nor time to establish a philosophical dialogue among themselves, even with colleagues working on the same theory or historical period. Although Pereda provides only anecdotal evidence for these claims, it is true that in general Latin American philosophers scarcely refer to their peers in their work.[11] So Pereda seems right in that there is an internal invisibility problem facing this branch of philosophy. About the external invisibility problem, Pereda also seems right since references to the works by Latin American philosophers rarely appear in major journals and books by European and US philosophers. In light of this evidence, Pereda's skeptical conclusion appears justified.

Other contemporary skeptics agree with Pereda. For example, Mexican philosopher Maite Ezcurdia (1966–2018) contends that the invisibility problems facing Latin American philosophers arise because of their poor

---

[11] Supporting Pereda's contentions is, for example, the monumental *Enciclopedia iberoamericana de filosofía* (Iberoamerican Encyclopedia of Philosophy), whose first volume appeared in Spain in 1987 (Robles Carcedo 1987). The essays in most of its volumes make little reference to works of Spanish and Latin American philosophers.

performance at certain kinds of originality that are desirable in philosophical work anywhere, and of which there are four: interpretative, argumentative, problem-making, and problem-solving originality. On her 2003 diagnosis, Latin American philosophers do have interpretative originality, as shown by the fact that on average they have been successful at interpreting the central works of Western philosophy. But they have done poorly at the other three kinds of originality, a fact that results in the invisibility problems raised by Pereda.

Although Ezcurdia's analysis of the types of originality that matter in a philosophical theory generally is insightful, there are some properties nearby that matter too. They include being authentic, peculiar, and tradition-generating. In 1968, Augusto Salazar Bondy of Peru offered a fine analysis of some of these properties in an influential book completely devoted to defending skepticism about Latin American philosophy against perspectivism, an opposite view considered below. As I interpret Salazar Bondy's subtle analysis of the properties most relevant to this debate, he equated originality with being creative or novel, authenticity with being genuine or non-spurious, and peculiarity with being autochthonous in the sense of having a relation to a certain region or country. Given these definitions, a philosophical work may be peculiar (e.g., if it is the product of a Latin American author) without being original (e.g., if it is not creative) or authentic (e.g., if it rehearses points made by others); a genuine work may lack originality and peculiarity, and so on. This picture might benefit from some adjustments, but it is good enough for our present purposes.

In 2007, Mexican philosopher Guillermo Hurtado (b. 1962) added to this list the property of originating a tradition or community of philosophical dialog. Since that is a very scarce property in Mexican and, more broadly, Latin American philosophy, he joined the skeptical camp (2006: 206 ff.; 2007: 24 ff.). Simplifying a great deal, his skeptical story has it that by adopting a "modernizing model" or approach to philosophy, many philosophers in Latin America have developed bad traits of intellectual character. These include a proclivity to form small groups and spend most of their time trying to learn some foreign philosophical doctrine, cite only foreign philosophers without paying much attention to regional peers, and adopt the latest philosophical theory of a major Western center quickly and thoughtlessly whenever they consider it fashionable. At the end of the day, in Latin American philosophy "each modernizing movement [gets] lost for the upcoming movement" (Hurtado 2006: 206), and there are neither traditions nor stable communities of philosophical dialogue. "But the foreign philosophers," observes Hurtado, "even those who visit our countries to deliver talks, very rarely quote us in their work. There is therefore no genuine dialogue . . ." (2006: 205).

Finally, Argentinean Eduardo Rabossi (1930–2005) joined the skeptical camp by making some remarks consistent with all of the above. Oddly enough for an analytic philosopher he nonetheless adopted the center/periphery distinction of dependency theorists and liberationists to charge that Latin American philosophers are periphery thinkers who have the self-image and attitudes of a *guacho* (in Argentinian slang, the word for anyone who is both an orphan and street urchin). These *guacho* philosophers of Latin America have systematically refused to acknowledge their own "philosophical parents," or to learn about them at all. As Rabossi puts it, the *guacho* "doesn't take them into account, he doesn't read them, he is not even interested in criticizing their defects or limitations; for him, his own philosophical past doesn't exist" (2008: 103, my translation).

If Rabossi is right, Latin American philosophers lack awareness of their own philosophical past and are unwilling to establish a dialogue with their local peers. It might not be surprising then if, as skeptics contend, their work is of low quality. But as we will see next, skepticism about Latin American philosophy has not gone without a number of replies.

10.3 Anti-Skepticism About Latin American Philosophy

Those who reject the skeptical challenges to Latin American philosophy have defended a number of different positions about what makes this area of philosophy distinct from other areas. In this section, I group their views under the general label 'distinctivism' and examine three varieties of it. First, I look closely at the perspectivism that Zea outlined in his debate with Salazar Bondy. Then I turn to Gracia's ethnic conception of Latino philosophy, and finally I outline my own view of Latin American philosophy as a type of applied philosophy. For the reasons discussed next, I argue that the latter view is not only defensible but scores better than the other two alternatives.

10.3.1   Perspectivism

We may label as 'perspectivism' the reply of Leopoldo Zea (Mexican, 1912–2004) to the skepticism about Latin American philosophy of Salazar Bondy. On Zea's view, peculiarity confers on Latin American philosophy all it might need to exist as a discipline with an acceptable quality. In fact, it already has peculiarity because its practitioners mostly come from Latin America, so they are bound to regard the standard problems of philosophy from a Latin American perspective. As a result, it does not matter that they imitate philosophers from other regions of the world: originality and authenticity will develop *por añadidura* ('as an addition'). Accordingly, Zea writes,

> The abstract issues [of philosophy] will have to be seen from the Latin American man's own circumstance. Each man will see in such issues what is closest to his own circumstance. He will look at these issues from the standpoint of his own interests, and those interests will be determined by his way of life, his abilities and inabilities, in a word, by his own circumstance. In the case of Latin America, his contribution to the philosophy of such issues will be permeated by the Latin American circumstance. Hence, when we [Latin Americans] address abstract issues, we shall formulate them as issues of our own. Even though being, God, etc., are issues appropriate for every man, the solution to them will be given from a Latin American standpoint. (Zea 1974/1943: 226)

Note that, according to this perspectivism, no philosophical work from a Latin American philosopher can fail to be peculiar, simply because of the geo-cultural origin of its writer. It would necessarily show some features of the circumstance of its creation. Furthermore, to avoid missing the skeptics' point, peculiarity must entail originality and authenticity because Latin American philosophy should have at least these three properties that figure in the skeptical challenge. Zea believes that he can dismiss the skeptical worries considered above by appeal to the *context of creation* of a given philosophical work.

Yet there is no good reason for thinking that peculiarity entails either originality or authenticity. After all, as defined above, 'peculiarity' seems more descriptive as a concept than 'originality' and 'authenticity,' which have strong evaluative components. It is simply false that from the peculiarity of Latin American philosophy, its being either original or authentic would invariably follow.[12] Perspectivism can only maintain that these other properties *might* come. It follows that perspectivism falls short of meeting the challenge of those skeptical of Latin American philosophy.

10.3.2   Latin American Philosophy as Ethnic Philosophy

If Jorge Gracia (Cuban American, b. 1942) is on the right track, the areas of philosophy of concern here make up a Latino philosophy which is a type of 'ethnic' philosophy. Unlike nonethnic philosophies, the ethnic ones have an open subject matter because in each case it is a relevant ethnos or group of people who decides what to include in it (Gracia 2008: 142–144). Thus if the Latino ethnos decides to include some major philosophical traditions of the West, then those traditions too would be part of Latin American philosophy, to which Gracia has previously referred as 'Hispanic philosophy,' but now calls 'Latino philosophy.'

Gracia thinks that this new conception avoids regarding any single property (language, geographical location, place of birth, etc.) as necessary and sufficient for inclusion in Latino philosophy. But he is wrong about this, since according to his proposal, it is the property of being included in the philosophy in question by the Latino people that is necessary and sufficient for any intellectual product (a tradition, a theory, an argument) to belong to Latino philosophy. In addition, if the Latino people decide that, say, David Sosa's work in philosophy of language or mind counts as Latino philosophy, that would make it belong to this type of philosophy. These results suggest that Gracia's ethnic conception of Latin American philosophy is a kind of meta-philosophical relativism according to which what counts as philosophy in certain areas is a matter of group opinion. Moreover, since Latinos themselves are of many different philosophical persuasions, we can hardly expect that they might one day converge on a list of what should count as their ethnic philosophy.

Another problem facing the ethnic-philosophy proposal resides in the line it draws between universally construed branches of philosophy

---

[12] On my view (2002, 2016), if perspectivism is true, there must be something Greek in Aristotle's theory of the syllogism, something German in Kant's normative theory, British in Mill's utilitarianism, and so on. Since such claims are at the very least open to doubt, it follows that perspectivism is false.

(metaphysics, epistemology, ethics, and the like) on the one hand, and a series of ethnically construed branches on the other (Latin American philosophy, African philosophy, Chinese philosophy, etc.). On Gracia's proposal, only on the latter construals of philosophy do the standards for being a philosophical work of a certain kind vary according to the opinion of the relevant ethnic groups. As I interpret Renzo Llorente's critique of that proposal, he objects that it is incompatible with the universalist conception of philosophy that Gracia himself wishes to keep for the standard areas of philosophy. Given that conception, Llorente (2013: 75) writes, "we should either reject Gracia's view that the ethnos enjoys a privileged position in determining what artifacts count as ethnic philosophy or else opt for a word other than philosophy to designate the corpus of works that are judged by the ethnos as forming a part of its philosophy,"

Nevertheless, these problems have not made it impossible for some Latino philosophers to endorse Gracia's ethnic-philosophy approach, in which they see some practical advantages. José Antonio Orosco (2016: 26) for example takes the approach to be friendly to the task that he considers fitting to Latino philosophers: namely, developing the philosophical perspective of their own ethnos, whether it be a Mexican ethnos, a Cuban ethnos, or whatever. This task in turn requires reflection on "questions about [Latino] identity, power, and citizenship in the United States." But, thus interpreted, Gracia's proposal opens the door to a reductionist view of Latin American and Latino philosophy according to which these disciplines should focus exclusively on matters of applied social and political philosophy. Although, as I have shown throughout this book, these matters have traditionally attracted considerable interest within the discipline –triggering many developments in the history of Latin American philosophy – philosophical inquiry is an inherently open-minded set of inquiries that are worth undertaking for their own sake because they take us closer to the truth. If the sole value of Latin American philosophy turns out instead to be only that of a mere means for social change, its inquiries would on my view cease to be philosophical and become ideological.[13]

---

[13] It is not uncommon for the socialists and liberationists of Latin America to assign to philosophy the sole role of helping advance the struggle against colonialism. But is the region today still in need of liberation from that historical evil? On my view, the answer depends on very complex historical, political, and socioeconomic matters

After all, philosophers commonly lack the knowledge necessary to develop scientifically acceptable theories of social change, and are thus susceptible to making unsupported empirical claims that can have negative consequences for Latin American philosophy, a discipline that is sometimes suspected of relying on armchair sociology and political science.[14] In connection with this criticism, there is another argument against the ethnic-philosophy view: it could have bad consequences for Latin American philosophy, since it might contribute to perpetuating those biases that undermine its standing in the profession – a practical problem often noted by Latino philosophers (e.g., the last chapter in Gracia 2000; Mendieta 1999; Sánchez 2011; Vargas 2007, 2010).

Finally, the ethnic-philosophy theorists cannot avoid a skepticism problem for Latin American philosophy, one concerning its quality. For their theory offers no clear way to decide what to include in this field. As a result, they make room for the existence of two classes of philosophy. On the one hand, there is philosophy properly construed with its different branches, each of which follows the rules of inclusion set by the consensus of the community of philosophers. On the other, there are a series of ethnic philosophies whose only standard of inclusion seems to be acceptance by an ethnos.

10.3.3 Latin American Philosophy as a Type of Applied Philosophy

In other works I have developed an alternative, anti-skeptical view (Nuccetelli 2001, 2004) according to which the label 'Latin American philosophy,' when broadly construed to include the philosophical thought of

that fall beyond the realm of what philosophers can settle from the armchair. If I am right, then the reductionists need the sort of evidence from history and the social sciences that they commonly ignore. For my views on Latin American socialism and liberationism, see Chapters 8 and 9, respectively.

[14] Susanna Siegel, for instance, while commenting on the "insularity" of Latin American philosophy in the United States, has recommended that its practitioners keep in mind "the fact that philosophical questions are genuinely distinct from many questions in neighboring fields in both the social sciences and the humanities ... " (Siegel 2014). That is, philosophers simply lack the resources to conduct adequate studies in such neighboring fields.

a number of academic and nonacademic philosophers, refers to a type of applied philosophy that deals with *characteristically* Latin American issues. To qualify for this branch of philosophy, a philosophical work must have some relation in content or method to a Latin American context. In all the chapters of this book, I have provided abundant evidence of numerous works that meet these two conditions. They are mostly devoted to issues of moral, social, and political philosophy and have been produced by both nonacademic and academic philosophers. Thus construed, Latin American philosophy comes out as a branch of applied philosophy and its existence is compatible with that of epistemology, metaphysics, moral theory, and other general branches of philosophy. To such general branches belong questions such as what there is, how we know about it (if we know it at all), and whether there is moral right and wrong. To Latin American philosophy belong questions of the sort discussed in this book and many more. Some such questions concern meta-philosophy; others practical ethics and political philosophy. Latin American philosophers may devote their efforts to general philosophy, applied philosophy, or both – as some actually do (including this writer). And of course an interest in applied philosophy need not include an interest in Latin American philosophy, since there are many other branches of applied philosophy.

Now this proposal should not be conflated with one published in the Montevideo newspaper *El Nacional* of Montevideo (October 2, 1840) by Juan Bautista Alberdi, who also seems to think of Latin American philosophy as applied philosophy. On his view, Latin Americans should avoid wasting their efforts in general philosophical matters and should limit their studies to issues of practical social and political philosophy that could offer some "positive benefit" to their nascent nations (Alberdi 1988/1840: 94–95). He wrote, "[Latin] America should practice what Europe thinks." Alberdi's remark here is of course in line with his Eurocentric philosophy, discussed in Chapter 4 of this book. But some scholars interpret it as implying that Latin Americans are less capable of doing general philosophy than their peers from major Western centers of philosophy. I believe that this interpretation, missing the context of the remark, somehow distorts what Alberdi had in mind.[15] In any case, there

---

[15] Pereda (2006), for example, claims that Alberdi's remarks "dishonor" Latin Americans. Read out of context, they do appear insulting. But context is needed here: Alberdi was responding to a request for a recommendation about the sort of philosophy course that

is no relevant analogy between my proposal and Alberdi's. After all, his was a proposal about what philosophy in Latin America should become, while mine is one about what Latin American philosophy, when understood in an interesting sense, actually has been and is. Again, no one any longer doubts that there is philosophy in Latin America. When someone asks 'Is there a Latin American philosophy?,' that person expresses curiosity about whether there is a characteristically or distinctively Latin American branch of philosophy. In light of what I have argued in this chapter, the correct response should be: it is a type of applied philosophy that conducts philosophical inquiry on issues that are related to Latin America.

10.4   The Upshot

Philosophers in Latin America tend to engage in self-regarding founda-tional debates concerning the nature, quality, and existence of a branch of philosophy named 'Latin American philosophy.' But the name of the branch is ambiguous because it may mean philosophy *in* Latin America or a *characteristically Latin American* philosophy. As a result, there is a great deal of equivocation in these debates. Putting the ambiguity of that name aside, on my view the right response to those skeptical about Latin American philosophy is to charge that they are too demanding: their demands are unreasonable in light of certain external factors that have affected, and still affect, the philosophical development of the region. Consider 'originality' or 'being tradition-generating.' Plausibly, there might be some internal and external factors other than the alleged vices of its practitioners that can explain why academic philosophy in Latin America may lack some of these properties, as the contemporary skeptics contend, or have them rarely, as Frondizi claimed in 1949. By "external factors," I mean factors concerning social and economic burdens that make the practice of philosophy in Latin America comparatively more difficult – together with an unfavorable inter-national division of resources of the kind that T. S. Kuhn (1962) described as

should be offered in a high school of Montevideo that was about to open in the 1840s, when questions about national organization were most pressing. In that context, it made perfect sense to propose a course in applied social and political philosophy because this branch of philosophy could address issues that were of central concern to these Latin Americans of post-Independence.

accounting for the infrequent changes of paradigm in the history of science.

Here Cannabrava, in spite of his extreme skepticism, provides a genealogical clue that is useful for understanding the problems facing philosophy in Latin America. As you may recall, his account invokes the fact that, before the 1930s philosophy in Latin America was subordinated to other interests, chiefly political science, literature, and the arts. Nineteenth-century positivism did not have the same impact in all the regions of the world that adopted that philosophy. Many Latin American positivists were also literary figures, as you may recall from the above discussion of positivism in Brazil or Chile. By contrast, in Western centers such as the UK during the same period, philosophy was developing in close relation with mathematics and the natural sciences. Unlike the major philosophical centers of the West, in Latin America the concerns of those who have been most original and tradition-generating were issues of practical moral and political philosophy. In addition, the failure of positivism in the region only fostered mistrust of science among intellectuals, which in turn accounts for the rapid spread of philosophical views that were hostile to science.

Among those who reject skepticism about Latin American philosophy, I have argued that they should avoid any form of ideological reductionism that confines the philosophy of the region to capturing the worldview of a supposed "ethnos" or considers it valuable only as an instrument to remedying some social injustices facing Latinos.

Latin American philosophy has the potential to avoid these defeating options if it continues to engage in reasoned argument about interesting philosophical questions – as illustrated in lingering debates over its foundations and the ethnic-group term that best identifies it.[16] It can also benefit from recognizing within its history the philosophical works of the so-called Latin American *pensadores* or *ensayistas* (thinkers or essayists) who have advanced many interesting philosophical issues and arguments. Among these nonacademic thinkers are some of the figures discussed in this book such as Bartolomé de las Casas, Juana de la Cruz, José Martí, and José Carlos Mariátegui. Like *philosophes* Michel de Montaigne and Miguel de

---

[16] Although I have not addressed the debate over the semantics of ethnic-group terms in this book, I offer outlines of the chief doctrines at stake in Nuccetelli (2001 and 2004).

Unamuno, the *pensadores* of Latin America have produced works chiefly on issues of applied ethics and political philosophy that are insightful and illustrative of the intellectual history of the region. Many of their works have all the properties the skeptics cannot find in the works of Latin America's academic philosophers. They include the properties of being tradition-generating and original, as well as having a visibility of the internal and the external kinds discussed in this chapter.

10.5   Suggested Readings

Corlett, J. Angelo. 2007. "Race, Ethnicity, and Public Policy," pp. 225–247 in *Race or Ethnicity? On Black and Latino identity*, ed. Jorge J. E. Gracia. Ithaca, NY: Cornell University Press.

Attempts to provide a definition of 'Latino' which, if adequate, might solve the problem of determining what Latino philosophy is. But Corlett's necessary and sufficient condition for counting in this group (namely, being genealogically related to people from Latin America) has proved controversial. See for instance Tammelleo (2011).

Frondizi, Risieri. 1949. "Is There an Ibero-American Philosophy?" *Philosophy and Phenomenological Research* 9: 345–355.

Together with Cannabrava (1949), the source for the early skepticism about Latin American philosophy discussed in this chapter.

Gooding-Williams, Robert. 2002. "Comment on J. J. E. Gracia's Hispanic/Latino Identity," *Philosophy and Social Criticism* 27(2): 3–10.

Takes issue with Gracia's conception of the meaning of the terms 'Hispanic' and 'Latino,' in ways relevant to determining what Hispanic and Latino philosophy are. I discuss this objection in Nuccetelli (2018).

Gracia, Jorge J. E. 2008. *Latinos in America: Philosophy and Social Identity*. Oxford: Blackwell.

Best source for tracing Gracia's conception of Latin American philosophy as a type of ethnic philosophy.

Hurtado, Guillermo. 2006. "Two Models of Latin American Philosophy," *Journal of Speculative Philosophy* 3: 204–213.

Consistent with Pereda (2006), this skeptical account focuses on Latin American philosophy's failure to be tradition-generating.

Pereda, Carlos. 2006. "Latin American Philosophy: Some Vices," *Journal of Speculative Philosophy* 3: 192–203.

Best source for the internal and external invisibility problems facing Latin American philosophy, according to the contemporary skeptics discussed above.

Miró Quesada, Francisco. 1978. "Posibilidad y límites de una filosofía lationamericana," *Revista de Filosofía de la Universidad de Costa Rica* XVI (43): 75–82.

Outlines the Salazar Bondy/Zea debate on the nature and quality of Latin American philosophy and proposes a compromise solution to this debate.

Nuccetelli, Susana. 2018. "Latino Philosophy," in Illan Stavans, ed., *Oxford Handbook of Latino Studies*. DOI:10.1093/oxfordhb/9780190691202.001.0001.

Argues that Latin American philosophy, as currently developing in the United States, has the potential to overcome some of the problems pointed out by contemporary skeptics about the nature and quality of the discipline. But it must avoid falling into some form of ideological reductionism.

Rabossi, Eduardo. 2008. *En el comienzo Dios creo el Canon. Biblia berolinensis. Ensayos sobre la condición de la filosofía*. Buenos Aires: Gedisa.

Offers a colorful narrative about the contingencies that the Founders faced in Argentina when they were trying to "normalize" the practice of philosophy – together with a similarly colorful statement of the author's skepticism about Latin American philosophy.

Stavans, Ilan. 2000. "Life in the Hyphen," pp. 3–26 in *The Essential Ilan Stavans*. New York and London: Routledge.

Provides a stipulative definition of 'Latino' and 'Hispanic' as terms that apply respectively to Spanish-speaking people living in the United States, and Spanish-speaking people living elsewhere. Stavans thus captures the current common but (as noted above) imprecise usage of these words, which proves particularly problematic when they are used as qualifiers of the term 'philosophy.'

Glossary

Absolutism. The view that there is at least one value (truth, life, knowledge, etc.) that never varies. It competes with RELATIVISM and UNIVERSALISM.

Aggregate happiness. In classical utilitarianism, the notion that what counts morally is the total balance of happiness over pain for most of those concerned.

Alterity. See OTHER.

Anadialectical method. The method that Enrique Dussel and some other LIBERATION PHILOSOPHERS pitch as better than the methods of Western philosophy. It purports to have both an analogical part wherein the philosopher realizes she is similar to the OTHER, and a dialectical part wherein she realizes she is also distinct from the OTHER.

Analytic philosophy. The prevailing style of philosophical thinking in the English-speaking world since the beginning of the twentieth century. It emphasizes the importance of conceptual analysis and reasoned argument in philosophical inquiry.

Apostolate. A group of Brazilian Comtean POSITIVISTS led by Miguel Lemos and Raimundo Teixeira Mendes, who reduced Comte's philosophy to a kind of anti-religious religion. They created a Brazilian Positivist Church for the purpose of practicing a so-called RELIGION OF HUMANITY.

Arielism. The LATIN AMERICANIST proposal in Rodó's book *Ariel*. It rejected positivist values while claiming exclusive Mediterranean roots for the culture of Latin America, thus amounting to a type of Eurocentric vision of Latin American identity.

Authoritarian republicanism. Bolívar's proposal for the political organization of some post-independence Latin American countries such as GRAN COLOMBIA. It envisions four powers: a judiciary power, an executive power headed by an elected president *serving for life*, a legislative power featuring a *hereditary senate*, and a MORAL POWER.

Black Legend. Some fictitious accounts of abuses of the Spanish conquest that circulated in Europe during the sixteenth century. Chiefly promoted by Britain, they were designed to undermine the image of its major colonial rival.

Bolivarism. The doctrine that the best form of polity for a people is the one that best promotes three basic values: AGGREGATE HAPPINESS, social safety, and political stability. See also AUTHORITARIAN REPUBLICANISM and *MESTIZAJE* MODEL.

Bonapartism. Marx's term for reactionary governments such as that of Napoleon Bonaparte in nineteenth-century France, who aimed at ruling with the dictatorial powers typical of monarchs. Marx regarded as Bonapartist Bolívar's style of politics and military action.

Categorical Imperative. According to Kant, the supreme principle of morality. Of his several formulations (which he controversially claimed to be equivalent), the HUMANITY-AS-AN-END-IN-ITSELF principle seems most plausible to many sympathetic readers of Kant's moral theory.

Caudillo(s). Rural chieftains who acquired political and military power in Latin America during the wars of independence and in the period of national organization that followed. They frequently engaged in internal wars and were accused of lawlessness, ungrounded political ambitions, and propensity to extreme violence.

Center–Periphery dichotomy. See DEPENDENCY THEORY.

Cholo(s). In Peru, *mestizo* people of Indian and Spanish ancestry.

Civilization-versus-barbarism dichotomy. Racist theory of the development of post-independence Latin America. According to Domingo F. Sarmiento's famous version, his native Argentina's *PAMPAS* and their inhabitants fostered barbarism while its cities and their inhabitants promoted civilization. The former should be resisted, the latter endorsed and supported.

Classical utilitarianism. A CONSEQUENTALIAST theory that evaluates the morality of an action according to whether it maximizes or diminishes utility, which is the total balance of happiness over suffering for all concerned. This theory may accept that LIBERAL DEMOCRACY is the form of polity that best promotes utility.

Communitarianism. A modern-day label for a family of doctrines that connect forms of polity with morality while assigning the chief role to tradition and social context. Communitarians usually emphasize the social role of persons, make normative claims concerning the value of community, and reject the emphasis on individual freedom characteristic of LIBERALISM.

Comtean positivism. August Comte's theory of social progress according to which the development of human thought and societies invariably progresses as described in his LAW OF THREE STAGES.

Consequentialism/Consequentialist. A set of moral theories, including CLASSICAL UTILITARIANISM, that use the value of outcomes as the basis for determining whether an action is morally mandatory, permissible, or forbidden.

Contractualism. A view in political philosophy that believes that liberal democracy best captures the self-interested, free choice that qualifying members of society would make under some ideal conditions.

Criollo(s). Persons of Spanish ancestry born in Latin America. Not to be confused with the term 'creoles,' which in US English denotes persons of mixed European and black descent.

Dependency theory. Any theory that explains underdevelopment as a necessary byproduct of the international division of labor inherent in capitalist development. As a result of that development, the countries at the "center" (i.e., the producers of industrial goods) prosper while those at the "periphery" (i.e., the producers of food and raw materials) suffer widespread poverty and stagnation. To break that vicious circle, the DEVELOPMENTALISTS who introduced this theory in the 1950s proposed protectionist economies in the periphery. But their successors in the 1970s and 1980s thought that replacing capitalism with socialism was the only alternative.

Developmentalism. A type of DEPENDENCY THEORY.

Distinctivism. The doctrine that philosophy can be peculiar to regions, persons, groups, or cultures. See also PERSPECTIVISM and UNIVERSALISM.

Distributive justice. The part of social justice concerned with what is fair in the allocation of benefits and burdens in society between individuals or groups.

Empiricism. The thesis that knowledge is based on observation and inference from observation.

Encomienda. A system of servitude and slavery of Amerindians that Spain used in its American colonies. In this system, the Amerindians were part of the land that was given to settlers by the Spanish crown. They were supposed to work for the settlers or pay tribute in exchange for instruction in Catholicism.

Estancia. Type of large cattle ranch found in South America. . See also *LATIFUNDISTA.*

Ethical egoism. A consequentialist normative theory holding that what determines whether an action is right or wrong for an agent is whether or not its results are in that agent's overall best interests.

Ethnocentrism. The bias of thinking that one's own culture or people is best.

Exteriority. See OTHER.

Favela. Shanty town or slum of Brazil's urban centers.

Federales. In post-independence Argentina, members of a party that advocated equal power for all provinces in the country. They fought against the rival party of *UNITARIOS.*

Gamonalism. A system of exploitation of the Andean Indians whereby they were forced to work under semi-servitude conditions by the owners of vast parcels of lands or by local chieftains.

Gaucho(s). In nineteenth-century Argentina, Southern Brazil, and Uruguay, an ethnic-group term for rural persons of mixed ethnic ancestry, usually Spanish and Amerindian, who roamed in vast uninhabited lands (especially the *PAMPAS*) and sometimes sought temporary work as cowboys or farmers in the *ESTANCIAs.* Analogous temporary, rural workers elsewhere in Latin America were called *llaneros* in Venezuela and Colombia, *huasos* in Chile, and *vaqueiros* in northern Brazil.

Guacho(s). Argentinian slang for an orphan, street urchin.

Gran Colombia. A republic in post-independence Latin America that, from 1819 to 1830, comprised the territories of the former Viceroyalty of New Granada. Today it would denote roughly the countries of Colombia, Ecuador, Panama, and Venezuela. See also AUTHORITARIAN REPUBLICANISM, BOLIVARISM, and BONAPARTISM.

Harmonic rationalism. Another name for the doctrine of KRAUSISM.

Humanity-as-an-end-in-itself principle. Kant's supreme moral rule prescribing that persons should always be treated as ends in themselves and never merely as means. See also CATEGORICAL IMPERATIVE.

Human right(s). A human agent's strong moral demand, usually thought to create a correlative moral duty or obligation on other human agents. See also NATURAL RIGHTS.

Iberian ultramontanism. In Latin America, the sort of worldview with roots in the Catholic Church and the colonial period that later acquired the reputation of being not only too conservative but also exceedingly retrograde.

Ideological contamination. The charge of Enrique Dussel and other LIBERATION PHILOSOPHERS that no philosophy is value-free. Especially directed against all Western philosophy.

Immodest feminism. A family of contemporary feminist theories in Latin America that take the distinctiveness of women as a premise for the argument that women and men should have different rights and duties. They also extend the scope of feminist inquiry from ethics and political philosophy to other branches of philosophy such as symbolic logic, epistemology, and philosophy of science. See also MODEST FEMINISM.

Impartialism. The thesis that every person counts as equal in moral value (neither more nor less than anyone else).

Incomplete-Independence theory. Invoked chiefly by Mexican POSITIVISTS, the doctrine that (i) some retrograde values of Spanish culture and Catholicism remained in Latin America after its political emancipation; and (ii) that those values amounted to an obstacle for post-independence Latin America to achieve prosperity and freedom. See also IBERIAN ULTRAMONTANISM.

Instrumental value. A value that a thing does not have intrinsically (see INTRINSIC VALUE), but as a means for something else.

Intrinsic value. A value a thing has in itself, independent of anything external to it. See also INSTRUMENTAL VALUE.

Invisibility problem. A skeptical problem facing philosophy in Latin America (see SKEPTICISM ABOUT LATIN AMERICAN PHILOSOPHY). It breaks down into External Invisibility (the thesis that philosophers do not regularly consider works by Latin American philosophers) and Internal Invisibility (the thesis that Latin American philosophers do not regularly consider each other's works).

Krausism. A neo-Kantian comprehensive system that in epistemology seeks a compromise between a priori, "conscience" knowledge of God, and a posteriori knowledge of the world. In metaphysics it postulates a divine harmony between humanity and nature, and in philosophy of religion vindicates a PANENTHEISM that explicitly rejects both monotheism and polytheism.

Lascasianism. A set doctrines of practical ethics developed in the sixteenth century as a reaction to the view that Amerindians are less human than those of European descent and may therefore exemplify the sort of people Aristotle had in mind with his THEORY OF NATURAL SLAVES.

Latifundista. The owner of a *latifundio* or large portion of land generally used for farming. See also *ESTANCIA*.

Latin Americanism/Latin Americanist. The thesis that Latin Americans have a valuable unique culture. See also ARIELISM and *MESTIZAJE* MODEL of identity.

Law of three stages. August Comte's deterministic conception of the development of human thought and societies. It holds that each of these invariably undergoes three successive stages: first a theological stage, second a metaphysical stage, and finally a positive stage. See also COMTEAN POSITIVISM.

Liberal democracy. A form of polity that (a) allows eligible citizens to make autonomous decisions on governmental policies through their participation in periodic, free elections of their representatives in the government; and (b) protects all residents' fundamental HUMAN RIGHTS. See also AUTHORITARIAN REPUBLICANISM and BONAPARTISM.

Liberalism. The political philosophy most common in Latin America after its independence from Spain and Portugal. Its representatives vindicated values such as civilization, prosperity, education, personal freedom and the like. See also POSITIVISM.

Liberation philosophy/liberation philosophers. A philosophical movement initiated in Argentina in the early 1970s by philosophers who had an instrumentalist conception of philosophy according to which it should contribute to the liberation of the oppressed, including liberation from IDEOLOGICAL CONTAMINATION. See also OTHER and ANADIALECTICAL METHOD.

Liberationist feminism. A contemporary version of IMMODEST FEMINISM fueled by the doctrines of LIBERATION PHILOSOPHY. See also MODEST FEMINISM.

Los científicos. In a strict sense, this term refers to the Mexican POSITIVISTS of the Liberal Party that supported the administration of Porfirio Díaz, also known as PORFIRIATO. In a broad sense, as used in this book, it refers to the third and most consequential wave of Mexican positivists.

Machismo. In Spanish, word for 'male chauvinism.' *Machismo* is a type of sexism in Latin America according to which men have greater normative worth than women.

Martí's Latin Americanism. It adds to LATIN AMERICANISM the Krausist thesis (see KRAUSISM) that, like any other group of people, Latin Americans too are members of the whole human family, with equal rights.

Marxism. A political philosophy first proposed in the nineteenth century by Karl Marx and his collaborator Friedrich Engels to account for capitalism's failure to maximize well-being and which recommended its replacement with socialism and eventually communism by means of a proletarian revolution. See also POSITIVISM and BONAPARTISM.

***Mestizaje* model.** The view that Latin America's collective identity is a mix of Afro-Latin Americans, Amerindians, and Europeans. This model competes with the TRANSPLANTATION THEORY OF IDENTITY.

Mestizofilia. *See MESTIZAJE* MODEL.

Método analéctico. See ANADIALECTICAL METHOD.

Modest feminism. The thesis of moral and political philosophy that women are equal to men in morally relevant respects and therefore deserve the same treatment in any relevant matter. See also IMMODEST FEMINISM.

Moral power. In Simón Bolívar's conception of the best polity for some Latin American countries, this is a branch of government charged with seeing that certain things, institutions, or states of affairs (a book, the media outlet, a play, etc.) are morally acceptable for society. Thus conceived, the government has four powers: executive, legislative, judiciary, and moral.

Moral worth. The intrinsic moral importance of a thing, sometimes called 'moral status,' 'moral standing,' and 'dignity' (for humans). See also RACISM, SEXISM, and SPECIESISM.

Mulatto(s). In colonial Latin America, a racial-group term used to refer to any person of mixed racial ancestry, usually European and African. See also *PARDO (S)* and *ZAMBO(S)*.

Natural law theory. The moral theory of Thomas Aquinas.

Natural law theory justification of democracy. The view that liberal democracy is the right political arrangement because it is the most conducive to respect for NATURAL RIGHTS.

Naturalism. The thesis that the natural world is *all there is* – so that there are no supernatural causes or entities. It entails SECULARISM.

Natural rights. The ancestors of HUMAN RIGHTS. If there are any such rights, humans have them just because they are human.

Nihilism. In moral philosophy, the view that that are no moral truths.

Normative theory. Usually a theory concerning the system of morality or of rationality. It may primarily be a VALUE-BASED THEORY or a THEORY OF RIGHT CONDUCT.

Originalism. The skeptical doctrine that holds that Latin American philosophy must fulfill the condition of being something new in order for it to be acceptable as a philosophy. See also PERSPECTIVISM. See also UNIVERSALISM.

Other. In LIBERATION PHILOSOPHY, anything that, from any perspective whatsoever, could be regarded as being oppressed: the poor, women, children, Latin America, Africa, and so on. Also called 'alterity' and 'exteriority.'

Pampas. Extended grasslands of Argentina. Until the turn of the nineteenth century, it was sometimes misnamed 'the desert,' a term with the racist connotation that only "savage" Amerindians inhabited this region. See also CIVILIZATION-VERSUS-BARBARISM DICHOTOMY.

Panentheism. A combination of pantheism and theism. See also KRAUSISM.

Pardo(s). In colonial Latin America, a racial-group term used to refer to any person of mixed racial ancestry who had some African blood. See also MULATTO(S) and *ZAMBO(S).*

Pardocracia. Simón Bolívar's derogatory way of referring to a government in the hands of the *PARDOS.*

Perfectionism. The belief that there is at least one human excellence or perfection, which should be promoted.

Perspectivism. Contra ORIGINALISM, this anti-skeptical doctrine about the existence and quality of Latin American philosophy holds that philosophers from Latin America are bound to regard the standard problems of philosophy from a Latin American perspective, which thereby renders this type of philosophy original.

Physicalism. The thesis that the physical world is all there is. It implies NATURALISM but is not equivalent to it.

Porfiriato. The rule of the Mexican dictator Porfirio Díaz, especially during his second administration of 1884–1911. See also *LOS CIENTÍFICOS* and POSITIVISM.

Positivism/Positivists. A family of European doctrines widely popular in Latin America during the latter part of the nineteenth century. They arrived in a first wave as COMTEAN POSITIVISM. But, more broadly construed, they involved a number of theories in social and political philosophy that shared their PROGRESSIVISM, such as MARXISM, CLASSICAL UTILITARIANISM, and SOCIAL DARWINISM. See also *LOS CIENTÍFICOS and PORFIRIATO.*

Positivist Nucleus. A group of Brazilian POSITIVISTS, led by Miguel Lemos and Raimundo Teixeira Mendes, the founders of the Brazilian Positivist Church, an institution devoted to the advancement of a secular creed.

Primacy of justice. The view that justice is the weightiest of all moral demands.

Principle of utility. The sole supreme moral rule according to CLASSICAL UTILITARIANISM, which holds that an action is the right one to take in a given situation only if it produces either the greatest happiness – or the least unhappiness – of the greatest number among all persons affected by it.

Progressivism – The thesis that perfectibility (i.e., any change for the better) is inevitable for certain entities, institutions, or states of affairs – for example, biological organisms, human thought, wealth, morality, and even celestial bodies. See also COMTEAN POSITIVISM.

Racial-democracy objection. An argument against the *MESTIZAJE* MODEL of Latin America's identity. It contends that that model falsely presupposes a racial equality in the region.

Racism. The bias that race determines MORAL WORTH. See also SEXISM and SPECIESISM.

Realism. The view that entities of a certain kind exist, and that they do so independently of minds and language.

Relativism. The view that all truths, values, or norms are contingent upon factors such as culture, class, history, and so on. It competes with ABSOLUTISM and UNIVERSALISM. Relativism about forms of polity takes the legitimacy of *any* political arrangement to depend on either culture, class, history, or something else.

Religion of humanity. Secularist creed first proposed by August Comte and that was well represented among his orthodox followers in Brazil during the late nineteenth century. See also APOSTOLATE and COMTEAN POSITIVISM.

Rodó's Latin Americanism. See ARIELISM.

Scientific feminism. A contemporary version of MODEST FEMINISM. See also IMMODEST FEMINISM.

Scientism. The thesis that science is the only path to knowledge of what there is. It implies EMPIRICISM but is not equivalent to it.

Scholastic method. A method of disputation in philosophy and theology that proceeds by formulating a thesis, raising objections to it, offering rejoinders that refute the objections, and proposing solutions to any remaining problems for that thesis. It relies heavily on appeal to scripture, Greek philosophers, and medieval theologians.

Secularism. A NATURALIST thesis that there is no supernatural agency. See also RELIGION OF HUMANITY and POSITIVISM.

Sexism. The bias that sex or gender determines MORAL WORTH. See also SPECIESISM and RACISM.

Skepticism about Latin American philosophy. The doctrine that either there is no Latin American philosophy or only a very small part of it, if any part at all, is of value. See also INVISIBILITY PROBLEM.

Social Darwinism. A family of determinist theories that invokes a seemingly Darwinian theory of natural selection to account for the success or failure of groups of people in the struggle for survival. Some versions have made racist claims, others have confused the descriptive meaning of 'fit for survival' with an evaluative, moral meaning.

Sociocracy. According to COMTEAN POSITIVISM, a government run by scientists, and the best form of polity in a mature society – which is one where human thought has reached the third, positive stage described in the LAW OF THREE STAGES.

Speciesism. The bias that species membership determines MORAL WORTH, which critics believe amounts to a bias akin to SEXISM or RACISM.

Theory of natural slaves. Aristotle's racist theory that some groups of people are barbarians by nature, and thus fit only for slavery. According to the theory, these people should not be freed since only conventional slaves can adapt to life as free individuals. . See also LASCASIANISM.

Theory of right conduct. The branch of NORMATIVE THEORY focused on right and wrong action. It takes judgments of right and wrong (e.g., Kant's CATEGORICAL IMPERATIVE) to be more fundamental than judgments of value. See also VALUE-BASED THEORY.

Transplantation theory of identity. Mostly popular in the nineteenth century, it holds that the collective identity of either Latin America or a specific Latin American country is European, for it resulted from a "transplantation" of Europeans into the region. This theory competes with the *MESTIZAJE* MODEL of Latin American identity.

Unitarios. During Argentina's national organization, the members of a political party known for its vindication of a strongly centralized form of republic with the capital in Buenos Aires. They fought to prevail over their rivals, the *FEDERALES*.

Universalism.   The doctrine that all philosophy is universal. See also DISTINCTIVISM.

Value-based theory. Any theory that takes one or more values to be explanatorily more basic than deontic concepts on the rightness or wrongness of actions.

Vasconcelos's Latin Americanism. A casting of LATIN AMERICANISM according to the *MESTIZAJE* MODEL of Latin American identity.

Zambo(s). A racial-group term introduced in colonial times to refer to any person of mixed Amerindian and African descent. (Now a racial slur, a taboo word.) See also *PARDO(S)* and MULATTO(S).

Bibliography

Abellán, J. L. 1989. "La dimensión krauso-positivista en Eugenio María de Hostos," *Cuadernos Americanos, Nueva Época* 7/8(4): 58–66.

Acosta, José de. 1604/1590. *The Natural & Moral History of the Indies*. London: Hakluyt Society.

Alberdi, Juan Bautista. 1886–1887. *Obras completas*. Buenos Aires: La Tribuna Nacional.

1900. *Cartas Quillotanas*. Buenos Aires: Talleres Gráficos Argentinos L. J. Rosso. https://archive.org/details/cartasquillotana00albeuoft/page/n3

1988/1840. "Ideas para presidir la confección del curso de filosofía contemporánea." In Oscar Terán, ed.,*Alberdi póstumo*.Buenos Aires: Puntosur, pp. 90–98.

1997. *Escritos Póstumos*. Buenos Aires: Universidad Nacional de Quilmes,

2017/1852. *Bases y puntos de partida para la organización política de la República Argentina*, ed. Matías Farías. Buenos Aires: Biblioteca del Congreso, https://bcn.gob.ar/uploads/BasesAlberdi.pdf.

Alberini, Coriolano. 1927. "Contemporary Philosophic Tendencies in South America," *The Monist* 37: 328–334.

Alberto, Paulina L. and Jesse Hoffnung-Garskof. 2018. "'Racial Democracy' and Racial Inclusion: Hemispheric Histories." In Alejandro De la Fuente and George Reid Andrews, eds., *Afro-Latin American Studies: An Introduction*. Cambridge, UK: Cambridge University Press, pp. 264–316.

Alcoff, Linda. 2005. "Latino vs. Hispanic: The Politics of Ethnic Names," *Philosophy and Social Criticism* 31: 395–408.

Allen, Nicolas. 2018, December 15. "Mariátegui's Heroic Socialism: An Interview with Michael Löwy," *Jacobin*. www.jacobinmag.com/2018/12/jose-carlos-mariategui-seven-interpretive-essays-peru-marxism-revolutionary-myth

Almeder, Robert. 1994. "Liberal Feminism and Academic Feminism?" *Public Affairs Quarterly* 8(4): 299–315.

Alvarez, Sonia. 1990. *Engendering Democracy in Brazil: Women's Movements in Transition Politics*. Princeton, NJ: Princeton University Press.

1998a. "Advocating Feminism: The Latin American NGO 'Boom,'" Global Solidarity Dialogue (website). www.antenna.nl/~waterman/alvarez2.html

1998b. "Latin American Feminisms 'Go Global': Trends of the 1990s and Challenges for the New Millennium," in Sonia Alvarez, Evelina Dagnino, and Arturo Escobar, eds., *Cultures of Politics/Politics of Cultures*. Boulder, CO: Westview Press, pp. 293–324.

Amory, Frederic. 1999. "Euclides da Cunha and Brazilian Positivism," *Luso-Brazilian Review* 36(1): 87–94.

Anderson, Jon Lee. 1997. *Che Guevara: A Revolutionary Life*. New York: Grove Press.

Andrade, G. and J. Lugo-Ocando. 2018. "The Angostura Address 200 Years Later: A Critical Reading," *Iberoamericana – Nordic Journal of Latin American and Caribbean Studies* 47(1): 74–82. DOI:http://doi.org/10.16993/iberoamericana.427

Andrews, George Reid. 2004. *Afro-Latin America: 1800–2000*. New York: Oxford University Press.

Anzaldúa, Gloria E. 2003. "La Conciencia de la Mestiza: Towards a New Consciousness," in Carole R. McCann and Kim Seung-Kyung, eds., *Feminist Thought Reader: Local and Global Perspectives*. New York: Routledge, pp. 179–187.

Ardao, Arturo. 1963. "Assimilation and Transformation of Positivism in Latin America," *Journal of the History of Ideas* 24: 515–522. (Reprinted pp. 150–156 in Nuccetelli and Seay 2004.)

Ardiles, Osvaldo, Hugo Assmann, Mario Casalla, et al. 1973. *Hacia una filosofía de la liberación lationamericana*. Buenos Aires: Bonum. www.academia.edu/16122091/Hacia_una_filosof%C3%ADa_de_la_liberaci%C3%B3n_latinoamericana

Arroyo Luna, Alejandro F. and Orlando Lima Rocha. 2013. *Filosofía en América Latina* (website). August 12. http://filosamericalatina.blogspot.com/

Assmann, Hugo. 1971. *Opresión-Liberación: desafío a los cristianos*. Montevideo: Tierra Nueva.

Bar-Lewaw, M. Itzhak. 1971. *La revista "Timón" y José Vasconcelos*. Mexico City: Casa Edimex.

Barreda, Gabino. 2003. "Oración Cívica." Speech given in Guanajuato, September 16, 1867. Biblioteca Virtual Universal (website). www.biblioteca.org.ar/libros/1112.pdf

Becker, Marc. "Mariátegui, the Comintern, and the Indigenous Question in Latin America," *Science & Society* 70(4) 2006: 450–479.

Bello, Andrés. 1997a. *Selected Writings of Andrés Bello*, ed. Iván Jaksić. New York: Oxford University Press.

1997b. "Commentary on 'Investigations on the Social Influence of the Spanish Conquest and Colonial Regime in Chile' by José Victorino Lastarria, 1844." In Bello 1997a, pp. 154–168 (excerpts reprinted in Burke and Humphrey 2007 as "Response to Lastarria on the Influence of the Conquest and the Spanish Colonial System in Chile," pp. 62–73).

1997c. "Monarchies in America." In Bello 1997a, p. 194.

1997d. "American Congress." In Bello 1997a, p. 213.

Bentham, Jeremy. 1988/1789. *Introduction to the Principles of Morals and Legislation*. Buffalo, NY: Prometheus Books.

Bethell, Leslie, ed. 1996. *Ideas and Ideologies in Twentieth Century Latin America*. Cambridge, UK: Cambridge University Press.

Beuchot, Mauricio. 1996. *The History of Philosophy in Colonial Mexico*. Washington, DC: The Catholic University of America Press.

Biscaia de Lacerda, Gustavo. n.d. "Philosophy and Political Movement," *Positivism: Secular, Social, Scientific* (blog). http://positivists.org/blog/brazil

Block, Ned. 1995. "How Heritability Misleads about Race," *Cognition* 56(2): 99–128.

Blum, Lawrence. 2009. "Latinos on Race and Ethnicity: Alcoff, Corlett, and Gracia." In Nuccetelli, Schutte, and Bueno 2009, pp. 269–281.

Boff, Leonardo. 1979. *Jesus Cristo Libertador*. Petrópolis, Brazil: Vozes.

1985. *Church, Charism and Power: Liberation Theology and the Institutional Church*. New York: Crossroad (references to excerpts in Márquez 2008, pp. 107–136).

1995. Science, Technology, Power, and Liberation Theology," pp. 123–130 in *Ecology and Liberation: A New Paradigm*. Maryknoll, NY: Orbis.

Boff, Leonardo and Clodovis Boff. 2000/1987. "A Concise History of Liberation Theology." In *Introducing Liberation Theology*, 13th ed. Maryknoll, NY: Orbis, www.landreform.org/boff2.htm

Boff, Leonardo and Virgil Elizondo, eds. 1990. *1492–1992: The Voice of the Victims*. London: SCM Press.

Bolívar, Simón. 1812. "The Cartagena Manifesto," *Manifesto Portal* (website). http://manifestoindex.blogspot.com/192011/04/cartagena-manifesto-1812-by-simon.htm

1951a. "Angostura Address," 1819. In Bolívar 1951b, pp. 103–122 (reprint in Burke and Humphrey 2007, pp. 1–21).

1951b. *Selected Writings of Bolivar*, ed. Harold A. Bierck, Jr. New York: The Colonial Press.

2004. "Jamaica Letter," 1815. In Nuccetelli and Seay 2004, pp. 105–119. http://faculty.smu.edu/bakewell/BAKEWELL/texts/jamaica-letter.html

Brading, D. A. 1991. *The First America: The Spanish Monarchy, Creole Patriots, and the Liberal State 1492–1861*. Cambridge, UK: Cambridge University Press.

Burke, Janet and Ted Humphrey. 2007. *Nineteenth-Century Nation Building and the Latin American Tradition*. Indianapolis/Cambridge, MA: Hackett.

2011. "The New Black Legend of Bartolomé de las Casas." In Gracia 2011, pp. 31–54.

Bushnell, David and John Callan James Metford. 2019. "José de San Martín: Argentine Revolutionary," *Encyclopaedia Britannica* (website). February 21, www.britannica.com/biography/Jose-de-San-Martin

Candelaria, Michael. 2012. "Introduction," pp. 1–20 in *The Revolt of Unreason: Miguel de Unamuno and Antonio Caso on the Crisis of Modernity*. Amsterdam/New York: Rodopi,

Canteñs, Bernardo J., "The Rights of the American Indians," pp. 23–35 in Nuccetelli, Schutte, and Bueno 2009.

Cappelletti, Angel J. 1991. *Filosofía argentina del siglo XX*. Rosario, Argentina: Universidad Nacional de Rosario.

2017. *Anarchism in Latin America*. Chico, CA: AK Press.

Carbonero Gamundí, María Antonia, and Silvia Levín, eds. 2014. *Injusticias de género en un mundo globalizado: conversaciones con la teoría de Nancy Fraser*. Colección Politeia, Rosario, Argentina: Homo Sapiens Ediciones.

Cardoso, Fernando Henrique and Enzo Faletto. 1969. *Dependencia y desarrollo en América Latina*. Mexico: Siglo XXI.

Castañeda, Jorge G. 1997. *Compañero: The Life and Death of Che Guevara*. New York: Alfred A. Knopf.

Cerutti Guldberg, Horacio. 1983. *Filosofía de la liberación latinoamericana*. Mexico City: Fondo de Cultura Económica, https://enriquedussel.com/txt/Textos_200_Obras/Filosofos_Mexico/Filosofia_liberacion-Horacio_Cerutti.PDF

1998. "Liberation Philosophy," in E. Craig, ed., *Routledge Encyclopedia of Philosophy*. London: Routledge. www.rep.routledge.com/article/ZA011.

Clark, Meri L. 2009. "The Emergence and Transformation of Positivism," pp. 53–67 in Nuccetelli, Schutte, and Bueno 2009.

2013. "The Good and the Useful Together: Colombian Positivism in a Century of Conflict," pp. 27–48 in Gilson and Levinson 2013.

Chavarría, Jesús. 1979. *José Carlos Mariátegui and the Rise of Modern Peru, 1890–1930.* Albuquerque: University of New Mexico Press,

1968a. "Excerpts," Conference of Latin American Bishops, Medellín, Colombia, September 6. www.povertystudies.org/TeachingPages/EDS_PDFs4WEB/Medellin%20Document-%20Poverty%20of%20the%20Church.pdf

1968b. "Poverty of the Church," Conference of Latin American Bishops, Medellín, Colombia, September 6, www.povertystudies.org/TeachingPages/EDS_PDFs4WEB/Medellin%20Document-%20Poverty%20of%20the%20Church.pdf

Columbus, Christopher. 1960. *The Journal of Christopher Columbus.* New York: C. N. Potter.

Cannabrava, Euryalo. 1949. "Present Tendencies in Latin American Philosophy," *Journal of Philosophy* 5: 113–119.

Conniff, Michael L., and Thomas J. Davis. 1994. *Africans in the Americas: A History of the Black Diaspora,* New York: St. Martin's Press.

Corlett, J. Angelo.2007. "Race, Ethnicity, and Public Policy," pp. 225–247 in. Jorge J. E. Gracia, ed., *Race or Ethnicity? On Black and Latino Identity.* Ithaca, NY: Cornell University Press.

Coutinho, Afranio. 1943. "Some Considerations on the Problem of Philosophy in Brazil," *Philosophy and Phenomenological Research* 4: 186–193.

Cruz Costa, Joâo. 1964. *A History of Ideas in Brazil: The Development of Philosophy in Brazil and the Evolution of National History.* Berkeley, CA: University of California Press.

Cruz Revueltas, J. C., ed.2003. *La filosofía en América Latina como problema.* Mexico City: Publicaciones Cruz.

Curiel, Ochy. 2007. "Los aportes de las afrodescendientes a la teoría y la práctica feminista: desuniversalizando el sujeto mujeres," pp. 163–190 in M. L. Femenías, ed., *Perfiles del feminismo Iberoamericano,* vol. 3. Buenos Aires: Catálogos.

Dana, Miriam Jerade. 2015. "Antisemitismo en Vasconcelos: antiamericanismo, nacionalismo y misticismo estético," *Mexican Studies/Estudios Mexicanos* 31 (2): 248–286.

De Beer, Gabriella. 1966. *José Vasconcelos and His World.* New York: Las Americas.

de la Cruz, Juana Inés. 1988/1691. "Respuesta a Sor Filotea" ("Reply to Sor Philothea"), pp. 166–243 in Octavio Paz, ed., *A Sor Juana Anthology.* Cambridge, MA: Harvard University Press.

1998/1681. *Autodefensa Espiritual: Letter of Sor Juana Inés de la Cruz to Her Confessor*. San Antonio, TX: Galvart Press.

De la Fuente, Alejandro and George Reid Andrews, eds. 2018. *Afro-Latin American Studies: An Introduction*. Cambridge, UK: Cambridge University Press.

Deutschmann, David, ed.1987. *Che Guevara and the Cuban Revolution: Writings and Speeches of Ernesto Che Guevara*. Sidney: Pathfinder/Pacific and Asia.

Devés Valdés, Eduardo. 2000. "Antecedentes del proyecto modernizador cepalino," pp. 287–304 in *Del Ariel de Rodó a la CEPAL (1900–1950)*. Buenos Aires: Editorial Biblos.

Dierksmeier, Claus. 2009. "Krausism," pp. 110–127 in Nuccetelli, Schutte, and Bueno 2009.

2019. *Qualitative Freedom – Autonomy in Cosmopolitan Responsibility*. Cham, Switzerland: Springer, open access. www.springer.com/gp/book/97830300 47221

Draper, Hal. 1968. "Karl Marx and Simón Bolívar: A Note on Authoritarian Leadership in a National-Liberation Movement," *New Politics* 7(1): 64–77, www.marxists.org/archive/draper/1968/winter/bolivar.htm

Dussel, Enrique. 1973a. *Caminos de liberación latinoamericana II: teología de la liberación y ética*. Buenos Aires: Latinoamérica Libros/CLACSO.

1973b. *Para una ética de la liberación latinoamericana*, vols. I and II. Mexico City: Siglo XXI.

1978. *Ethics and the Theology of Liberation*, Maryknoll, NY: Orbis (references to selection in Nuccetelli and Seay 2004, pp. 92–98).

1980/1973. *Philosophy of Liberation*. Maryknoll, NY: Orbis (references to selection in Márquez 2008, pp. 148–161).

1994. *Historia de la filosofía latinoamericana y filosofía de la liberación*. Bogota: Nueva América.

1995. *Teología de la liberación: Un panorama de su desarrollo*. Mexico City: Potrerillos Editores.

1996. "Note on Liberation Theology," pp. 275–286 in Bethell 1996.

Engels, Friedrich. 1996/1879. "The Part Played by Labour in the Transition from Ape to Man," *Marxists Internet Archive*, www.marxists.org/archive/marx/works/1876/part-played-labour/

Etcheverri, Catriel. 2007. *Salvador Allende: La revolución desarmada*. Buenos Aires: Capital Intelectual.

Farías, Matías. 2017. "Prólogo," pp. 7–54 in Alberdi 2017/1852.

Feinmann, Jose Pablo. 1996. *Filosofía y Nación: Estudios sobre el pensamiento argentino*. Buenos Aires: Ariel.

Fernández Retamar, Roberto. 1976. "La crítica de Martí," pp. 11–29 in *Para una teoría de la literatura hispanoamericana*. Mexico City: Editorial Nuestro Tiempo. 1989. *Caliban and Other Essays*. Minneapolis: University of Minnesota Press, 2007. "Sus últimos días," pp. 9–15 in Noble 2007.

Fitzpatrick-Behrens, Susana. 2016. "The Catholic Church and Dictatorship," pp. 398–413 in Garrard-Burnett, Freston, and Dove 2016.

Ford, Thayne R. 1998. "Stranger in a Foreign Land: Jose de Acosta's Scientific Realizations in Sixteenth-Century Peru," *The Sixteenth Century Journal* 29(1): 19–33.

Fornet-Betancourt, Raúl. 1997–2015. "El pensamiento de José Martí. Estudio introductorio: Vida y líneas generales de su pensamiento," in José Luis Gómez-Martínez, ed., *Proyecto Ensayo Hispánico*, www.ensayistas.org/filoso fos/cuba/marti/marti2.htm

Freire, Paulo. 1993/1970. *Pedagogy of the Oppressed*. New York: Continuum.

Frondizi, Risieri 1943a. "Tendencies in Contemporary Latin-American Philosophy," pp. 35–48 in *Inter-American Intellectual Interchange*. Austin, TX: Institute of Latin American Studies, University of Texas.

1943b. "Contemporary Argentine Philosophy," *Philosophy and Phenomenological Research* 4: 180–187.

1949. "Is There an Ibero-American Philosophy?" *Philosophy and Phenomenological Research* 9: 345–355.

1951. "On the Unity of the Philosophies of the Two Americas," *The Review of Metaphysics* 4: 617–623.

Fuentes, Carlos. 1988. "Prologue" pp. 13–28 in Rodó 1988/1900.

1992a. *El espejo enterrado*. Mexico: Fondo de Cultura Económica.

1992b. *The Buried Mirror*. Boston, MA: Houghton Mifflin.

Fuller, Amy. 2015. *Between Two Worlds: The Autos Sacramentales of Sor Juana Inés de la Cruz*. Cambridge, UK: Modern Humanities Research Association.

Funes, Patricia. 2006. *Salvar la nación: cultura y politica en los años veinte*. Buenos Aires: Prometeo.

Garrard-Burnett, Virginia, Paul Freston, and Stephen C. Dove, eds. 2016. *The Cambridge History of Religions in Latin America*. New York: Cambridge University Press.

Garrido, Manuel, Nelson R. Garrido, Luis M. Garrido, and Margarita M. Garrido, eds. 2009. *El legado filosófico español e hispanoamericano del siglo XX.*Madrid: Cátedra.

Gilligan, Carol. 1982. *In a Different Voice: Psychological Theory and Women's Development*. Cambridge, MA: Harvard University Press.

Gilson, Gregory D. and Irving W. Levinson, eds. 2013. *Latin American Positivism: Theory and Practice*. Lanham, MD: Lexington Books.

Gimenez, Martha. 1989. "'Latino? Hispanic?' Who Needs a Name? The Case against a Standardized Terminology," *International Journal of Health Services* 19: 557–571.

Giorgis, Liliana. 2010. "José Martí: recuperación y vigencia de 'Nuestra América,'" pp. 141–152 in Adriana María Arpini, ed., *Diversidad e integración en nuestra América: Independencia, Estados nacionales e integración (1804–1880),*, vol. 1. Buenos Aires: Editorial Biblos.

Gómez-Martínez, José Luis, ed. 1997–2015. "Martí, José (1853–1895)," in *Proyecto Ensayo Hispánico*, www.ensayistas.org/filosofos/cuba/marti/index.htm

Gooding-Williams, Robert.2002. "Comment on J. J. E. Gracia's *Hispanic/Latino Identity*," *Philosophy and Social Criticism* 27(2): 3–10.

Gracia, Jorge J. E. 1993. "Hispanic Philosophy: Its Beginning and Golden Age," *Review of Metaphysics* 46: 475–502.

2000. *Hispanic-Latino Identity: A Philosophical Perspective*. Oxford: Blackwell.

2008. *Latinos in America: Philosophy and Social Identity*. Oxford: Blackwell.

Gracia, Jorge J. E., ed. 2011. *Forging People: Race, Ethnicity, and Nationality in Hispanic American and Latino/a Thought*. Notre Dame, IN: University of Notre Dame Press.

Gracia, Jorge J. E. and Elizabeth Millán-Zaibert, eds. 2003. *Latin American Philosophy for the 21st Century: The Human Condition, Values, and the Search for Identity*. Buffalo, NY: Prometheus.

Gray, Richard Butler. 1962. *José Marti, Cuban Patriot*. Gainesville, FL: University of Florida Press.

Guevara, Ernesto. 1967. "Message to the Tricontinental," April 16 (references to reprint in *Che Guevara Internet Archive*, www.marxists.org/archive/guevara/works.htm)

1987/1962a. "A New Culture of Work," pp. 116–127 in Deutschmann 1987.

1987/1962b. "The Cadres: Backbone of the Revolution," pp. 127–133 in Deutschmann 1987 (references to reprint in the *Che Guevara Internet Archive*, www.marxists.org/archive/guevara/works.htm)

1987/1965. "Socialism and Man in Cuba," pp. 197–214 in Deutschmann 1987 (references to reprint in the *Che Guevara Internet Archive*, www.marxists.org/archive/guevara/works.htm)

Gutiérrez, Gustavo. 1973/1971. *A Theology of Liberation*. Maryknoll, NY: Orbis, (references to excerpts pp. 93–106 in Márquez 2008).

1993. *Las Casas: In Search of the Poor Jesus Christ*. Maryknoll, NY: Orbis.

1999. "The Task and Content of Liberation Theology," pp. 19–38 in Christopher Rowland, ed., *The Cambridge Companion to Liberation Theology*. Cambridge, UK: Cambridge University Press.

Haack, Susan. 1993. "Epistemological Reflections of an Old Feminist," *Reason Papers* 18: 31–43.

1998. *Manifesto of a Passionate Moderate: Unfashionable Essays*. Chicago: University of Chicago Press.

Haight, Roger. 1998. "Liberation Theology," in E. Craig ed., *Routledge Encyclopedia of Philosophy*. London: Routledge. www.rep.routledge.com/articles/thematic/liberation-theology/v-1

Hale, Charles A. 1996. "Political Ideas and Ideologies in Latin America, 1870-1930," pp. 133–206 in Bethell 1996.

Hale, Charles A. 2004. "Edmundo O'Gorman, Mexican National History and the 'Great American Dichotomy.'" *Journal of Latin American Studies* 36(1): 131–145.

Halperín-Donghi, Tulio. 1993. *The Contemporary History of Latin America*, ed. and trans. John Charles Chastein. Durham, NC and London: Duke University Press.

Hanneken, Jaime. 2012. "José Carlos Mariátegui and the Time of Myth," *Cultural Critique* 81: 1–30.

Haya de la Torre, Víctor Raúl. 1973/1943. "No estamos listos aún para la democracia?" pp. 101–108 in Robert J. Alexander, ed., *Aprismo: The Ideas and Doctrines of Víctor Raúl Haya de la Torre*. Kent, OH: Kent State University Press (references to reprint in Nuccetelli and Seay 2004, pp. 138–142).

Held, Virginia, ed. 1993. *Justice and Care: Essential Readings in Feminist Ethics*. Boulder, CO: Westview Press.

Helg, Aline.2003. "Simón Bolívar and the Spectre of Pardocracia: José Padilla in Post-Independence Cartagena," *Journal of Latin American Studies* 35: 447–471.

Hennelly, Alfred T. 1990. *Liberation Theology: A Documentary History*. Maryknoll: NY: Orbis.

Himelblau, Jack J., ed. 1994. *The Indian in Spanish America: Centuries of Removal, Survival, and Integration*. Lancaster, CA: Labyrinthos.

Hindess, Barry. 1995. "Marxism," pp. 312–332 in Robert E. Goodin and Philip Pettit, eds., *A Companion to Contemporary Political Philosophy*. Malden, MA: Blackwell.

Hooker, Juliet. 2017a. *Theorizing Race in the Americas: Douglass, Sarmiento, Du Bois, and Vasconcelos*. New York: Oxford University Press.

2017b. "Anti-Imperial, but Not Decolonial? Vasconcelos on Race and Latin American Identity." https://pdfs.semanticscholar.org/b267/c1f67765b5fba8 1269606cff894885f19c08.pdf?_ga=2.106692032.255566675.1591125580-1061535041.1591125580

Horan, Elizabeth. 2010. "Whose José Martí?" *American Quarterly* 62(1): 181–189.

Hurtado, Guillermo. 2006. "Two Models of Latin American Philosophy," *Journal of Speculative Philosophy* 3: 204–213.

2007. *El búho y la serpiente: ensayos sobre la filosofía en México en el siglo XX*. Mexico City: UNAM.

2010. "El diálogo filosófico interamericano como un diálogo para la democracia," *Inter-American Journal of Philosophy* 1: 1–17.

Jaksić, Iván. 1989. "The Sources of Latin America Philosophy," *Philosophical Forum* 20: 141–157.

1996. "The Machine and the Spirit: Anti-Technological Humanism in Twentieth-Century Latin America," *Revista de Estudios Hispánicos* 30: 179–201.

2001. *Scholarship and Nation-Building in Nineteenth-Century Latin America*. Cambridge, UK: Cambridge University Press.

2011. "Race and National Political Culture," pp. 85–98 in Gracia 2011.

2015. "Philosophy in Chile," in Edward Zalta, ed., *Stanford Encyclopedia of Philosophy*. Stanford, CA: CSLI. https://plato.stanford.edu/entries/philoso phy-chile/

James, Daniel. 2001. *Ché Guevara: A Biography*. New York: Rowman & Littlefield.

Jiménez García, Antonio and Nelson R. Orringer. 2009. "Del krausismo al krausopositivismo," pp. 67–78 in Garrido et al. 2009.

Jorrín, Miguel and John D. Martz. 1970. *Latin-American Political Thought and Ideology*, Chapel Hill, NC: University of North Carolina Press.

Kain, Philip J. 2011. *Marx and Ethics*, Oxford: Clarendon Press.

Kant, Immanuel. 1948/1785. *Groundwork of the Metaphysic of Morals*. London: Hutchinson University Library.

Keating, Joshua. 2013. "Was Bolivar a 'Bolivarian'?" *Foreign Policy*, March 6. https://foreignpolicy.com/2013/03/06/was-bolivar-a-bolivarian/

Krause, C. Chr. F. 1871. *Ideal de la Humanidad para la vida, con introducción y comentarios por Julián Sanz del Río*. Madrid: Imprenta de F. Martínez García. (2nd ed. available online at www.cervantesvirtual.com/obra-visor /ideal-de-la-humanidad-para-la-vida–0/html/

Krause, Will. 1990. "Marxism," pp. 160–198 in *Contemporary Political Philosophy: An Introduction*. Oxford/New York: Oxford University Press.

Kreimer, Roxana n.d. (a). "Es sexista reconocer que hombres y mujeres no son idénticos? Una evaluación crítica de la retórica neurofeminista," Universidad Nacional de Tucumán, undated MS. Available via Facebook group "Feminismo científico." https://es-la.facebook.com/groups/feminis mocientifico/permalink/273421369955768/

n.d. (b). "Evidencias en contra del 'techo de cristal,'" Universidad Nacional de Tucumán, MS, undated MS. *Feminismo científico* (website), https://feminismo cientific.wixsite.com/misitio/techo-de-cristal-evidencias-en-cont

Kuhn, Thomas S. 1962. *The Structure of Scientific Revolutions*. Chicago: University of Chicago Press.

Kymlicka, Will. 2002. *Contemporary Political Philosophy: An Introduction*. New York: Oxford University Press.

Las Casas, Bartolomé de. 1990. *Memorial of Remedies for the Indies*, V. N. Baptiste, ed.Culver City, CA: Labyrinthos.

1992a/1537. *Bartolome de las Casas: The Only Way*, H. Rand Parish, ed. Mahwah, NJ: Paulist Press.

1992b/1542. *A Short Account of the Destruction of the Indies*. London: Penguin.

1993. *Witness: Writings of Bartolomé de las Casas*. George Sanderlin, ed. Maryknoll, New York: Orbis Books.

Las Casas, Bartolomé de and Juan Ginés de Sepúlveda. 1994/1550. "Aquí se contiene una disputa o controversia," pp. 372–379 in Himelblau 1994 (trans. pp. 39–54 in Nuccetelli and Seay 2002).

Lastarria, José Victorino. 2007/1842. Investigaciones sobre la influencia social de la conquista i del sistema colonial de los españoles en Chile. *Memoria Chilena*, Biblioteca Nacional de Chile. www.memoriachilena.gob.cl/archi vos2/pdfs/MC0008961.pdf. (References to reprint in Burke and Humphrey 2007, pp. 81–91.)

1875. *Lecciones de política positiva*. Paris: Librería de A. Bouret e Hijo.

2000/1878. *Literary Memoirs*. Ed. Frederic M. Nunn. Oxford/New York: Oxford University Press (miscellaneous writings from several periods. Spanish title: *Recuerdos literarios. Datos de la historia literaria de la América española y del progreso intelectual de Chile*. Santiago: Librería de M. Servat, 2nd edition, 1885).

León-Portilla, Miguel. 1963. *Aztec Thought and Culture*. Norman, OH: University of Oklahoma Press.

2016. "Extending Christendom: Religious Understanding of the Other," pp. 62–76 in Garrard-Burnett, Freston, and Dove 2016.

Levinson, Irving W. 2013. "Positively Disastrous: The Comtian Legacy of Mexico," pp. 109–132 in Gilson and Levinson 2013.

Liss, Sheldon B. 1984. *Marxist Thought in Latin America*. Berkeley, CA: University of California Press.

Llorente, Renzo. 2009. "Marxism," pp. 170–184 in Nuccetelli, Schutte, and Bueno 2009.

2011. "The Amauta's Ambivalence: Mariátegui on Race," pp. 228–248 in Gracia 2011.

2013. "Gracia on Hispanic and Latino Identity," *The Journal of Speculative Philosophy* 27 (1): 67–78.

2018. *The Political Theory of Che Guevara*. London: Rowman & Littlefield.

Lopes Franco, Costa Luiza, Ana Beatriz Dillon Esteves, Roxana Kreimer, Noel Struchiner, and Ivar Hannikainen. 2019. "Gender Stereotypes Underlie Child Custody Decisions," *European Journal of Social Psychology* 3: 548–559.

López, Rick Anthony. 2010. *Crafting Mexico: Intellectuals, Artisans, and the State after the Revolution*. Durham, NC: Duke University Press.

López-Morillas, Juan. 1981. *The Krausist Movement and Ideological Change in Spain, 1854–1874*. Cambridge, UK: Cambridge University Press.

Love, Joseph L. 1996. "Economic Ideas and Ideologies in Latin America since 1930," pp. 207–274 in Bethell 1996.

Löwy, Michael. 1992. *Marxism in Latin America from 1909 to the Present: An Anthology*. Atlantic Highlands, NJ: Humanities Press.

2007. *The Marxism of Che Guevara, Philosophy, Economics, Revolutionary Warfare*, 2nd ed. Lanham, MD: Rowman & Littlefield.

Lukes, Stephen. 1987. *Marxism and Morality*. Oxford: Oxford University Press.

Mahbubani, Kishore. 1998. *Can Asians Think?* Singapore: Times Books International.

Macklin, Ruth. 2009. "Global Inequalities in Women's Health: Who Is Responsible for Doing What?" *Philosophical Topics: Global Gender Issues* 37(2): 93–108.

Maffie, James. 2009. "Pre-Columbian Philosophies," pp. 9–22 in Nuccetelli, Schutte, and Bueno 2009.

2013. *Aztec Philosophy: Understanding a World in Motion*. Boulder, CO: University Press of Colorado.

Mañach, Jorge. 1950. *Martí: Apostle of Freedom*. New York: Devin-Adair.

Marchesi, Aldo. 2018. "The Subjective Bonds of Revolutionary Solidarity: From Havana to Ñancahuazú (Bolivia) 1967," pp. 69–100 in *Latin America's Left: Rebellion and Cold War in Global 1960s*. Cambridge, UK: Cambridge University Press.

Mariátegui, José Carlos. 1922. "'Indologia' por José Vasconcelos," *Variedades*, Lima, October 22. www.marxists.org/espanol/mariateg/oc/temas_de_nuestra_america/paginas/indologia.htm

1925. "La escena contemporánea," *The Internet Marxists Archive*, www.marxists.org/espanol/mariateg/ 191925/escena/06.htm

1971/1928. *Seven Interpretive Essays on Peruvian Reality*. Austin, TX: University of Texas Press (Marxists Internet Archive, www.marxists.org/archive/mariateg/works/7-interpretive-essays/index.htm)

1996. *The Heroic and Creative Meaning of Socialism: Selected Essays of José Carlos Mariátegui*, ed. Michael Pearlman. Atlantic Highlands, NJ: Humanities Press.

1996/1923. "The World Crisis and the Peruvian Working Class," pp. 3–8 in Mariátegui 1996.

1996/1929. "The Indigenous Question," pp. 94–109 in Mariátegui 1996.

2004a/1928. "The Problem of the Indian," pp. 239–243 in Nuccetelli and Seay 2004.

2004b/1928. "The Religious Factor," pp. 243–253 in Nuccetelli and Seay 2004.

Marinello, Juan. 1975. "The Cuban Revolutionary Party: Jose Marti's Exemplary Creation," Speech at the Lazaro Pena Theater, Central Organization of Cuban Trade Unions, December 5. www.walterlippmann.com/docs1123.html

Marini, Ruy Mauro. 1977. *Dialéctica de la dependencia*. Mexico: Era. www.marini-escritos.unam.mx/024_dialectica_dependencia.html

Marks, Greg C. 1992. "Indigenous Peoples in International Law: The Significance of Francisco de Vitoria and Bartolomé de las Casas," MA thesis, pp. 131–151 in *The Australian Yearbook of International Law*. Australia National University.

Márquez, Iván, ed. 2008. *Contemporary Latin American Social and Political Thought: An Anthology*. Lanham, MD: Rowman & Littlefield.

Martí, José. 1871. *El presidio político de Cuba*. Madrid: Imprenta Ramón Ramírez, https://revista-iberoamericana.pitt.edu/ojs/index.php/Iberoamericana/article/viewFile/2597/2785

1873. "The Spanish Republic and the Cuban Revolution," February 15, pp. 32–42 in Martí 1999.

1977. *Our America by José Martí: Writings on Latin America and the Struggle for Cuban Independence*, ed. Philip S. Foner. New York/London: Monthly Review Press.

1997–2015/1884a. "Maestros ambulantes," *La América*, in Gómez-Martínez 1997–2015, www.ensayistas.org/antologia/XIXA/marti/marti3.htm

1997–2015/1884b. "Mente latina," *La América,* in Gómez-Martínez 1997–2015, www.ensayistas.org/antologia/XIXA/marti/marti4.htm

1997–2015/1894a. "El plato de lentejas," *Patria,* January 2, 1894, in Gómez-Martínez 1997–2015. www.ensayistas.org/antologia/XIXA/marti/marti6 .htm

1999. *José Martí Reader: Writings on the Americas,* eds. D. Shnookal and M. Muñiz eds., 1st ed. Hoboken, NJ: Ocean Press.

1999/1883. "The Memorial Meeting in Honor of Karl Marx," *La Nación,* March 29, 1883, reprint in Martí 1999, pp. 43–45.

1999/1885. "Indians in the United States," October 25, 1885, pp. 51–58 in Martí 1999.

1999/1889. "Mother America," *El Partido Liberal,* December 19, 1889, pp. 101–110 in Martí 1999.

1999/1891a. "With All, for the Good of All," November 26, 1891, reprint, pp. 132–144 in Martí 1999.

1999/1891b. "Our America," *La Revista Illustrada,* January 1, 1891, pp. 111–121 in Martí 1999.

1999/1893. "My Race," *Patria,* April 16, 1893, pp. 160–162 in Martí 1999 (references to "Mi raza," in Gómez-Martínez 1997–2015).

1999/1894b. "The Truth about the United States," *Patria,* March 23, 1894, pp. 172–176 in Martí 1999.

1999/1895a. "Letter to the New York Herald," *New York Herald,* May 2, 1895, reprint pp. 241–252 in Martí 1999.

1999/1895b. "Manifesto de Montecristi," *Revolutionary Party,* March 15, 1895, reprint pp. 177–186 in Martí 1999.

1999/1895c (with Máximo Gómez). "Manifesto de Montecristi," Cuban Revolutionary Party Address, March 25, 1895, pp. 177–186 in Martí 1999.

Martinez-Saenz, Miguel. 2004. "Che Guevara's New Man: Embodying a Communitarian Attitude," *Latin American Perspectives* 31(6): 15–30.

Marx, Karl. 1935/1851–1852. *The Eighteenth Brumaire of Louis Napoleon.* Moscow: Progress Publishers (references to edition in *The Marxists Internet Archive,* www.marxists.org/archive/marx/works/1852/18th-brumaire/)

1858. "Bolívar y Ponte," *The New American Cyclopedia,* Vol. III (references to edition in the *Marxists Internet Archive.* www.marxists.org/archive/marx/ works/1858/01/bolivar.htm)

1967/1867. *Capital.* London: Lawrence & Wishart.

1968/1845. "Theses on Feuerbach," pp. 181–185 in Karl Marx and Friedrich Engels, *Selected Works* (one-volume edition). London: Lawrence and Wishart (references to edition in *The Marxists Internet Archive*, www.marxists.org/archive/marx/works/1845/theses/theses.htm)

1970/1875. *Critique of the Gotha Programme*. Moscow: Progress Publishers (references to edition in *The Marxists Internet Archive*, www.marxists.org/archive/marx/works/1875/gotha/)

Marx, Karl and Friedrich Engels. 1968/1845. "The Communist Manifesto," pp. 31–61 in Karl Marx and Friedrich Engels, *Selected Works* (one-volume edition). London: Lawrence and Wishart.

Matute, Alvaro. 1997. "El historiador Edmundo O'Gorman (1906–1995). Introducción a su obra y pensamiento histórico," *Mexican Studies/Estudios Mexicanos* 13(1): 1–20.

McLaren, Peter. 2000. *Che Guevara, Paulo Freire, and the Pedagogy of Revolution*. Lanham, MD: Rowman & Littlefield.

Medina, Vicente. 2013. "The Innocent in the Just War Thinking of Vitoria and Suárez: A Challenge Even for Secular Just War Theorists and International Law," *Ratio Juris* 26(1): 47–64.

Mendieta, Eduardo. 1999. "Is There Latin American Philosophy?" *Philosophy Today* 43: 50–61.

2016. "Philosophy of Liberation," in Edward Zalta, ed., *Stanford Encyclopedia of Philosophy*. Stanford, CA: CSLI.

Merrim, Stephanie, ed. 1991. *Feminist Perspectives on Sor Juana Inés de la Cruz*. Detroit, MI: Wayne State University Press.

https://plato.stanford.edu/entries/liberation/

Merquior, J. G. 1982. "More Order than Progress? The Politics of Brazilian Positivism," *Government and Opposition* 17(4): 454–468.

Miliani, Domingo. 1963. "Utopian Socialism, Transitional Thread from Romanticism to Positivism in Spanish America," *Journal of the History of Ideas* 24: 523–538.

Mill, John Stuart. 1979/1863. *Utilitarianism*. Indianapolis: Hackett.

Miller, Nicola. 1999. *In the Shadow of the State: Intellectuals and the Quest for National Identity in Twentieth-Century Spanish America*. London: Verso.

2008. *Reinventing Modernity in Latin America: Intellectuals Imagine the Future, 1900–1930*. New York: Palgrave MacMillan,

Miró Quesada, Francisco. 1974. *Despertar y proyecto del filosofar latinoamericano*. Mexico City: Fondo de Cultura Económica,

1976. *El problema de la filosofía latinoamericana*. Mexico City: Fondo de Cultura Económica,

1978. "Posibilidad y límites de una filosofía lationamericana," *Revista de Filosofía de la Universidad de Costa Rica* XVI(43): 75–82.

Mitchell-Walthour, Gladys L. 2018. *The Politics of Blackness: Racial Identity and Political Behavior in Contemporary Brazil*. Cambridge, UK: Cambridge University Press.

Moore, G. E. 1953. "What Is Philosophy?" pp. 1–40 in *Some Main Problems of Philosophy*. London: Allen & Unwin.

1993/1903. *Principia Ethica*, ed. Thomas Baldwin. Cambridge, UK: Cambridge University Press.

Morales-Franceschini, Eric. 2018. "Latin American Liberation Theology," *Global South Studies: A Collective Publication with the Global South*. May 9. https://global southstudies.as.virginia.edu/key-thinkers/latin-american-liberation-theology

Nathanson, Stephen. 1998. *Economic Justice*. Upper Saddle River, NJ: Prentice Hall.

Noble, Cristina, ed. 2007. *José Martí: La primera revolución cubana*. Buenos Aires: Capital Intelectual.

Noddings, Nel. 1984. *Caring: A Feminine Approach to Ethics and Moral Education*. Berkeley and Los Angeles: University of California Press.

Novak, Michael. 1984. "The Case against Liberation Theology," *The New York Times Magazine*, October 21. www.nytimes.com/1984/10/21/magazine/the-case-against-liberation-theology.html

1986. *Will It Liberate? Questions about Liberation Theology*. Lanham, MD: Madison Books.

Nubiola, Jaime. 1998. "C. S. Peirce and the Hispanic Philosophy of the Twentieth Century," *Transactions of the Charles S. Peirce Society* 34(1): 31–49.

Nuccetelli, Susana. 2001. "'Hispanics,' 'Latinos,' and 'Iberoamericans': Naming or Describing?" *Philosophical Forum* 32: 175–188.

2002. *Latin American Thought: Philosophical Problems and Arguments*. Boulder, CO: Westview Press.

2004. "Reference and Ethnic-Group Terms," *Inquiry* 6: 528–544.

2017/2013. "Latin American Philosophy: Metaphilosophical Foundations," in Edward Zalta, ed., *Stanford Encyclopedia of Philosophy*. Stanford, CA: CSLI. http://plato.stanford.edu/entries/latin-american-metaphilosophy/

2016. "Latin American Philosophers: Some Recent Challenges to Their Intellectual Character," *Informal Logic* 36(2): 121–135.

2017. "What the 'Nina'-Film Controversy Shows about African Heritage in the Americas," *The APA Newsletter on Hispanic/Latino Issues in Philosophy*, October: 4–7, https://cdn.ymaws.com/www.apaonline.org/resource/collection/60044C96-F3E0-4049-BC5A-271C673FA1E5/HispanicV17n1.pdf

2018. "Latino Philosophy," in Illan Stavans, ed., *Oxford Handbook of Latino Studies*. Oxford: Oxford University Press. DOI:http://dx.doi.org/10.1093/oxfordhb/9780190691202.001.0001.

2018/2013. "Latin American Ethics," pp. 2970–2979 in Hugh LaFollette, ed., *International Encyclopedia of Ethics*. Cambridge, MA: Wiley-Blackwell. DOI:10.1002/9781444367072.wbiee648

Nuccetelli, Susana and Gary Seay, eds. 2004. *Latin American Philosophy: An Introduction with Readings*, Upper Saddle Brook, NJ: Prentice Hall.

Nuccetelli, Susana, Ofelia Schutte, and Otavio Bueno, eds. 2009. *Blackwell Companion to Latin American Philosophy*. Oxford: Wiley-Blackwell.

O'Gorman, Edmundo. 1961/1960. *The Invention of America: An Inquiry into the Historical Nature of the New World and the Meaning of its History of America: An Inquiry into the Historical Nature of the New World and the Meaning of its History*. Bloomington: Indiana University Press.

2017/1960. "Art or Monstrosity," in Carlos Alberto Sánchez and Robert Eli Sánchez Jr., *Mexican Philosophy in the 20th Century*. New York: Oxford University Press.

Orosco, José Antonio. 2011. "José Vasconcelos, White Supremacy and the Silence of American Pragmatism," *Inter-American Journal of Philosophy* 2(2): 1–13.

2016. "The Philosophical Gift of Brown Folks: Mexican American Philosophy in the United States." *APA Newsletter on Hispanic/Latino Issues in Philosophy* 15 (Spring): 23–28.

Ortega y Gasset, José. 1983/1910. "Pedagogía social como programa político," pp. 503–521 in *Obras Completas*, vol. 1. Madrid: Alianza.

Paz, Octavio. 1961. *The Labyrinth of Solitude: Life and Thought in Mexico*. New York: Grove Press.

1988. *Sor Juana: Or, the Traps of Faith*. Cambridge, MA: Harvard University Press.

Paz Salinas, Maria Emilia. 1997. *Strategy, Security, and Spies: Mexico and the US as Allies in World War II*. University Park, PA: Penn State Press.

Pereda, Carlos. 2006. "Latin American Philosophy: Some Vices," *Journal of Speculative Philosophy* 3: 192–203.

Petrella, Ivan, 2016. "The Intellectual Roots of Liberation Theology," pp. 359–371 in Garrard-Burnett, Freston, and Dove 2016.

Pitts, Andrea and Adriana Novoa, eds. 2014. "Moving Philosophies: Bridging Latin American and U.S. Latino/a Thought." *Inter-American Journal of Philosophy* 5(1).

Piossek Prebisch, Lucía. 2008. *Argentina: identidad y utopía*. Tucumán, Argentina: EDUNT Editorial.

Prebisch, Raúl. 1971. *Change and Development – Latin America's Great Task: Report Submitted to the Inter-American Development Bank*. New York: Praeger (references to selection in Márquez 2008, pp. 200–207).

Rabossi, Eduardo. 2003. "Filosofar: profesionalismo, profesionalidad, tics, y modales," pp. 34–44 in Cruz Revueltas 2003.

    2004. "Notes on Globalization, Human Rights, and Violence," pp. 139–155 in Ricardo J. Gómez, ed., *The Impact of Globalized Neoliberalism in Latin America: Philosophical Perspectives*. Newbury Park, CA: Hansen House Publishing.

    2008. *En el comienzo Dios creo el Canon. Biblia berolinensis. Ensayos sobre la condición de la filosofía*. Buenos Aires: Gedisa.

Ratzinger, Joseph (Cardinal). 1984. "Instruction on Certain Aspects of the 'Theology of Liberation,'" Congregation for the Doctrine of the Faith, www .vatican.va/roman_curia/congregations/cfaith/documents/rc_con_cfaith_ doc_19840806_theology-liberation_en.html

Ripoll, Carlos. 1984. *José Martí, the United States, and Marxist Interpretation of Cuban History*. New Brunswick, NJ and London: Transaction Publishers.

Ripoll, Carlos and Raymond Carr. 1988. "Marx & Martí," *The New York Review of Books*, December 8, www.nybooks.com/articles/1988/12/08/marx-marti/

Rivera, Faviola. 2016. "Liberalism in Latin America," in Edward Zalta, ed., *Stanford Encyclopedia of Philosophy*. Stanford, CA: CSLI. https://plato .stanford.edu/entries/liberalism-latin-america/

Rivera Berruz, Stephanie. 2018. "Latin American Feminism," in Edward Zalta, ed., *Stanford Encyclopedia of Philosophy*. Stanford, CA: CSLI. https://plato .stanford.edu/entries/feminism-latin-america/

Rivera Cusicanqui, Silvia. 1996. "Los desafíos para una democracia étnica y genérica en los albores del tercer milenio," pp. 17–84 in Silvia Rivera Cusicanqui, ed., *Ser mujer indígena, chola o birlocha en la Bolivia postcolonial de los años 90*. La Paz: Ministerio de Desarrollo Humano.

    2002. "Ch'ixinakax utixiwa: A Reflection on the Practices of Discourses of Decolonization," *The South Atlantic Quarterly* (Winter): 96–109, www.adivasir esurgence.com/wp-content/uploads/2016/02/Silvia-Rivera-Cusicanqui-Chixinakax-Eng1.pdf

Robles Carcedo, Laureano, ed. 1987. *Filosofía iberoamericana en la época del Encuentro, Enciclopedia Iberoamericana de filosofía*, vol. 1. Madrid: Editorial Trotta.

Rodó, José Enrique. 1988/1900. *Ariel*. Austin, TX: University of Texas Press.

Rodríguez de Lecea, Teresa. 1997. "Una entrevista con Edmundo O'Gorman," *Historia Mexicana* 46(4): 955–969.

Roig, Arturo Andrés. 1969. *Los krausistas argentinos*. Puebla, Mexico: Editorial José M. Cajica (references to selection in Gómez-Martínez 1997–2005, www .ensayistas.org/filosofos/argentina/roig/etica/etica18.htm)

Andrés1981. *Teoría y crítica del pensamiento latinoamericano*. Mexico City: Fondo de Cultura Económica. www.ensayistas.org/filosofos/argentina/roig/teoria/ introduccion.htm

Andrés1984. "Cuatro tomas de posición a esta altura de los tiempos," *Nuestra América* 11: 55–59.

Andrés1998. "Etica y liberación: José Martí y el 'hombre natural,'" in *Etica del poder y moralidad de la protesta: La moral latinoamericana de la emergencia*. Mendoza, Argentina (references to reprint in Gómez-Martínez 1997–2015, www.ensayistas.org/filosofos/argentina/roig/etica/etica18.htm)

Andrés2000. *Etica del poder y moralidad de la protesta. La moral latinoamericana de la emergencia*. Athens: Proyecto de Ensayo Hispánico, www.ensayistas.org /filosofos/argentina/roig/etica/

Andrés2003. "Necesidad de una segunda independencia," *Cuadernos Americanos Segunda Época* 100(4): 11–41.

Romanell, Patrick. 1943. "The Background of Contemporary Mexican Thought," *Philosophy and Phenomenological Research* 4: 121–134.

1952. *Making of the Mexican Mind: A Study in Recent Mexican Thought*. Freeport, NY: Books for Libraries Press.

Romero, Francisco. 1943. "Tendencias contemporáneas en el pensamiento hispanoamericano," *Philosophy and Phenomenological Research* 2: 127–133.

1944. "Sobre la filosofía en Iberoamérica," pp. 147–157 in *Filosofía de la persona y otros ensayos*. Buenos Aires: Losada.

1949. "Las ideas de Rivadavia," pp. 109–124 in *Ideas y figuras*, 2nd ed. Buenos Aires: Losada.

Romero, José Luis. 1998. *El pensamiento político latinoamericano*. Buenos Aires: A-Z Editora,

Salazar Bondy, Augusto. 1967. "El pensamiento de Mariátegui y la filosofía marxista," pp. 311–342 in *Historia de las ideas en el Perú contemporáneo: El proceso del pensamiento filosófico*, vol. 2. Lima: Francisco Moncloa Editores.

1968. *Existe una filosofía de nuestra America?* Mexico City: Siglo XXI.

Salles, Arleen. 2011. "Rodó, Race, and Morality," pp. 181–202 in Gracia 2011.

Sánchez, Carlos Alberto. 2011. "Philosophy and the Post-Immigrant Fear," *Philosophy in the Contemporary World* 18(1): 31–42.

Sandel, Michael J. 1982. *Liberalism and the Limits of Justice*, 2nd ed. Cambridge, UK: Cambridge University Press.

Santayana, George. 1989/1900. *Interpretations of Poetry and Religion*. Cambridge, MA: MIT Press.

Sanz del Río, Julián. 2003. "Introducción y comentarios," in Krause 1871 (references to online version, *Biblioteca Virtual Universal* http://biblioteca.org.ar/libros/89759.pdf)

Sarmiento, Domingo F. 1850. *Recuerdos de Provincia*. Santiago de Chile: Julio Belin y Co, www.librosenred.com/libros/recuerdosdeprovincia.html

1853. *Las Ciento y Una*. Buenos Aires: L. J. Rosso.

1978/1883. *Conflicto y armonía de las razas en américa (conclusiones)*. Humanities Committee, Center of Latin American Studies, Faculty of Philosophy and Letters, Autonomous University of Mexico, www.cervantesvirtual.com/obra/conflicto-y-armonias-de-razas-en-america–0/

1998/1845. *Facundo or, Civilization and Barbarism*. New York: Penguin.

2017/1866. *Vida de Abraham Lincoln*. Barcelona: Biblok Book Export.

Scannone, Juan Carlos. 2009. "La filosofía de la liberación: historia, características, vigencia actual," *Teología y vida* 50 (1–2): 59–73. https://scielo.conicyt.cl/scielo.php?script=sci_arttext&pid=S0049-34492009000100006#n05

Schulman, Sam. 1948. "Juan Bautista Alberdi and His Influence on Immigration Policy in the Argentine Constitution of 1853," *The Americas* 5(1): 3–17.

Schutte, Ofelia. 1991. "Origins and Tendencies of the Philosophy of Liberation in Latin American Thought: A Critique of Dussel's Ethics," *The Philosophical Forum* 22: 270–295.

1993. *Cultural Identity and Social Liberation in Latin American Thought*. Albany, NY: State University of New York Press,

1998. "Cultural Alterity: Cross-Cultural Communication and Feminist Theory in North-South Contexts," *Hypatia* 13(2): 53–72.

2011a. "Engaging Latin American Feminisms Today: Methods, Theory, Practice, " *Hypatia* 26(4): 783–803.

2011b. "Undoing 'Race': Martí's Historical Perspective," pp. 99–123 in Gracia 2011.

Schutte, Ofelia and María Luisa Femenías. 2009. "Feminist Philosophy," pp. 397–411 in Nuccetelli, Schutte, and Bueno 2009.

Segato, Rita Laura. 2003. *Las estructuras elementales de la violencia*. Buenos Aires: Prometeo and Universidad Nacional de Quilmes.

Sierra, Justo. 1969/1900–1902. *The Political Evolution of the Mexican People*. Austin, TX: University of Texas Press.

Siegel, Susanna. 2014. "Reflections on the Use of English and Spanish in Analytic Philosophy." *Informes del Observatorio / Observatorio Reports*. Cambridge, MA: Instituto Cervantes, Harvard University, http://cervante sobservatorio.fas.harvard.edu/sites/default/files/006_informes_ss_analy tic_philosophy.pdf.

Simon, Joshua. 2017. *The Ideology of Creole Revolution: Imperialism and Independence in American and Latin American Political Thought*. Cambridge, UK: Cambridge University Press.

Singer, Peter. 2009. "Speciesism and Moral Status," *Metaphilosophy* 40(3–4): 567–581.

Sobrino, Jon. 1978/1976. *Christology at the Crossroads*. Maryknoll, NY: Orbis.

Stavans, Ilan.1998. "Introduction," pp. vii–xxxii in Sarmiento 1998/1845.

Stavans, Ilan, ed. 1997. *The Oxford Book of Latin American Essays*. New York/Oxford: Oxford University Press.

2000. "Life in the Hyphen," pp. 3–26 in *The Essential Ilan Stavans*. New York and London: Routledge.

2011. *José Vasconcelos: The Prophet of Race*. New Brunswick, NJ: Rutgers University Press, http://muse.jhu.edu/book/2208

Sterba, James P. 1996. "Understanding Evil: American Slavery, the Holocaust, and the Conquest of the American Indians," *Ethics* 106(2): 424–448.

Subercaseaux, Bernardo. 1980. "Liberalismo positivista y naturalismo en Chile (1865–1875)," *Revista de Crítica Literaria Latinoamericana* 6(11): 7–27.

Sunkel, Osvaldo and Pedro Paz. 1975. *El subdesarrollo latinoamericano y la teoría del desarrollo*. Mexico: Siglo XXI. https://repositorio.cepal.org/bitstream/handle/11362/1604/S33098159S1_es.pdf

Swanson, Philip. 2003a. "Civilization and Barbarism," pp. 69–85 in Swanson 2003b.

Swanson, Philip, ed. 2003b. *The Companion to Latin American Studies*. Oxford: Oxford University Press.

Symington, James W. 1988/1900. "Foreword," pp. 7–12 in Rodó 1988/1900.

Talbot, William. 2005. *Which Rights Should Be Universal?* Oxford: Oxford University Press.

Tammelleo, Steve. 2011. "Continuity and Change in Hispanic Identity," *Ethnicities* 11 (4): 536–554.

Tardieu, Jean-Pierre. 2015. "El negro y 'La raza cósmica' de José Vasconcelos (1925)," *Boletín Americanista* 2(71): 155–169, https://dialnet.unirioja.es/descarga/articulo/5503120.pdf

Terán, Oscar. 1995. "Mariátegui: el destino sudamericano de un moderno extremista," *Punto de vista* 7 (51): 15–29, https://www.ahira.com.ar/ejemplares/51/

2004. *Las palabras ausentes: Para leer los escritos póstumos de Alberdi*. Buenos Aires: Fondo de Cultura Económica.

Todorov, Tzvetan. 1992. *The Conquest of America: The Question of the Other*. New York: Harper Torch.

Torres, Camilo. 2016. *Camilo Torres Restrepo, profeta de la liberación: antología (teológica) política*, eds. Lorena López Guzmán, and Nicolás Armando Herrera Farfán. Buenos Aires: Editorial El Colectivo.

Townsend, Camilla. 2006. *Malintzin's Choices: An Indian Woman in the Conquest of Mexico*. New Mexico: University of New Mexico Press.

Vincent, Mauricio. 2012. "Che Guevara: The Philosopher," *El Pais*, May 17, https://elpais.com/elpais/2012/06/17/inenglish/1339954013_189905.html

Vales, José Francisco. 1996. "La influencia de la cultura alemana en la formación del pensamiento de José Martí," *Iberoamericana* 20(1): 5–25.

Vargas, Manuel. 2007. "*Real* Philosophy, Metaphilosophy, and Metametaphilosophy: On the Plight of Latin American Philosophy," *CR: The New Centennial Review* 7(3): 51–78.

2010. "On the Value of Philosophy: The Latin American Case," *Comparative Philosophy* 1(1): 33–52.

Vargas Lozano, Gabriel. 2010. "El Ateneo de la Juventud y la Revolución Mexicana," *Literatura Mexicana* 21(2), www.scielo.org.mx/pdf/lm/v21n2/v21n2a3.pdf

Vasconcelos, José. 1926. *Indología: una interpretación de la cultura iberoamericana*. Barcelona: Agencia Mundial de Librería.

1997/1925. *The Cosmic Race: A Bilingual Edition*. Baltimore, MD: The Johns Hopkins University Press.

2011/1925a. "Mestizaje," pp. 45–90 in Stavans 2011 (reprint of Vasconcelos 1997/1925, pp. 7–40).

2011/1926. "The Race Problem in Latin America," Norman Wait Harris Memorial Foundation Lecture, University of Chicago, pp. 91–111 in Stavans 2011.

Vásquez, Manuel A. and Anna L. Peterson. 2016. "Progressive Catholicism in Latin America: Sources and Its Evolution from Vatican II to Pope Francis," pp. 372–397 in Garrard-Burnett, Freston, and Dove 2016.

Vinson, Ben III. 2018. *Before Mestizaje: The Frontiers of Race and Caste in Colonial Mexico*. New York: Cambridge University Press.

Vitoria, Francisco de. 1991. *Vitoria: Political Writings*, eds. Anthony Pagden and Jeremy Lawrence. Cambridge, UK: Cambridge University Press.

von Vacano, Diego A. 2011. "Zarathustra Criollo: Vasconcelos on Race," pp. 203–226 in Gracia 2011.

2012. *The Color of Citizenship: Race, Modernity and Latin American/Hispanic Political Thought*. Oxford: Oxford University Press.

Wittgenstein, Ludwig.1970. *Zettel*. Berkeley and Los Angeles: University of California Press,

Wolff, Jonathan. 2017. "Karl Marx," in Edward Zalta, ed., *Stanford Encyclopedia of Philosophy*. Stanford, CA: CSLI. https://plato.stanford.edu/entries/marx/

Woll, Allen L. 1976. "Positivism and History in Nineteenth-Century Chile: Jose Victorino Lastarria and Valentin Letelier," *Journal of History of Ideas* 37(3): 493–506.

Wood, Allen. 1981. *Karl Marx*. London: Routledge.

Yugar, Theresa A. 2014. *Sor Juana Inés de la Cruz: Feminist Reconstruction of Biography and Text*. Eugene, OR: Wipf and Stock.

Zea, Leopoldo. 1974/1943. *Positivism in Mexico*. Austin, TX: University of Texas Press.

1993. "Vasconcelos y la utopia de la raza cósmica," *Cuadernos Americanos* 37(1): 23–36.

2004. "Positivism and Porfirism in Latin America," in F. S. C. Northrop, ed., *Ideological Differences and World Order: Studies in the Philosophy and Science of the World's Cultures*. New Haven, CT: Yale University Press (reprinted pp. 198–218 in Nuccetelli and Seay 2004).

Zweig, Arnulf. 1967. "Karl Christian Friedrich Krause," pp. 263–265 in *Encyclopedia of Philosophy*, vol. 3, ed. Paul Edwards. New York/London: Macmillan.

Index of Names and Subjects